MR. CALM AND EFFECTIVE

EVALUATING THE PRESIDENCY OF BARACK OBAMA

by

Michael Haas

Professor of Political Science

Nobel Peace Prize Nominee

PUBLISHINGHOUSE FOR SCHOLARS

LOS ANGELES

Library of Congress Cataloging-in-Publication Data

Haas, Michael 1938-
    Mr. Calm and Effective: Evaluating the Presidency of
    Barack Obama
    p. cm.
    Includes bibliographic references and index.

    ISBN-12 978-0-9839626-1-8 (paper)
    ISBN-12 978-0-9839626-0-1 (hardcover)
    Library of Congress Control Number: 2011944170

I 1. Obama, Barack H. (Barack Hussein) 1961- 2. Obama,
    Barack—Philosophy 3. Presidents—United States—
    Elections—History—Politics and government—
    Economics 4. War on terrorism 5. Multiculturalism—
    United States 6. Political culture—United States 7. De-
    mocracy—United States—History—21st century 8. Pro-
    gressivisim (United States politics)—History—21st centu-
    ry II. Haas, Michael, 1938-

First published in 2012
Publishinghouse for Scholars
P.O. Box 461267, Los Angeles, CA 90046

There was a bright candidate named Barack Obama,
Whose quest to be president brought curious drama.
    Then a Senator named McCain
    Tried to oppose his campaign,
Provoking calmness befitting the Dalai Lama.

Table of Contents

Preface

In January 2011, Praeger Publications brought out my book *Barack Obama, The Aloha Zen President: How a Son of the 50th State May Revitalize America Based on 12 Multicultural Principles*. The book attempts to explain that President Obama's personality and political philosophy were primarily shaped in Honolulu, Hawai'i, where he lived most of his life until the age of 18. The reason for the book was that I noticed how friends, journalists, and pundits completely misconstrued him because of a monocultural bias. They could not imagine anyone from a different cultural background from themselves and repeatedly misjudged him from their own perspectives.

Soon after publication of my book, review copies were sent to the major newspapers. But no reviews were forthcoming. Other biographies, with very conventional outlooks, were reviewed. Both the biographers and their reviewers failed to correctly perceive Obama, again because they operated from a Mainland American/Western perspective. Some pundits expressed surprise, even chagrin, that he did not act in an expected manner. I then began to write, in letters to the editor, emails, and Internet comments, that his behavior was that of a typical local Honolulu boy, citing my book. My commentaries were published on various websites, but that did not evoke the kind of corrective "aha" moments that I had hoped.

Nevertheless, when I presented the thesis of my book to audiences of college professors and students in Los Angeles, the response was overwhelmingly positive. A repeated comment was "Why didn't we know this before?" I felt as if I were re-launching Obama's re-election campaign, though my presentation was entirely objective, aimed at explaining the president's background and approach to politics. One such talk, alongside Michael Dukakis, is posted on the Author Events tab of *www.publishinghouse4scholars.com*.

I also wrote opinion essays for editorial pages (known as op-eds) on various topics that came up during the Obama presidency, interpreting them from both Hawai'i and political

vii

science perspectives, having been stimulated by questions after my talks or by unfolding events. They were sent to the major newspapers as well. None were published.

Accordingly, I decided to collect what I wrote into the present book. In doing so, I provide more historical and theoretical background than a short op-ed would permit. I would like to acknowledge helpful suggestions regarding Japanese culture from Beverly Keever of the University of Hawai'i and on Obamacare from Millard Zisser.

The present book starts with two chapters that summarize the essence of *Barack Obama, The Aloha Zen President.* I then comment on sources of opposition to his presidency. Next, key aspects and events in his presidency are discussed in depth. Accomplishments as president are presented in the final chapter.

The appendix has two summaries of important contrasts between Obama and his critics. A third appendix reviews some of the most prominent biographies, identifying their aims and biases.

The overall purpose is to dispel misconceptions about Barack Obama and to place his presidency into an historical context as a visionary thinker who has accomplished much more than almost anyone believed possible. At same time, he has had many critics, so as a scholar I also feel responsible to evaluate his record objectively. Whether I do so appropriately is for the reader to determine.

Michael Haas

MR. CALM AND EFFECTIVE

EVALUATING THE PRESIDENCY
OF BARACK OBAMA

Chapter 1
The Aloha Zen President

Barack Obama is the most misunderstood president in American history. Prominent journalists have asked, "Who is Barack Obama? What are his core beliefs? Where did he acquire his philosophy of life and politics? What explains his performance as a candidate and actions as president?"

Most observers have no idea how to answer correctly. They search for influences on his life—from his parents, grandparents, and his wife, to educational experiences and historical milestones. But they ignore one major influence because they have never lived in Honolulu, where he was born. They have no idea that Barack Obama absorbed a unique culture while growing up in the Aloha State. They cannot link his governance style to the special place where he and his family lived during his formative years—Hawai'i. Baffled by his personality and his values, they judge him from their own perspectives and remain puzzled. Appendix C, a review of his biographies, explains wherein they go astray.

That's why I felt the necessity to publish *Barack Obama, The Aloha Zen President: How a Son of the 50th State May Revitalize America Based on 12 Multicultural Principles* (Praeger 2011). I wanted to explain not only how Hawai'i shaped President Obama but also how to understand the Aloha State itself as an embodiment of the multiculturalism that he represents. And that's why in part I am writing this book—to explain sociocultural reasons that account for President Barack Obama's crucial decisions and policies.

Hawai'i has a very different culture from the continental United States. Obama's background in multicultural Hawai'i is central to his personality and philosophy because he says so and others close to him agree, as the following observations attest:

- The opportunity that Hawai'i offered—to experience a variety of cultures in a climate of mutual respect—became an integral part of my world view, and a basis for the values that I hold most dear. – *Barack Obama*

- You do not understand Barack Obama until you understand Hawaiʻi. – *Michelle Obama*
- There is no doubt that the residue of Hawaiʻi will always stay with me, that it is part of my core, and that what's best in me, and what's best in my message, is consistent with the tradition of Hawaiʻi. – *Barack Obama*
- I think it was Hawaiʻi that made him so broad and spacious and that forced him really to learn how to talk to different kinds of people and to not make assumptions about who they are or what they need. – *Barack Obama's half-sister, Maya Sotero-Ng*
- The multicultural nature of Hawaiʻi helped teach me how to appreciate different cultures and navigate different cultures. – *Barack Obama*
- What people often note as my even temperament I think draws from Hawaiʻi. – *Barack Obama*
- If you really want to know who Barack Obama is, you have to understand the culture of inclusivity. You need to go to Hawaiʻi. – *Professor Kathleen Hall Jamieson, University of Pennsylvania*
- The essence of Hawaiʻi has always been that we come from far and wide, that we come from different backgrounds and different last names, and yet we come together as a single ʻohana [family] because we believe in the fundamental

commonality of people." – *Barack Obama*

- We have a sense that beneath the surface of things, all of us share a common set of hopes, a common set of dreams and a common set of values. That's what the Islands have always been about. – *Barack Obama*
- Hawai'i is a fabulous model for the kind of America I hope this campaign will bring about, a place where different cultures can come together in harmony, and a place that rises above the barriers that divide us. – *Barack Obama*
- I try to explain to [America] something about the Aloha Spirit. I try to explain to them this basic idea that we all have obligations to each other, that we're not alone, that if we see somebody who's in need, we should help. – *Barack Obama*
- President Obama has brought a more relaxed sensibility to his public appearances, an Aloha Zen, a comfortable calm that reflects a man who seems easy going, not so full of himself – *David Gergen, Harvard University*
- When you come from Hawai'i, you start understanding that what's on the surface, what people look like, that doesn't determine who they are. And that the power and strength of diversity, the ability of people from everywhere, whether they're black or white, whether they're Japanese-American or Korean-American or Filipino-American or whatever they are, they are just Americans, that all of us can work together and all of us can join together to create a better country. It's that spirit, that I'm absolutely convinced, is

3

what America is looking for right now. – *Barack Obama*

- Here [in Hawaiʻi] we're a single ʻohana—one family. We remember that beneath the surface, behind all the different languages and some very long names, we all share the same hopes, the same struggles and the same aspirations. And we've learned that we're more likely to realize our aspirations when we pursue them together. That's the spirit of Hawaiʻi. It's what made me who I am. – *Barack Obama*

Barack Obama's Multicultural Background

Those who know Barack Obama best explain what few others have fathomed—that President Barack Obama desires political change **and** cultural change, both needed in order for America to live up to fundamental ideals in a country that has gone astray from its basic creed—as a shining city on a hill, a beacon that once provided hope to the globe, and now may do so for the rest of world with a man of vision from the Aloha State. Obama wants America to recapture its virtuous past and embrace the future. The culture and life in Hawaiʻi is his model.

The purpose of *Barack Obama, The Aloha Zen President* is to demonstrate a different multicultural reality from that found anywhere else in the world, one based on an intercultural philosophy rooted in principles that represent an amalgam of the best elements of American, Native Hawaiian and Japanese cultures. Hawaiʻi's successful integration of many races is in fact the model on which school desegregation was based in the 1954 Supreme Court decision *Brown v Board of Education.*

The book illustrates how Hawaiʻi's intercultural philosophy, often known as the Aloha Spirit, developed over time, changed bitter ethnic rivalries and suspicions into a more harmonious direction, and as a result how politics, society, and everyday life have benefited, even though problems, as

4

everywhere, remain. Each of fifteen chapters in that book links Barack Obama, as a boy and as president, to the multicultural reality of the Fiftieth State. There are many, many connections between how he thinks and where he is from.

Those who have always lived in the same culture may not understand what happens when someone moves to a place with a different culture. But I know: When I went to Honolulu in 1964, I experienced "culture shock." During thirty-five years in Hawai'i, I became assimilated to a very different culture, one that I idolize and praise today.

But I experienced "culture shock" again when I retired from my position as University of Hawai'i political science professor to live in Los Angeles. Someone born in Honolulu, who lived there for most of his first 18 years would have experienced a similar "culture shock" upon arriving on the U.S. Mainland. That's what happened to Barry Obama as he left for college in 1979. Although he has learned to navigate life in Chicago and Washington and on the campaign trail, he has never changed his core ethical beliefs, as identified in Chapter 2 below.

The multicultural ethos that now prevails in Hawai'i emerged from a historical context fundamentally unlike that of the U.S. Mainland. Although I describe the development of that ethos in Chapter 2, the historical context needs to be explained first, as Barack Obama's vision was shaped therein.

From Monarchy to Racist Governance

The multicultural ethos began with the indigenous people of Hawai'i, the Native Hawaiians, who navigated thousands of miles from what is now known as Tahiti and discovered a chain of volcanic islands in about 800. They lived in isolation until the mid-16th century, when Spanish ships passed through but kept their discovery a secret. When Captain James Cook arrived in 1778, the cat came out of the bag, and the Islands entered a long history of foreign exploitation.

First, sandalwood was cut down and exhausted. Whalers came to re-stock their ships and spread their diseases. Sugarcane and pineapple were grown until farming those crops became unprofitable in the competitive world market. The American military, which began to occupy bases in 1875, has not paid rent for squatting on the land since the monarchy fell. And tourists have now come to squander the best beaches and despoil the land for hotels and golf courses.

But the most exploited resources have been the people. White businesses first tried to force the native people to work in agriculture. When most Native Hawaiians refused, White owners recruited workers from China, Japan, the Philippines, and elsewhere. They hoped that White economic interests would prevail politically.

The Kingdom of Hawai'i was respected as a sovereign country by European powers. But in 1893, White leaders in collusion with U.S. Marines overthrew the monarchy by establishing a Republic until the annexation of Hawai'i by the United States in 1898.

The democratic framework established by the United States meant that Whites would eventually lose power to the various non-White groups. When plantation workers recruited from Japan were first allowed to vote in 1954, they joined their sons and daughters in voting out White Republican racist elements. And they have remained mostly in control of political power ever since statehood was granted in 1959.

The Culture of the Islands
Because rule by White Americans before statehood was racist, there was no incentive for non-Whites to assimilate to the values of the ruling Caucasian elites. Instead, the cultures of Native Hawaiian and Japanese were retained intact throughout the first half of the twentieth century. They have continued to assert the best elements of their cultures. Mainlanders moving to the Islands since statehood have adapted to what I call the multicultural ethos, not just to survive economically and socially but because the payoff is a gentler and more respectful existence that is the envy of the world, accounting for the unexcelled ethnic harmony that prevails in the Aloha State.

The parameters of the culture of Hawai'i extend widely within the society. In matters of language, a Creole tongue in the Islands developed among workers on the plantations. Racist overlords were not interested in teaching English to the field workers, who spoke Chinese, Japanese, Portuguese, and other languages and came home tired from work. Their kids, however, went to English-language schools and played after school. To communicate across linguistic divides, they picked up words in various languages along with English and developed a Creole patois that linguists identify as having an entirely distinct language, with its own grammar and syntax. Today, all youngsters learn the Creole, which may even be spoken more often than English itself. Words from that delightful language, known technically as Hawai'i Creole English, are occasionally spoken by Barack Obama—accompanied by a big smile and often with a "shaka" sign.

The relaxed and humorous way of speaking Creole reinforces the multicultural ethos. Formal English speakers eventually learn the joy of speaking commonly used words from the Island language. Meanwhile, Hawai'i has more bilingual speakers than any other state, since those with ancestries from China, Japan, and the Philippines continue to speak their ancestral languages at home even to the fifth and sixth generations.

Linguistic diversity ensures media diversity in Hawai'i. The first English-speaking settlers, missionaries from New England, encouraged Native Hawaiians to make their tongue a written language and print newspapers. Chinese, Filipino, and Japanese newspapers also arose. Those who spoke only English never realized how the non-English media criticized their racism and undermined their legitimacy. With the advent of radio and television, broadcasters seeking advertising from a predominantly non-White population have had to cater to non-English listeners. Accordingly, Media Council Hawai'i arose as America's first multiethnic pressure group to stop racist programming by newcomers.

Barry Obama was a member of the literary club at his school, Punahou, and perhaps that is why his *Dreams from My Father* (1995) shows exceptional writing ability. But Caucasian writers, whether Jack London or Somerset Maugham, have given the world a very false impression of the Islands. In a word, they depicted the local population in a racist manner. While Barry was at school, a literary revolution began, one in which those with Chinese, Native Hawaiian, Japanese, and Philippine backgrounds began to write about their lives in

7

Hawai'i. The classic *All I Asking for Is My Body* (1975) by Milton Murayama provides both Creole in the title and a window into Island life as experienced by the local population. Whether Barry read that book is unknown, but those who do so can derive a better idea of how life in Hawai'i is really experienced by the local population.

Language and words end up in music. Evident in his selection of music for his inauguration, the varied musical tastes of Barack Obama are typical within the Islands, where different cultures easily intermingle. Whites may take a fancy to Korean or Native Hawaiian dance. Japanese may excel at symphonic music and opera. Those of one ethnic background readily attend music concerts of other ethnic backgrounds. What is called "Hawaiian music" on the U.S. Mainland pays homage to musical instruments and a musical genre invented in the Islands. But there are many more forms that often fuse in unusual ways. Island music demonstrates, perhaps more than any other medium, how much joy the people of Hawai'i experience by learning from other cultures. The inclusivity of Island culture is perhaps best demonstrated through diverse musical habits learned from childhood in a land where half the births are from fathers and mothers of differing ethnic backgrounds.

The mutual admiration society of Hawai'i took awhile to spill over into politics. The struggle to overcome White-imposed racism was strengthened by trade union organizers who formed America's first multiethnic unions. In 1974, a Japanese American became governor, doubtless serving as Obama's political role model. Soon the politics of Hawai'i began a post-racial transformation, as after Governor George Ariyoshi came Native Hawaiian John Waihe'e, followed by Filipino Ben Cayetano and two Caucasian governors in recent years. Although ethnic bloc voting existed during the era of White racist rule, and persisted to some extent after statehood, in recent years what has become obvious is that winners in elections are increasingly those who embody the multicultural ethos of Hawai'i. Newcomers have little appeal because they just do not seem to belong.

Once in power, the non-White majority was challenged to remove the residue of institutional racism. Civil rights complaints on behalf of Filipinos, filed while Barry Obama was in his late teens, played a role in opening the doors for the last of the ethnic groups to leave the plantations. And the end of racist rule has meant that there is no evidence of ethnic profiling or discrimination by police or the courts nowadays. Social mobility in Hawai'i, as everywhere, lags behind the dismantling of institutional racism.

The general recognition of the tragic loss of sovereignty by the Native Hawaiian people has led to important innovations, including the re-establishment of the Native Hawaiian language in education as well as study centers at the University of Hawai'i and elsewhere. Barry Obama saw the beginning of what is called the "Hawaiian Renaissance," a movement that is similar to his effort to mobilize support at the grass roots during his 2008 election campaign.

Conclusion

The book *Barack Obama, The Aloha Zen President* concludes that there is an apparent contradiction to Obama's politics. On the one hand, he stands for humanistic ideals. On the other hand, he tries to be inclusive by bringing together those with differing perspectives to find "common ground." That's how life proceeds and politics works in the Aloha State, where mutual respect is a crucial norm, and incremental progress is achieved through consensus building without haste.

But on the U.S. Mainland, politics commonly operates by cutting deals that betray high principles. New policies evoke strong opposition from a variety of interests who refuse to give up their power, their profits, and their prejudices.

Obama's number one priority has been to change the culture in Washington. Yet one man cannot change the culture of a nation. To get Congress to pass his priorities more quickly, he would have to employ hardball politics. But for Obama, culture trumps politics. He would rather be true to his core values than to achieve his campaign promises disrespectfully. His basic belief is that social problems are best solved by people cooperating together—through compromise. For Obama, the role of government is to help people regain community. He says that he wants America to be united, seeking democracy, justice, progress, and prosperity.

The apparent contrast between his campaign success and later performance as president has puzzled and surprised many observers. Washington was not ready for a transformative president. Obama promised to replace the old politics of division with a new spirit of bipartisanship. Before his election, he had not been in Washington long enough to cultivate close friendships in the capitol. Elected without needing support from entrenched power centers, he has disappointed his supporters by not finding a way to overcome hyperpartisanship linked to vested interests.

President Obama continues to operate as a son of the Fiftieth State, following multicultural principles, however alien they are to Washington politics. He will continue as a self-styled "extreme pragmatist." Yet there is a tension between his Japanese-inspired confident diffidence and his practice of Hawaiian Aloha. As president, Obama has demonstrated much more of the former than the latter.

The purpose of the present book, accordingly, is to show how Obama's acceptance of Hawai'i's multicultural ethos has been applied in his presidency and the political context in Washington. My task begins with a definition of the multicultural ethos that has guided Barack Obama as president, especially why he refuses to get into the gutter with those who attack him (Chapter 2). I then explain how the election of a Black president signals the rise of a new current in the American electorate (Chapter 3). Ideologies of his major opponents are identified next (Chapters 4-7), thereby sharpening the contrast with Obama's centrist political philosophy. I then reveal why Democrats lost in 2010 but Obama may win in 2012 (Chapter 8). I follow by discussing specific policies—economics, health care, and foreign policy (Chapter 9-14). The final chapter identifies wherein President Obama has achieved successes but has been blocked from fulfillment of many 2008 campaign promises.

The first two appendices sharpen distinctions made in previous chapters. The third appendix reviews biographies of Barack Obama so that the reader will become familiar with why he has been misinterpreted by many writers. The bibliographic essay, which follows the appendices, will enable readers to locate references for more detailed study of various themes developed in the book.

Overall, the present volume is essential for understanding Barack Obama, the forty-fourth president of the United States. Along the way, the book reveals what most observers have missed—how his Aloha Zen talents might transform Washington and even America if anyone cared to pay attention to them. Accordingly, the next chapter identifies his basic values—his ethics.

Chapter 2
Obama's Ethics

As a candidate, Barack Obama charmed voters. As president, he has appeared to be an entirely different person, not what New York and Washington pundits expected. Yet he is the same person, so what accounts for the difference in perceptions?

The answer, as explained in detail below, is that Obama is a true son of the Fiftieth State, where a multicultural ethos prevails that is entirely different from the standards condoned in Washington—so different that he often seems inexplicable to his critics on the Mainland. That's the source of his charm.

Hawai'i's multicultural ethos is an amalgam of three cultures—Christian, Native Hawaiian, and Japanese. The Aloha Spirit of the indigenous people of Hawai'i has merged with the Bushido Code of the traditional Japanese to the extent that they are consistent with the social gospel of Christianity. Before identifying principles of that ethos, what is important to know is how they developed over time, particularly while Obama lived in Honolulu.

Development of the Multicultural Ethos
Native Hawaiian culture developed for a thousand years before the arrival of Captain James Cook in 1778, followed by European commercial vessels and, during the 1820s, by missionary settlers from New England. Visitors and settlers alike initially assimilated to Hawaiian culture, including its language, while Native Hawaiians adopted progressive practices but not the mindsets of the foreigners. They continued to practice what we now call the Aloha Spirit, and became influenced by compassionate elements of Christianity.

When the Islands were unified under the rule of Kamehameha the Great in 1795, all land was held in common by the monarchy. Karl Marx, who heard anthropological accounts about Hawai'i, considered the Islands as the paradigm case for what he called "primitive communism."

Up to the middle of the nineteenth century, Native Hawaiians practiced communal agriculture. There was no private property. Instead, the local chieftains allowed families to live and work on the land productively, sharing food together with their neighbors, whether derived from agriculture, animal husbandry, or fishing.

Private property was established in 1848 on the advice of White advisers to the king so that there would be collateral (land) for Mainland banks to loan to companies seeking to develop sugarcane plantations. The communal culture persisted thereafter, even though its economic basis did not. Agricultural laborers were imported but isolated from the cultural mainstream on plantations that were remote from the towns. Most workers came from Japan. Prevented from learning English, they lived apart from their Caucasian bosses. Accordingly, they brought and maintained their own traditional culture, including the Bushido Code of the samurai warrior.

The White commercial establishment had close ties with American businesses and politicians. They tried to impose Mainland culture after 1893, when they organized the coup that toppled the Hawaiian monarchy. Then in 1898, they persuaded Washington to annex the Islands without a plebiscite.

During the period of the Territory of Hawai'i (1900-1959), when the President of the United States appointed the governor, Mainland-oriented Americans enforced racist practices in government and on the agricultural plantations. Whites subordinated non-Whites economically and politically. Because Japanese and Native Hawaiians resented subordination, they resisted monoculturalization but accepted the legal framework of American capitalism and democracy while accepting Christian values similar to their own.

During the first half of the twentieth century, Japanese and Native Hawaiians adopted different political responses to White rule. The indigenous population, unhappy about the loss of sovereignty, relied on special treatment by White governors of the Territory of Hawai'i, who were mostly appointed by Republican presidents.

Japanese on the plantations, however, sought to better conditions of work through strikes. During World War II, they were recruited into the Democratic Party by trade union lead-

14

ers. As a result, Native Hawaiians and Japanese became political rivals.

In 1952, American law first allowed those born in Japan to become citizens. Two years later, Japanese Democratic candidates were elected to the Territorial legislature in a landslide. They have largely controlled Island politics ever since, at first to the chagrin of Native Hawaiians. Japanese brought their traditional culture into the center of political power, where they expected that their norms of behavior would be respected.

After statehood in 1959, however, increasing numbers of Mainland Caucasians and immigrant Filipinos have diluted the numerical preponderance of Japanese Americans. The result in the 1970s, while Barry Obama was growing up, was a culture clash between Caucasians, Filipinos, Japanese, and Native Hawaiians that erupted into the political arena.

One element in the culture clash was an assertion of the special culture and political plight of the indigenous people of the Islands known as the "Hawaiian Renaissance." The values stressed are often known as the Aloha Spirit.

Mary Kawena Pukui's definition of "Aloha" became so well respected that in 1986 the Hawai'i State Legislature adopted her formulation as the Aloha Spirit Law. The statute encourages courts and the highest elected and appointed officers of the state to give due consideration to that spirit in making decisions.

Mary Pukui identified her concept of Aloha in five Hawaiian words—*akahai, lōkahi, 'olu'olu, ha'aha'a,* and *ahonui.* Her English equivalents of the five terms are kindness expressed as tenderness, unity expressed as harmony, agreeableness expressed as pleasantness, humility expressed as modesty, and patience expressed as perseverance. The virtues have some similarity to traits to which young Barack was exposed while living in Indonesia, especially humility and patience. Native Hawaiians originally came from Indonesia, though that was millennia ago.

While living in Hawai'i for 35 years, however, I experienced a more complex cultural environment than Mary Pukui's idea of Aloha. Because I lived in Honolulu and worked at the Mānoa campus of the University of Hawai'i, I

15

encountered more Japanese than Native Hawaiians over the years. To adjust, as I made friends with non-Whites and Caucasians who had already assimilated to the culture of the Islands, I engaged in very enjoyable intercultural learning.

What I discovered was that after statehood, and particularly during the era of Governor George Ariyoshi (1974-1986), local-born Japanese talked about Hawai'i as a "special place" that should avoid becoming like the Mainland. Japanese Americans repeatedly insisted that others should respect their "cultural heritage," referring to Japanese values but not contesting the concept of Aloha.

Many Japanese Americans began to rally behind the view that they were "locals," that is, that they had much in common with Native Hawaiians and other non-Whites. They perceived that the recent surge of Whites from the Mainland after statehood was a threat because they had not yet assimilated to values widely shared by the non-White population.

For Japanese, the most highly valued principles of the Bushido Code are benevolence, courage, honesty, honor, loyalty, rectitude, and respect. What happened after statehood was that Japanese values gradually merged with Native Hawaiian values to form what I characterize as principles of "Hawai'i's multicultural ethos." The principles are enumerated and explained below.

While young Barry Obama grew up, the set of principles known as the Aloha Spirit expanded into a multicultural ethos of twelve principles that eventually brought about a peaceful modus vivendi in which members of all cultures now learn from and respect one another, including their political differences.

Today, Barack Obama personifies that multicultural ethos. Meanwhile, the remaining forty-nine states, beset by culture wars from the 1960s, have yet to develop much beyond a monocultural bias in which the norm is to assimilate to a Mainland culture that has becoming increasingly crass. Obama's primary reason for running was to change the way Americans are perceived and perceive themselves.

Hawai'i's Multicultural Ethos

Mary Pukui's concept of Aloha consists of five pillars. Combined with Japanese values, I have identified twelve principles:

1. **Seductive friendliness**. Most visitors to Honolulu are intoxicated by the Aloha they encounter, since almost everyone smiles when they talk. As Hawai'i's current governor Neil Abercrombie puts it, Obama's mannerisms and voice have been described as "loose and inviting" and "mesmerizing." According to the president, "No place else . . . could have provided me with the environment, the climate, in which I could not only grow but also get a sense of being loved." Aloha is something very deep inside Islanders. Although he is often accused of being impersonal, Obama truly wants to befriend Republicans and others who oppose his policies.

2. **Inclusiveness**. Whereas Mainlanders still practice social segregation, in Hawai'i everyone is invited and welcome. No group is left out. Although various ethnic groups have their own societies to organize cultural events in the Islands, they are open to everyone. Those of mixed-race ancestry go to events of their own cultural groups as well as those of their mixed-race friends. For Obama, "the multicultural nature of Hawai'i helped teach me how to appreciate different cultures and navigate different cultures, out of necessity." For Kathleen Hall Jamieson of the University of Pennsylvania, "If you really want to understand who Barack Obama is, you have to understand the culture of inclusivity. You need to go to Hawai'i." The president, according to those in the White House, has delayed decisions until he could find consensus. With respect to Congress, he would have been happier if Democrats welcomed Republican input in crafting reforms during the first three years of his presidency. Support for reforms can unravel when Congressional party control shifts, so Obama has played an important role by seeking and achieving compromises.

3. **Charismatic humility**. In dealing with others, attitudes of arrogance, pretentiousness, and superiority, which set up hierarchies between people, are disapproved in Hawai'i. Island unpretentiousness is truly awe-inspiring. On the night of his election, he was so humbled that he cancelled fireworks

17

and refused his wife's invitation for a "high-five." Obama, the self-styled "unlikely" president, repeatedly admits his mistakes as endemic to being human, believing that "It is hard to find your individual potential or sense of self-worth unless you are also concerned about the collective potential and self-worth of others." His interest in right-wing views is genuine, and he brushes off undeserved attacks with simple facts. In contrast, Mainlanders often exhibit arrogance and thereby burn their bridges.

4. **Joviality**. For some, President Obama is too prone to amusement; others wonder why he does not laugh at himself. Yet his tendency to smile when asked nasty questions during interviews demonstrates that he takes mischaracterizations lightly. Self-deprecating Island humor is hard to describe to Mainlanders, as everyone is gently ribbed for their flaws and thereby learns to laugh at the human condition. In comparison, Mainlanders are much too serious, unable to laugh at their own foibles when identified by others.

5. **Respectfulness**. One of the worst things one can do in Hawai'i, particularly among Japanese, is to show disrespect. Nobody is supposed to openly contradict anyone else. Cultural perspectives are so diverse among ethnic groups in Hawai'i that everyone is likely to have profound if unexpected insight. As Obama puts it, "People in Hawai'i generally don't spend a lot of time, you now, yelling and screaming at each other. I think that there is just a cultural bias toward courtesy and trying to work through problems in a way that makes everybody feel like they're being listened to. And I think that reflects itself in my personality as well as my political style." Bill O'Reilly, though a critic of Obama's policies, has praised him for being respectful. Republicans who treat Obama with respect will go farther toward solving problems than those who cling to catchwords and phrases. But many Mainlanders are prone to criticize disrespectfully and want Obama to lash out at critics.

6. **Nonconfrontationalism**. Conflicts in Hawai'i are rarely expressed openly. Native Hawaiian culture stresses the need for those with major differences to calm down and engage in "talk story," that is, quiet dialog involving neutral intermediaries. In domestic affairs, Democratic pundits wonder

18

why Obama will not "fight" for his principles when they are attacked, wanting him to act as if he were born on the Mainland. Instead, Obama's reluctance to do battle is because he fundamentally refuses to get in the mud, preferring conversation. As he puts it, "We must talk and reach for common understandings precisely because all of us are imperfect and can never act with the certainty that God is on our side." Ill-mannered confrontational political rallies, which began on the Mainland in the turbulent 1960s, have never been accepted in Hawai'i. In international affairs, however, he has been confrontational as a last resort, a point dealt with in the last point (enforcement) below.

7. **Communitarianism**. Caring for others and generosity without expectation of reciprocity are valued interpersonal norms that operate beyond one's family and ethnic group in Hawai'i. The Aloha State has transcended the racist caste system that operated on the plantations by accepting the wisdom that most solutions to public problems can be effected in the private sector—that is, outside government—by building community between diverse interests. Reflecting on the culture of Hawai'i, President Obama has said, "We have a sense that beneath the surface of things, all of us share a common set of hopes, a common set of dreams and a common set of values. That's what the Islands have always been about." Republicans who look carefully at Obama's policies will see that he has advocated solutions that involve a minimal governmental framework to facilitate problem solving in society at large. Chrysler and General Motors, for example, were not "bailed out" until they first came up with plans to self-restructure. Many other examples underscore his unwillingness to subscribe to rigid ideologies of the right and left. As noted by Obama, Mainlanders often believe in rugged individualism, valuing those who are stubbornly independent. But he sees his role as trying to build a sense of community amid a broken political culture.

8. **Harmony**. Particularly among Japanese, Islanders tend to avoid negative news, people, and situations, that is, to avoid bad karma. According to Barack Obama, "Hawai'i is a fabulous model for the kind of America I hope this campaign will bring about, a place where different cultures can come

together in harmony, and a place that rises above the barriers that divide us." His propensity to compromise comes from his Island roots. Sometimes meetings in the White House involve heated discussions, with some persons left demoralized. In such cases, President Obama will talk to disconsolate advisers afterward in order to calm them down so that they can proceed constructively ahead, thereby removing a burden from their shoulders. Mainlanders, in contrast, are far too negative.

9. **Serenity**. For Mainland observers, Obama's most puzzling characteristic is his calm, unflappable demeanor and unexcitable steadiness. Quick movements in a hot climate result in excessive perspiration, so Islanders are accustomed to move slowly, even gracefully, and taking others into consideration along the way. The quiet solitude present in Japanese restaurants carries over to signs in gym saunas and on public busses that warn not to make loud or unnecessary noise. Without meditation and "downtime," according to Obama, "you start making mistakes or you lose the big picture." Despite setbacks and disappointments, Obama characterizes himself as "serene." Although displeased by unfair attacks, he will never lose the zen personality that he acquired while living in Honolulu. For Mainlanders, conflict is seen as normal, so they are often quite irritable, hoping to use anger as a control mechanism for keeping others in bounds—but that never works in Hawai'i.

10. **Piety**. Many people in Hawai'i are intensely spiritual without being religious; they live their beliefs without pontification. Native Hawaiians have a spiritual connection with the air, land, ocean, and other people; they believe in a divine power that provides life-sustaining energy, and they employ special ceremonies to bless a variety of undertakings. Japanese stress the values of honor, loyalty, and rectitude. Barack Obama's anthropologist mom, Stanley Ann Dunham, exposed him to truths behind many different religions, and he was friendly with Buddhists in Honolulu. He embraces the social gospel of Black churches, which stress the Second Commandment. From the Vermont Avenue Baptist Church in Washington, D.C., he confided in January 2010, "It's faith that keeps me calm. It's faith that gives me peace." That's why he sees common values with the more religious members

of the Republican Party. But Mainlanders tend to be irreverent or cast aspersions on religious views of others.

11. **Humanism**. In Hawai'i, people come before principles. Universalistic approaches that ignore individual cases enjoy little favor. Both Native Hawaiians and Japanese value benevolence and measure others by that standard. Dogma is eschewed. Zero-sum decisions are avoided because one size will not fit all in a diverse society. For that reason, Obama says that he is an "extreme pragmatist." His view of the bank bailouts, as approved after he became president, was stated in the following terms: "It's not about helping banks—it's about helping people." Obama's measure of successful public policy is how people benefit. That's why he broke tradition by visiting coffins of Americans slain in Afghanistan before he reoriented the war policy. Mainlanders are often so dogmatic that they cannot agree on how to solve problems together.

12. **Enforcement**. Any culture must have boundary maintenance—ways to prevent the erosion of basic values by enforcing conformity. Those living in Hawai'i take great pride in the uniqueness of their own ethnic cultures as well as the ethos that binds everyone together. There is a general recognition that Hawai'i must be preserved against inroads from the chaotic Mainland, though those in the Aloha State highly respect the better traits of Mainlanders, which Obama identified in his Inaugural Address as "personal responsibility, optimism and faith . . . [and] honesty and hard work, courage and fair play, tolerance and curiosity, loyalty and patriotism."

The principal way to enforce Island culture is ostracism, an effective technique on small islands. Those who move to Hawai'i but resist assimilation to the multicultural ethos generally leave within a few years, mostly because they make few friends at work or near home. Similarly, Obama parted company with Reverend Jeremiah Wright because he was "divisive." Islanders often stick to their closest friends and avoid difficult people, a practice that President Obama has increasingly exhibited to the surprise of those who expected him to be more gregarious. As a result, he has been unable to assert leadership when his influence could have mobilized support.

If ostracism does not work in Hawai'i, vigorous resistance will. Serious infractions of the ethos activate stronger responses, often courageous actions, as when Native Hawaiians sailed to Kaho'olawe Island in 1976 to protest the U.S. military's use of ancestral lands for target practice.

A samurai instinct emerges when fundamental values are threatened. In zen culture, the samurai is brave, generous, upright, faithful, manly, self-respecting, self-confident, and willing to engage in self-sacrifice. Through massive mobilizations in the form of demonstrations and strikes, union members and their supporters in the Islands restrained management in the years immediately after World War II for violating multicultural principles.

Obama, who learned how to box as a boy in Indonesia, is no pacifist. His pursuit of Al-Qaeda has meant increased troops in Afghanistan, drone attacks inside Pakistan and elsewhere, and a ninja-type sneak attack on Osama Bin Laden.

He has threatened vetoes over restrictions on his ability to close Guantánamo and any deficit reduction plan that fails to increase taxes on the rich. There are boundaries to his willingness to compromise, but none have yet been exercised.

Nevertheless, as Obama has noted, the culture of Hawai'i is more forgiving of cultural clumsiness. After all, nobody in the Aloha State is truly expert at intercultural learning. There is always something new to learn, so what counts is to demonstrate an openness and a sensitivity to do so.

Disseminating the Multicultural Ethos
Barack Obama practices the principles of Hawai'i's multicultural ethos. The most memorable opportunity to spread Aloha occurred on March 18, 2008, during the presidential campaign leading up to his election, when he was pressed to dissociate himself from Jeremiah Wright, the pastor of his church who was quoted as saying "Damn America!" Obama's speech in Philadelphia made the point that Blacks and Whites see racial problems from different perspectives. The genius of his remarks was to demonstrate that racial problems could be solved if everyone had compassion for those unlike themselves.

A second opportunity arose unexpectedly in Tucson during January 2011. A gunman opened fire on January 8 outside a supermarket, killing and wounding several bystanders, including Congressional Representative Gabrielle Giffords. Immediately afterwards, left-wing pundits outraged conservatives by charging that the uncivil posturing by the Tea Party during 2009 and 2010 bore responsibility for the gunman's resort to arms. On January 12, when Barack Obama spoke at the memorial service in Tucson, he firmly declared that conservatives were not responsible in any way. He also displayed his Aloha by making extensive comments about the victims, exhorting all Americans to bring about a better cultural milieu.

Republicans, in response, agreed to sit alongside Democrats in Congress during the president's address on January 25 as a sign that they were eager to go beyond divisive, intemperate rhetoric. But divisive issues arose, as ever, in the new Congress. The effort at civility continued under the surface during 2011. Republicans who had been obstinate in negotiations over the debt limit began to chime that they sought "common ground" with the president. According to Kathleen Hall Jamieson, very few insults were heard in Congress throughout the rest of 2011.

President Barack Obama has been recognized as a masterful public speaker. Whereas his predecessor often governed by sound bite, Obama's speeches are carefully crafted and persuasively argued, often serving to close debate by stating policies thoroughly and definitively. What shines through his words are his ethical principles, which were formed as he grew up. According to his autobiography, his birth relatives shaped his personal values during his earliest years. But his social outlooks were acquired from friends and peers while a teenager in Honolulu.

As president, Obama has found few "teachable" opportunities to spread Aloha while focused on big problems. His outreach to the Republicans and to other countries has involved spreading Aloha by example, as demonstrated in later chapters of this book. After an administration that accentuated fear of terrorism, voters in 2008 primarily welcomed Barack Obama as a messenger of hope.

23

Some (but certainly not all) New York pundits who judge Barack Obama have a particular problem in reacting to his behavior. They tend to believe that New York has the ideal culture and that all other cultures are imperfect copies of New York culture. If his actions and temperament differ from what they expect, they view him as somehow deficient, a point to be further developed in discussing how he is critiqued by Progressive Democrats in Chapter 6. Although Obama spent almost as much time in New York as in Indonesia, and one of his biographers even suggests that his experience in Manhattan was formative, he is obviously not a New Yorker.

Most Americans do not realize that Barack Obama's personality and values were shaped by a profound cultural experience available only in Hawai'i. Since his inauguration, Americans have perhaps become more accustomed to the Aloha Zen President as a role model for ethical integrity. Although he remains personally popular, he has been frustrated amid the bad karma of Washington.

When a new president represents a new slice of America on the political stage, there is bound to be some confusion about him. The history of the United States reveals that the country has accepted new personalities from different backgrounds in stride. Political succession, as described in the next chapter, is nothing new in diverse America.

Chapter 3
Political Succession in 2008

The election of Barack Obama provoked speculation that the United States had entered into a new era of post-racial politics. But there is a long history in American politics for members of a once-powerful political majority to espouse rage rather than reason as a new group comes into office. As an astute observer of the political landscape, President Obama surely knows that some of his hysterical opponents are undergoing cognitive dissonance, that is, exhibiting strange ways to adjust to the new reality of a shift in the locus of political power to an African American president.

In the past, political succession in Washington occurred whenever one generation or one political party replaced another in a position of political power. Obama's election marks both the arrival of a younger generation in the center of power and the succession of forty-three White presidents by the first minority, a mixed-race African American. As the percentage of non-Whites increases to a majority in population by the mid-21st century, a succession to an Hispanic president may become inevitable.

Today, the hysteria about Obama is particularly fierce among those who have grown up in the belief that Blacks are inferior to Whites. The rage is strongest among those who fear that something sinister will happen, since a Black person might retaliate against centuries of oppression by Caucasians. However, the history of political succession in the United States demonstrates that such discontent eventually subsides. Cooler heads prevail, as democratic principles are cherished.

Previous Political Successions
Some major political successions of the past provoked even more political extremes. The debate over the adoption of the American constitution was so heated that on July 4, 1788, civil war nearly broke out when 1,000 Antifederalists marched into Providence, Rhode Island. Similar demonstra-

tions were held in Albany, New York, and Philadelphia, Pennsylvania.

Later, when the Federalists held office, Antifederalists continued harassment. Because the two factions sympathized with opposite sides in the French Revolution, the Federalist Congress and President John Adams sought to terrify their political opponents by the Sedition Act of 1798, which made criticism of the president a federal crime. Their excesses spelled defeat in the election of 1800.

In 1804, with Federalists out of office, their leader Alexander Hamilton was shot dead in a duel by Antifederalist Thomas Jefferson's Vice President, Aaron Burr, a conflict piqued by verbal slurs. Hamilton had dueled many times before to protect his honor. The Federalists finally disbanded in 1814, after defeats in the intervening years and the unity that emerged after the War of 1812.

By 1817, the new majority party, the Democratic-Republicans, enjoyed what historians have called "the era of good feelings." Until 1824, the dominant political party was united if factionalized and had no competitor.

In the 1824 election, the Democratic-Republicans split into four factions, none receiving a majority in the electoral college. The task of selecting a president was then constitutionally assigned to the House of Representatives. The division ended when the faction of Henry Clay swung its votes to John Quincy Adams, who in turn named Clay as his Secretary of State.

Andrew Jackson, who was furious over the deal, won in 1828 on behalf of the Democratic Party. He celebrated his victory as class succession. A Kentuckian from the "frontier," he characterized his defeat of Adams as a victory over Eastern aristocrats. He promptly fired college-educated bureaucrats, replacing them with his campaign supporters on the basis of the principle "To the victor belong the spoils."

The next major succession took place in 1860, when the candidate of the Republican Party defeated the Democrats. Even before Abraham Lincoln took office, southern states were seceding, and the Civil War soon began. After the war, the rallying cry "The South shall rise again!" first came to fruition with Lincoln's assassination.

Although the Republican Party was dominant for the next seventy-two years, Democrat Grover Cleveland was elected twice (in 1884 and 1892) in nasty campaigns. One opponent attacked him for fathering a child out of wedlock, which Cleveland then admitted.

Woodrow Wilson, who became president in 1912 due to a split among Republicans, provoked such ire that Republican Senators nixed his idea of American world leadership in the League of Nations by refusing to ratify the Treaty of Versailles at the end of World War I. Republicans then reclaimed the presidency in 1920, 1924, and 1928.

Franklin Roosevelt put the Republicans out to political pasture in 1932. Some of his opponents soon branded him a "dictator" and a "socialist." Intemperate protests and rhetoric continued through his early presidency, when perhaps politically there was "nothing to fear but fear itself." But voters repeatedly knew who best spoke for their interests in three subsequent re-elections.

The succession to Republican Dwight Eisenhower, the first with ancestry outside Britain and Holland, was relatively smooth in 1952. Democrats had also been courting him.

John Kennedy's election in 1960 involved two forms of succession. He was the first Catholic. And he made clear that he represented a new generation, born in the twentieth century. The Irish had taken over Boston back in 1885, though Catholic Alfred E. Smith had been defeated for president in 1928. Anti-Catholic slurs dogged Smith but faded after Kennedy was elected.

The next major political successions took place at local levels. African Americans were elected mayors of major American cities, beginning in Cleveland, where Carl Stokes was elected in 1967. In response, some Whites moved to the suburbs, but their earlier departure from big cities had ensured the victory of Stokes and many other Black can-didates for mayor. Whites who stayed in the cities learned that nothing much changed for the worse, as some had feared.

As Obama doubtless recalls, the first non-White governor of any state, George Ariyoshi, came to power in Hawai'i quietly during 1974. He completed a social revolution by displacing a succession of White governors. Twenty years earlier, the rising tide of Japanese American Democrats had to overcome desperate White Republican efforts to brand them as Communist fellow travelers, even having the House Un-American Activities Committee investigate Democrats as traitors. At one point, future Senator Daniel Inouye said, in response to incessant attacks, that he lost one arm fighting the Nazis and he would gladly lose the other arm to fight the Communists.

After Ariyoshi, governors of Native Hawaiian and Filipino ancestry were elected, and chances for Whites were considered passé until a Caucasian governor, Jewish Republican Linda Lingle, was elected in 2002. By then the old battles had been forgotten by a new generation of issue-oriented voters, who in 2010 elected bearded Democrat Neil Abercrombie, despite memories of his onetime hippie flirtations, against a Samoan in the primary and a Native Hawaiian in the general election that year. Signs of a post-racial politics are obvious in Hawai'i today.

By the 2008 election, Blacks had been elected as U.S. Senator and governor of Massachusetts (Edward Brooke, 1967-1979; Deval Patrick, 2007-), a Chinese had been elected governor of Washington (Gary Locke, 1997-2005), a Mexican as governor of New Mexico (Bill Richardson, 2002-2008), and an East Indian governor of Louisiana (Bobby Jindal, 2008-). Of course, Charles Curtis, a Native American, had been Herbert Hoover's Vice President (1929-1933). Today, ethnic and religious barriers to political power seem of the distant past at federal and state levels.

Although gays have not arisen as mayors of any big city, one was elected in Palm Springs during 2008. That succession occurred almost two decades after heated anti-gay rhetoric by Florida's Anita Bryant in the 1970s provoked a gay backlash that involved political mobilization of gays and lesbians. The election in San Francisco of openly gay Harvey Milk to San Francisco's Board of Supervisor in 1977 was the first breakthrough for gays. His tragic assassination in 1978 may have been a more personal decision by an unbalanced politician but occurred in the midst of the rhetorical turmoil of the era.

Women have also undergone succession, though with little backlash. In 1916, Jeannette Rankin was the first female to be elected to Congress. The first female governor, Nellie Tayloe Ross, was elected in Wyoming during 1924. The first female candidate for Vice President of a major political party, Geraldine Feraro, ran in 1984.

Nancy Pelosi broke through a glass ceiling after her elevation at the first female Speaker of the House of Representatives in 2007. Subsequently, she has been pilloried as a "San Francisco Democrat," an anti-gay Republican epithet of opprobrium yet stated in code rather than blatantly.

Hillary Clinton, who came close to being nominated as the Democratic standard bearer for president in 2008, was edged out by African American Barack Obama. Political succession seemed inevitable in 2008, as Republicans settled on nominee John McCain, who was so clearly unpopular with the conservative base of his party that many stayed home on election day after he selected Sarah Palin as his running mate.

During the 1980s and 1990s the rising numbers of Mexicans in California, mostly American-born and legal immigrants, spurred Republican leaders to espouse anti-immigrant ballot proposals that were seen by Latinos as offensive. Inevitable payback resulted at the polls, as family-value-oriented Mexicans have overwhelmingly voted for the Democratic Party ever since. The Republicans' best chance to regain power came in 2003, when an immigrant celebrity with a distinctive accent, Arnold Schwartzenegger, was elected governor.

Although Antonio Villaraigosa lost in the Los Angeles mayoralty election of 2001, he won in a close election in 2005, and was reelected mayor without serious opposition in 2009. By then, the die had been cast that Mexican Americans had become a power to be reckoned with in local, state, and even national elections. Opposition to the increasing voting strength of Mexicans, which has provoked restrictive legislation in Arizona and elsewhere, is destined to be vanquished whenever their demographic rise reaches a critical mass, as in California and New Mexico. Fearing that the Mexican vote will inevitably become a majority in some states, some politicians have even called for a revision of the Fourteenth

Amendment so that Mexican children born in the United States of undocumented aliens will not become automatic American citizens and head for the ballot box at age 18.

Backlash to Obama

Barack Obama should not be surprised by the nonsense articulated by extreme opponents. He is accused of hating Whites and of advocating socialist or Nazi-type reforms. Some have wanted to determine where exactly he was born and even whether he is circumcised.

As *The Daily Show* humorist Larry Wilmore once reflected, some Whites fear that they are losing their country. Wilmore's advice: "Well, the first step is to acknowledge that they are literally losing their country." Demographically, that is.

For some, Obama's election may signify a final end to the Civil War, but a few renegade sympathizers with the Confederacy and other fringe elements are still fighting to keep alive an American tradition of mindless protest, questioning his right to be president and suggesting impeachment.

According to various sources, Obama's election is associated with an increase in anti-Black Internet traffic and a rise in hate groups, including at least fifty new militia training groups and several "citizen's courts." "Grand juries" have even issued indictments against President Obama for treason. "Sovereign citizens" have arisen, claiming that Whites have more rights than non-Whites.

Yet Obama's perspective is that race relations is "a subset of a larger problem in our society, which is we have a diverse, complicated society where people have a lot of different viewpoints." Polls on race relations conducted at the end of President Obama's first hundred days in office found that two-thirds of Americans characterized race relations as "good." Twice as many Blacks thought so compared to their view in July 2008.

By November 2009, with health care legislation languishing in Congress, 53 percent (65 percent among Blacks) still decried ethnic and racial divisions in the country. Some 83 percent of Democrats praised Obama for uniting the country. In contrast, 77 percent of Republicans said the opposite while some of their leaders were sewing distrust and fear. Obama's approval rating among Whites then was 39 percent, though 90 percent among Blacks. Poll results, in other words, lack sufficient stability to permit definitive inferences about race relations in America. President Obama's view is that policy differences account for dissatisfaction with his job performance, not race. The popularity of Herman Cain among Republicans in 2011 trumped the race card.

Whereas ultra-conservative racists are unhappy with a Black man as president, coherent disagreements also have been expressed by African Americans interviewed on Tavis Smiley's television program. Blacks have complained that Obama does not pay attention to the unique problems of African Americans. Yet a fellow Black, Attorney General Eric Holder, has breathed life into the Civil Rights Division of the Department of Justice. Unquestionably, pandering to one's own ethnic group after a political succession would serve as a serious provocation to extremists and might imperil further success by non-Whites in the political system.

Conclusion

Barack Obama never campaigned as a Black candidate for president. The media pinned that label on him, though he identified himself to be the son of a White woman from Kansas and a Black man from Kenya. He declared himself as an African American on the 2010 census, but in actuality he is the nation's first multiethnic or multiracial president. The first time he stressed his European roots was on May 23, 2011, when he visited Moneygall, Ireland, an ancestral hometown. Genealogists identify his non-Kenyan background as Cherokee, Dutch, English, French, German, Irish, and Welsh. He is more Black than White.

Meanwhile, Obama focuses on fulfilling his campaign promises and engages in compromise to get legislation passed. Rather than an extremist, he proves that the political center, as usual, wins out in the end.

And during the run-up to the 2012 election, two Mormon candidates are running for the Republican nomination (John Huntsman and Mitt Romney). Their religion has mentioned infrequently in public discussions.

Yet even those who vilify President Obama at Tea Party rallies avoid attacking him on the basis of race, instead using indirect epithets. That very reluctance gives the clearest evidence of the rise of post-racial politics in the United States, which began many years before in the Aloha State.

Nevertheless, racial prejudice is still a cloud that hangs over many aspects of everyday life in the United States. "Only in America," a song played after his acceptance speech at the Democratic National Convention on August 29, 2008, sums up the breakthrough that Barack Obama's election has contributed to American political and social life.

Those who felt most uncomfortable the new president, nevertheless, searched for a can of worms to open. As described in the following chapter, they questioned circumstances of his birth.

Chapter 4
Birtherists

Barack Hussein Obama II was born in Honolulu on August 4, 1961. According to most interpretations of the Fourteenth Amendment to the Constitution of the United States, he is a natural-born American citizen. His mother was an American citizen, but his father had a British passport, as Kenya was then a colony of Britain and not yet an independent country. President Chester Alan Arthur, similarly, was born of an American mother, whereas his father was not an American citizen.

During the election campaign that led to the victory of Barack Obama in 2008, a member of Hillary Clinton's campaign reportedly hinted that Obama may not have been born in the United States. In response, his Certificate of Live Birth was retrieved on June 6, 2007, and the document was posted on the Internet. I reprinted the document just prior to the first page of the text of *Barack Obama, The Aloha Zen President.*

When Republicans considered the possibility of nominating John McCain, they had to grapple with the fact that he was born in Panamá. Similarly, Mexican-born George Romney was once a candidate for president. Because their parents were Americans, that was enough to shrug off most doubt that they were citizens of the United States, though the issue was never resolved with any certainty.

The Goal: Delegitmize Obama

But that was not the end of the matter. After Obama was elected, detractors identified in the press as "birthers" claimed that the Certificate of Live Birth was not independently authenticated and was not the original but instead a document that could have been faked. They could not accept him as an American, despite his Kansas accent, because his father was from Kenya.

Announcements in both Honolulu newspapers corroborated Obama's birth. Various people have confirmed his birth in press accounts. A journalist even went to the Hawai'i

33

Health Department one day to inspect an alphabetized public computer log of birth records. "Barack Hussein Obama II" was listed in the binder for 1960-1964 for anyone to see.

Then Donald Trump began to pontificate sympathy for the "birther" fringe during March 2011, seemingly as an opening salvo in an attempt to run for president in 2012. The more he broadcast his doubts, the higher the skepticism that Barack Obama had no right to be president.

A substantial percentage of Republicans and even a few Democrats continued to remain suspicious until May 2, 2011, when the president had his original birth certificate released to the public. Accordingly to opinion polls, the percentage of "birthers" dropped significantly after the announcement.

The Wrong Document

Yet a birth certificate is a secondary source about birth. Ironically the "birthers" never sought the primary source—the hospital record of Obama's mother for the time when she gave birth.

To outdo the "birthers," I called the hospital where he was born in Honolulu, now called the Kapiʻolani Medical Center for Women & Children, to find out whether a copy of the hospital record was available for inclusion in my book, *Barack Obama, The Aloha Zen President*. The response was that only Barack Obama could arrange its release. When I contacted the White House, I received no response.

The reason why I pursued the hospital record may be of interest. I had been told at an early age that I was adopted. I also was informed of the name of the hospital where I was born. My original birthname, with the same surname as that of my birthmother, was assigned in the hospital. Three months after my birth, a court accepted a petition from my adoptive parents to change my birthname. After the Final Order of Adoption, my current birth certificate was issued with my present first and last names.

Because of privacy issues related to adoption, I could not obtain my original birth certificate until I first learned my birthname. To do so, I first had to learn my birthmother's identity. Her name was available in the court document that changed my name. One day, accompanying my adoptive father in a visit to his safe deposit box, I saw that court document. Almost blind, he was searching for something else, and I found the document serendipitously.

Knowing my birthmother's name and the name of the hospital where I was born, I next asked my personal physician to request a copy of my birthmother's hospital record. As expected, the hospital record had my original birthname. I then asked the state health department where I was born for a copy of my original birth certificate, which I now have—an ugly, dark print from microfilm.

A Re-Birth

In other words, the "birthers" were fools. They wanted to cause suspicion yet lacked a scholar's penchant for original sources. They were looking for the wrong document all along. Their naïveté exposed their mischief. Their caper with Barack Obama stopped, at least for the time, when he posted his original birth certificate on May 2, 2011.

Then in October 2011 they had a re-birth. Showing a common anti-immigrant theme in their efforts, they decided to question two persons who might be chosen as Republican vice presidential candidates—Florida Senator Marco Rubio and Louisiana Governor Piyush "Bobby" Jindal. Why? Because their parents were not citizens of the United States at the time of their birth. Both candidates are therefore dual citizens. One surreal irony is that Jindal has urged passage of a law requiring presidential candidates to make their birth certificates public.

In December the re-birth refocused on Barack Obama. The Georgia Secretary of State received five challenges to having his name on the ballot as a candidate for president. The absurd drama is expected in other states, resulting as usual in rulings dismissing the allegations.

Whereas some Republicans have dismissed the "birthers," others have not. Partly as a result, a fundamental split in the Republican Party has come to light, as the following chapter explains.

Chapter 5
Social Darwinist Republicans

Charles Darwin's theory of natural selection was derived from an observation of finches in the Galápagos Islands and later generalized to all biological species. His principal claim was that species survive by adapting to environmental conditions. Those that fail to adapt successfully die out, a process known as "natural selection." Thus, biological history records the "survival of the fittest."

When Darwin applied his theory to humans, religious authorities resisted the idea that the human race may have developed gradually from nonhuman animals rather than being created by God. But they did not discount the possi-bility that those going to heaven are spiritually the fittest: Jehovah's Witnesses, for example, claim that only 144,000 will be admitted to heaven on Judgment Day.

The term "Social Darwinism" was coined by Thomas Huxley in 1860 in his review of Darwin's published scientific findings. For a Social Darwinist, groups of similar humans, such as ethnic groups, will die and fail to reproduce if they are too weak to survive in a social struggle for existence. Accordingly, the weak should be allowed to die off in order to ensure the survival of a hardier human race, superior to what came before.

There are at least two types of Social Darwinism. The **libertarian** version sees the struggle for existence as best achieved without intervention by government. Classical eco-nomics is an orthodoxy that eschews government regula-tion of the economy, such that the most competitive busines-ses will prevail over the inefficient in a free, self-correcting mar-ketplace; individuals and countries focused on pursuing their economic self-interest will succeed over those who do not. Milton Friedman and Ayn Rand are among the contem-porary exponents of libertarianism, favoring governmental deregula-tion of economic and social life so that self-interest will pre-vail over sentimentality. They oppose government "handouts" for creating "dependency." In many respects they are anarchists and isolationists.

Triumphalist Social Darwinists want government to intervene so that groups with the most power and resources can establish hegemony over others, such as by business subsidies and tax incentives and military adventures abroad. Adolf Hitler had a similar view: He considered Germans as the superior and virtuous race, and he sought to ride rough-shod over other races, particularly the Jews, to establish a "natural" hierarchy of privilege. Colonialism and imperialism are other forms of triumphalism. American neo-conservatives tend to be triumphalists.

During Senate testimony a few weeks before American withdrawal of military forces from Iraq, Defense Secretary Leon Panetta noted that the exit was because Iraq, a sovereign state, demanded the withdrawal date. Triumphalist Republicans, such as John McCain, disagreed strongly with the idea of leaving Iraq without American military protection, as if Washington is where decisions on the fate of other countries must be decided. Ron Paul and the libertarians, however, were opposed to any American role in Iraq in the first place.

Today, the tension between libertarianism and triumphalism is considerable. But both share the goal of enabling the human race to improve by marginalizing the inefficient and inferior. Both use Social Darwinism as a pseudo-scientific cover for elitism.

Social Darwinism in American Politics

Although Republicans began as a party determined to end or limit slavery, by the end of the nineteenth century the party was backed by big business elites. Catering to the needs of successful businesses, they gave short shrift to the poor and working classes. Republican William McKinley, a triumphalist, did not believe in a totally free market. He achieved fame from the McKinley Tariff, which set high tariffs on imported goods to protect American industry from outside competition.

Theodore Roosevelt, who became president in 1901 after McKinley's assassination, was not a Social Darwinist. As president, Roosevelt backed anti-trust legislation to curb excesses of the largest companies, which were trying to establish monopolistic control of the economy by mergers and other means to destroy competition. Although the Re-publican Party preferred William Howard Taft as Roosevelt's successor, Taft vigorously enforced anti-trust legislation.

Democrat Woodrow Wilson was elected in the three-way race of 1912 (including Roosevelt as a third-party candidate) and was reelected in 1916. Although Wilson also supported regulation of the economy, he was a segregationist, a variant of triumphalist Social Darwinism.

During the 1920s, the Republican Party operated as the Social Darwinist party, favoring big business, and won three presidential elections. In 1929, when the Great Depression emerged, libertarian President Herbert Hoover left economic recovery to the workings of the unregulated market. The economy continued to decline, so Hoover was easily defeated in 1932 by Franklin Delano Roosevelt.

Contrary to Social Darwinism, President Roosevelt intervened heavily in the economy to create jobs, protect unions, and to establish Social Security. He adopted the economic philosophy of John Maynard Keynes, who argued that government spending could "prime the pump" to revive the economy. Roosevelt was reelected three times. After his death, Harry Truman became president and continued policies for the "common man." In 1948, Truman was re-elected in a three-way race against candidates of the segregationist Dixie-crat Party and the Republican Party.

Republicans tried to masquerade their business bias in 1952 by picking war hero General Dwight Eisenhower to run for president. Although they opposed the welfare state in Social Darwinist terms as propping up the weakest and therefore most undeserving members of society, Eisenhower was only a triumphalist on the battlefield. He had also been courted by the Democrats. He even chastised the growing power of the "military-industrial complex" when he left office in 1960, having learned the extent to which big businesses believed that they could feed at the public trough by establishing military-related firms in nearly every Con-gressional district to produce goods or services supposedly relevant to national security, thereby ensuring passage of larger and larger defense budgets.

Democrats returned in 1960 with John Kennedy as their standard bearer. After his assassination, Lyndon Johnson became president and was elected in his own right in 1964. As president, he worked for passage of landmark civil rights legislation, Medicare, and tried to end poverty through Great Society programs. To Social Darwinist Republicans, his government "giveaways" to the poor remain an anathema.

Then came Richard Nixon, who as president from 1969-1975 supported legislation for clean air, clean water, and even proposed universal health care. His triumphalist "dirty tricks," used to win re-election in 1972, eventually infuriated even members of his own party. Gerald Ford then served as president after Nixon's resignation in 1974, but he was hamstrung by Democratic majorities in Congress and cast a record number of vetoes. Then non-ideological Ford was defeated by humanistic Democrat Jimmy Carter, who served only one term—from 1977 to 1981.

The Return of Social Darwinism

Republicans have never admitted that Social Darwinism is their philosophy. Ronald Reagan's successful campaign for the presidency in 1980 occurred during a recession. His economic solution was libertarian "supply-side economics," one feature of which was a tax cut for all, including the wealthy. The rich were expected to invest surplus income, producing a trickle-down effect that would result in jobs. The less fortunate would presumably be hired as demand in-creased. Although Reaganomics also sought to deregulate business from government restrictions (since "government was the problem, not the solution"), Reagan insisted on maintaining a social safety net. To boost the economy, Keyne-sian economics was utilized in the form of greatly increased military spending. Reagan's dynamic and warm personality masked the underlying Social Darwinism of his economic and social policies. But he also approved tax increases.

Until recently, Republicans have sought an attractive candidate to mesmerize voters so that their Social Darwinist philosophy would remain undetected. George Herbert Walker

Bush tried to do so by talking about a "kindler, gentler" style of governance. But there was no substance to his catchphrase, and he was defeated in 1992 by Democrat Bill Clinton. Re-elected in 1996, Clinton continued the policy of deregulation after Republicans gained Congressional control in 1994, and he even modified welfare to their liking.

Clinton's successor, George W. Bush, talked about "compassionate conservatism" during the 2000 election campaign but reverted to Social Darwinist trickle-down libertarian economics while asserting triumphalist "shock and awe" aggression abroad.

Those disgusted with Bush elected Barack Obama by a landslide in 2008, particularly after it become clear that reckless deregulation had resulted in an unraveling of the economy—that Bush's Social Darwinist deregulatory politics resulted in economic disaster.

Current Social Darwinism

President Barack Obama favored a Keynesian "stimulus" bill to create jobs in infrastructure projects. He continued bank bailouts and temporarily seized control of Chrysler and General Motors. Despite the intentions of Obama's "stimulus" bill, unemployment remained high because banks, fearing Darwinian insolvency, continued foreclosing homeowners and refused to make loans to homeowners and small businesses. And corporations stingily followed suit.

Republicans then harped on Obama for instituting "job-killing" socialism and dangerously increasing the national debt, though they did not object during the era of Bush's overspending, which ran up the budget deficit to $10 trillion while the rich enjoyed generous tax cuts. And they did not decry Bush's nationalization of Fannie Mae and Freddie Mac, the two major mortgage loan companies.

Similar to Reagan's trickle-down solution for job creation, Republican opponents of Obama insisted on continuing tax cuts for the rich as an antidote to the sluggish economic recovery. But the Reagan era occurred when socialist economies were separate from the capitalist world. In the post-Cold War global economy, many new jobs created by rich American business executives have been located overseas.

41

Universal health care was Obama's number one domestic priority, and Republican opposition was fierce. Thinking in a Social Darwinist mode, one criticism was about a nonexistent proposal for "death panels."

In the 2010 election, Republicans gained control of the House of Representatives. Soon after his election as Speaker of the House of Representatives, John Boehner said,

> For those who can compete and do well, fine. Some Americans can't compete. I think we have a responsibility as a people to help those who can't compete. But do we have a responsibility to help those who won't compete? I would have serious doubts about that.

Boehner, thus, articulated classic Social Darwinism.

True, Boehner has shed tears for the less fortunate, but they are consigned by fellow Social Darwinists to the fate of "natural selection." Survival of the richest has now become the Republican Party's official policy.

The Republican threat to shut down government, thus, is iconic—a symbol of the Darwinian struggle for existence, whereby the rich and powerful bulldoze the less affluent and powerless into submission by threatening to lower their benefits in the name of re-establishing principles of libertarian classical economics. The Republican demand to slash government spending is aimed directly at the elderly, the poor, and even the middle class, whom they consider the least productive members of society.

Among Republican cuts proposed in early 2011 were those to community health centers, fire and police departments, clean water projects, the Army Corps of Engineers, crime victim funds, and recipients of Medicaid, Medicare, and Social Security. Left to a Darwinian fate would be those who would lack health services, firefighting, policing of unsafe communities, uncontaminated water, flood prevention, and restitution on the part of crime victims. And deeper cuts were promised.

Then, during a debate among Republicans vying for the presidential nomination during September 2011, Social Darwinist views toward health care came into plain view when Ron Paul was asked whether he would let an uninsured person die after suddenly falling into a coma. Although some in the Tea Party audience cried out, "Let them die," Paul first blamed the sick person for not taking out health insurance and then suggested that a charity would somehow learn about the case and pick up the tab. Yet neither Paul nor any of the other Republican candidates castigated those in the audience for Paul's offhanded suggestion. And they failed to appreciate that such cases happen frequently, forcing hospitals to absorb costs and raise fees for everyone else.

Fie on Obamacare, according to Social Darwinists, as guaranteed health insurance will enable hypochondriacs and malingerers to stay away from work, pretending they are sick. Unemployment insurance, they have said, lets bad workers enjoy a vacation on everyone else. Republicans lust to end the "nanny state" and to stop "giveaways"—except, of course, the triumphalist imperative to provide subsidies to oil companies and other profit-making businesses.

Social Darwinist Republican triumphalists believe that economic policies of government should help those who are successful. Let them have tax breaks never imagined during the Reagan era. Lower regulatory barriers. Subsidize big corporations. Award government contracts to successful businesses. Cut welfare. Every man (sexist term intended) for himself!

But Social Darwinism also predicts that any country can fail competitively because of inadequate infrastructure and support for its middle class. Republican Social Darwinists have exhibited fear more than hope for the future of the United States, while Obama has offered a hopeful long-range view of the American economy by promoting infrastructure jobs, clean energy, "high-tech" industries, and tax cuts for the middle class.

President Barack Obama perhaps understands the ill effects of Social Darwinism more than any previous president. His early experiences in Honolulu have sharpened his opposition to efforts of elites to pretend that they have a scientific basis for mistreating the less fortunate. In Hawai'i, trade union organizers on behalf of non-White laborers ended racism on the plantations and catapulted Democrats to become the permanent majority party by the mid-twentieth century. Memories of White-imposed racist rule from annexation to statehood consign Republicans, who then overtly held Social Darwinist views, to a small minority in Hawai'i, today.

At least John Boehner was honest in issuing his manifesto of Social Darwinism. Today, the Republican Party has openly become a club for libertarians and triumphalists. The triumphalist lust for torture and anti-war libertarianism clearly fit the mold.

Contradictions between the two Social Darwinist strands, further explored in Chapter 7, remained during mid-2011 as Congress deliberated whether to ax subsidies to productive oil companies and the military-industrial complex while hoping to cut benefits for those who conscientiously contributed to Medicare and Social Security during their working years in the expectation that their benefits would be honored. Then, on September 8, 2011, some giggled and guffawed during a presidential speech that encouraged Congress to pass a law to create jobs. They believed they had triumphed over Obama.

Exposing Social Darwinism for what it is may end its popularity. Yet that is exactly what many Republican candidates have espoused in seeking the nomination. The elitist view that some are more deserving than others is antithetical to not just to the Aloha Spirit but also the American Dream and the American Way. And any form of Darwinism should alienate religious fundamentalist supporters.

But some Democrats have also found fault with President Barack Obama because he seems too Republican for their taste. An evaluation of his presidency would be incomplete without a discussion of the Progressive Democrats, as in the next chapter.

Chapter 6
Progressive Democrats

Throughout President Barack Obama's first years in office, he was attacked by the right as well as the left. Criticisms from conservatives were to be expected, but those from the left have been very annoying to the president.

For example, Ronald Brownstein of the *Los Angeles Times* has accused Obama of being "too cool." Katrina vanden Heuvel, editor of *The Nation*, has repeatedly accused President Obama of lacking "leadership." Princeton Professor Cornel West believes that Obama is a "Black puppet of corporate Plutocrats"—in other words, an Uncle Tom.

Their comments are typical of the group known as "Progressive Democrats," which was founded during July 2004. After Democratic Dennis Kucinich's unsuccessful campaign for the presidential nomination that year, his Deputy National Campaign Manager, Tim Carpenter, joined others in organizing Kucinich supporters into a more permanent faction within the Democratic Party. In some states, Progressive Democrats hold separate meetings from those of the mainline Democratic Party clubs. Steven Cobble and Michelle White are the official co-founders of Progressive Democrats of America.

Brownstein finds fault with Obama for failing to show anger and passion; in other words, to "fight" for principles. He and other progressives are unaware that the president subscribes to principles of Hawai'i's multicultural ethos, in which displays of emotion are regarded as signs of selfishness and even weakness. Those who want Obama to blow his top from time to time, in other words, are asking him to behave in a manner that would be considered immature and rude in Hawai'i.

Vanden Heuvel articulates a more serious criticism, claiming that Obama is "not a leader." She has done so on television, and she repeated her accusation at a Los Angeles Times Festival of Books panel on April 30, 2011. After the panel I asked her what she specifically wanted Obama to do in projecting leadership. In response, her reply was "Give speeches!" I then noted that Obama gives speeches. (And damn good ones at that!)

Unable to refute the fact that Obama gives good speeches, vanden Heuvel next complained that Obama concedes early in bargaining with Republicans. When asked for the source of her information, she walked off the stage without answering. Her colleague quickly promised to come down to the floor of the auditorium to provide an answer. But, face to face, he refused to disclose any sources, thereby casting serious doubt on the credibility of her claim. What many Progressive Democrats claim is that Obama accepts moderate proposals instead of pushing for extreme solutions. Obama gains majority support among Democratic moderates, who do not subscribe to the extreme progressive agenda.

As other Progressive Democrats and pundits have argued, vanden Heuvel doubtless wants Obama to be a bully like Lyndon Johnson. Or to lecture like George W. Bush. But not to "cave in" to Republicans. But for Obama, reflecting on the genius of Ronald Reagan's popularity, leadership is not about the president acting confident and firm but instead about "helping the American people feel confident."

Progressives, I have found, do not accept the fact that their agenda is largely being held up by Congress, not the president. They want the president to somehow get tough with moderate Democratic members of Congress to support causes that will make them unpopular in their districts. Indeed, during 2010 moderate Democrats feared defeat if they signed onto left-wing legislation opposed by their centrist constituents. Thus, Progressive Democrats were demanding that Obama urge moderate Democrats to commit political suicide. The 2010 election clearly disproved the progressive rant.

What Progressive Democrats do not realize is that Obama comes from Hawai'i, where those from the East Coast are considered much too "pushy." Brownstein, vanden Heuvel, West, and many other progressives want Obama to be like them, while he doubtless considers their suggestions to be impolitic and vulgar. After all, they are attacking his personality.

46

The culture of Hawai'i, which is responsible for unexcelled ethnic harmony, is fundamentally **non**confrontational. That's the most important reason why uncompromising progressives are out of sync with the White House. Confrontational behavior is contrary to Obama's nature. He instead seeks comity and compromise, knowing that reforms that really stick have something for all sides.

Cultural Differences

The most strident progressive attack on President Barack Obama appeared within a well-publicized tirade published on May 18, 2011, when Professor Cornel West accused President Barack Obama of growing up "in a White context." He further asserted that "All he [Obama] has known culturally is White."

Obviously Cornel West had not learned anything about Barack Obama's "context" as a resident of predominantly non-White Honolulu. But West is not alone. The *New York Review of Books* has published reviews of books about Obama written by biographers who have repeatedly made the same mistake (see Appendix C), ignoring that Obama lived most of his first eighteen years in Honolulu, where adoption of "Mainland culture" is opposed a majority non-White population. And Jakarta, where he spent four years from ages 6 to 10, is hardly a bastion of White culture.

In a subsequent interview, Cornel West's onetime Princeton colleague Melissa Harris-Perry correctly pointed out that West himself has lived primarily within "White culture." Indeed, she implies, West is no different from other Blacks in the United States, who sadly lost their African cultural heritage long ago. (If anyone is influenced by African culture, it is Obama, who has visited his ancestral Kenya.) Thanks to a conversation that I had with her in March 2011, she is also aware of the importance of Obama's life in Hawai'i, where Native Hawaiian and Japanese cultures have fused into what I call "Hawai'i's multicultural ethos" (see Chapter 2). I made the same point by email to West, but I received no response.

Thinking about Obama within a "White/Black" cultural context, thus, shows cultural bias. Among those who point out that the president's philosophy and temperament reflect his Island multicultural experience are Jonathan Alter (citing statements by Emil Jones and Eric Whitaker), Michael Dukakis, Kathleen Hall Jamieson, Michelle Obama, Maya Sotero-Ng (the president's half-sister), Jeff Zeleny, and authors of chapters in my recent book *Barack Obama, The Aloha Zen President*. They agree that Obama is a typical son of the multicultural Fiftieth State.

As noted in Chapter 1, Barack Obama has said many times that his basic values were shaped while growing up in Honolulu. He has also said that he hoped that America could become more like Hawai'i. And, on the campaign trail, he sensed that the American public wants the same.

The public is well aware that the very mode of West's angry, intemperate discourse is contrary to that of Barack Obama. West has much to learn from Obama's calm, friendly demeanor, his "Aloha Zen."

Barack Obama exudes the culture of the Aloha Spirit—values from a place where dogmatic efforts to steamroller the views of one group over another are identified with the racism of the plantation era when White-owned sugarcane businesses literally cracked the whip over non-White laborers. The plantation era has even been described as "feudal."

After statehood, the non-White majority took control of Hawai'i state government. Ever since, the tone for interaction has been set by representatives of Native Hawaiian and Japanese cultures, who frown on Mainland conflict-oriented divisiveness.

It would be wrong to say that Obama grew up in an anti-White racial context, however, because most Mainlanders who move to the Islands quickly learn to adapt to a very different culture. Mainlanders who move to Hawai'i may find that they are initially perceived as suspicious, insular, arrogant, disrespectful, dogmatic, negative, and confrontational (see Appendix A). Such a demeanor backfires in the Aloha State. They will fail to make friends, turn off colleagues and customers, and will be ostracized on the job as well as socially until they adapt to the entirely different culture of the Aloha State.

Nevertheless, Cornel West's ejaculation of Progressive Democrats' policy discontent that evolved into a personal attack might have served as a defining moment in efforts to evaluate President Barack Obama. Observers might have taken advantage of the opportunity to learn more about the culture of Hawai'i, which is the very antithesis of the culture that West both loathes and represents.

But West raised another issue: Leftist critics of President Barack Obama insist that he has betrayed his identity as a card-carrying progressive. Yet Obama is not and never was a Progressive Democrat. Their critique is a "straw man" projection of their own views onto him.

However, there are two issues wherein Obama agrees with progressives and has threatened vetoes—Congressional restrictions on how the executive branch should handle Guantánamo and tax increases for the rich. But Obama does not want to cast vetoes. He wants results.

According to David Axelrod, Obama's number one priority is to change the culture of Washington so that Democrats and Republicans will work together to solve the country's problems. He reiterated that goal in a *60 Minutes* interview on December 4, 2011. His moderate partisanship is rooted in Hawai'i's multicultural ethos, which he learned during his early years in Honolulu. Compromises in Hawai'i are achieved across cultural lines. To gain acceptance, politically and socially, one must take into consideration the distinctive value systems of the principal ethnic groups (Caucasians, Chinese, Filipinos, Japanese, and Native Hawaiians) by finding common ground. In Washington, he has tried to bring moderates of both parties together.

Progressives and Obamacare
During the debate on health care legislation, which occupied Congress nearly a year (from mid-2009 to spring 2010), progressives demanded "public option" or even "single payer" solutions. Due to their intransigence, they held up passage of the law in the House of Representatives for three months after the Senate had approved.

Then one day, Barack Obama invited Dennis Kucinich, leader of the progressives, onto Air Force One to gain his support for the pending legislation, the Patient Protection and Affordable Health Care Act. As a result, Kucinich dropped his opposition, and the bill later christened "Obamacare" finally passed on March 21, 2010. Reportedly, Kucinich was persuaded that Obamacare might be a first step toward his preferred option, "single payer" health care.

A few months later, I met Dennis Kucinich at a fundraiser and quietly asked him if he knew why Obama was so keen on the health care bill. When Kucinich replied that he did not know why, I pointed out that the original proposal was based on the Hawai'i health care plan, which covered his grandmother and might even have covered Obama himself from the age of 14. I also pointed that I am from Hawai'i, and I am still covered by the plan, which I praised. Kucinich was astonished. He had never heard anything about the Hawai'i plan before. In other words, the progressive endorsement of "single payer" was based on ideology rather than a serious study of the workable Obamacare alternative to "single payer."

When Republicans took control of the House of Representatives in 2011, they quickly passed a bill to abolish Obamacare. Kucinich then appeared pleased, as his pet scheme—single payer—might eventually emerge as a more viable alternative if Obamacare failed. But, of course, Republicans would never adopt a "single payer" scheme, and the Democratic-controlled Senate never took up the measure. Progressive Kucinich, in other words, repudiated Obamacare under cover of Republican opposition.

Early in 2011, I encountered more ideological blindness among Progressive Democrats after I nominated myself for a seat in the California Democratic Convention as a representative from my district in the Assembly, the lower house of the state legislature. I informed two progressive organizations of my self-nomination and hoped to be elected.

One day, I received a telephone call. A person of some authority was seeking to determine whether I would be part of a progressive slate of candidates for the district. As she went down a list of issues, I agreed with every progressive policy but one. I did not realize that members of the slate were required to support a "single payer" scheme similar to the British and Canadian models. I instead backed Obamacare as a less expensive health care plan, basing my judgment on long experience of being covered by the Hawai'i health care plan, which was the original model for Obamacare.

She then decided to screen me further by arranging a conference call with all the other members selected for the slate. During that conversation I repeated my preference for Obamacare, though not necessarily opposition to "single payer." Nobody during the conversation disputed my explanation that Obamacare would cost less than "single payer." They obviously had not thought through the pros and cons of Obamacare, preferring to subscribe to a fixed ideology established long before Obamacare was under consideration in Congress. As a result, I was not accepted on the slate. I then ran on my own and lost. (More on Obamacare appears in Chapter 10.)

The California progressives in my district, in other words, operated in a Leninist manner. Endorsement of their creed had to be all or nothing, with no real discussion permitted. One progressive with whom I spoke suggested that America's health care should be similar to that of France and Germany. Another advised me that progressives supported "single payer" so that insurance companies would get out of the health care business. Yet nonprofit insurance companies are central to the French and German health care plans.

Subsequently, I attended a social occasion that brought together many Los Angeles County Democrats. When I approached some progressives who knew my views on Obamacare versus single payer, a New York expatriate said, "I don't want to talk to you." Similar to vanden Heuvel, she walked away as if in a huff.

I then talked to the chair of the senior caucus of the California Democratic Party. His comment was that progressives had infuriated the party by being so uncompromising.

A later experience is worth retelling. Progressive Democrats of Los Angeles maintain a listserv through Yahoogroups, wherein members can make comments and engage in Internet dialog. Because of my left-of-center views, I decided to join. To announce a booklaunching event of my book *Barack Obama, The Aloha Zen President*, I decided to post a notice on the listserv during February 2011.

A torrent of opposition then emerged, with a consensus of opinion that no true progressive would attend such an event, since they believed Obama to be one of the worst presidents in American history, differing little from his predecessor. And indeed they failed to show up. Without hearing what I had to say, they were eager to besmirch an objective presentation that promised to explain Obama's personality and political philosophy. In mid-June, Obama's communications director Dan Pfeiffer, appearing personally before the progressive organization Netroots, encountered similar hostility. I have found the same "Keep Out" signs on two other listservs of Progressives, who clearly are not interested in friendly debate or discussion.

Who Are the Progressive Democrats?
During the listserv dialog just noted, several persons admitted to being democratic socialists. Some want to run a candidate in Democratic Party primaries of 2012 to oppose Obama.

During mid-2011 the dissatisfaction of progressives toward Obama took a new turn. A *Facebook* page "I Really Hated Bush But Obama Is Actually Worse" was launched. One posting indicated that a onetime Obama supporter is no longer a Democrat. Amid considerable invective and name-calling, the only policy criticisms were the adoption of Obamacare, approval of tax cuts for the rich, the increase in troops to Afghanistan, and the Libyan intervention. None of the criticisms attempted careful reasoning.

Regarding tax cuts for the rich, the writer joined many other Progressive Democrats in criticizing the Tax Relief, Unemployment Insurance Reauthorization, and Job Creation Act of 2010. In that legislation, a Bush-era reduction in tax rates for the top income group was indeed retained. But Republicans would not extend unemployment benefits unless the tax cuts continued. In other words, progressives who decried the extension of tax cuts for a few thousand rich persons cared nothing about what would happen to millions of unemployed Americans. Similarly, progressives have shown opposition to drone attacks and torture but little sympathy for the victims, including children—including the 64 who were imprisoned at Guantánamo, those who were abused at Abu Ghraib, or innocents killed in indiscriminate attacks. Progressive Democrats thereby show their true colors as "limousine liberals" by ignoring the plight of those less fortunate.

Progressives as Clicktivists

Progressives were taken by surprise in mid-2011, when Berkeley-based blogger Micah White began to plan a movement that later emerged on September 22 as Occupy Wall Street, a protest against the way 1 percent of the popula-tion has gained financially while the remaining 99 percent has stagnated. White, who decried the progressive effort to organize "petition drives that capitalize on current events . . . [by] clicking a few links," felt that real political change requires mobilization in the street.

Accordingly, Progressive Democrats began to send out emails urging members to join protests not only in a New York park under the banner Occupy Wall Street but in other venues across the country. Rather than promoting a Progressive agenda, however, assemblies of hundreds of disaffected did not rally behind any specific agenda. Instead, they engaged in dialog, hearing the views of anyone who chose to participate while agreeing on only one theme—that the rich had been engaging in class warfare by hijacking the political system for decades. The political establishment, thus, was eager to clear the parks and the streets before participants reached consensus on a platform for change. But the movement is expected to mushroom in spring 2012.

Conclusion

Many Progressive Democrats have little interest in compromise or dialog. As a result, they are not capable of persuading anyone else of their views, some of which are otherwise quite worthy of consideration. They oppose dialog, the hallmark of the Occupy Wall Street/99 Percent movement.

When Progressive Democrats and Tea Party libertarians uncompromisingly insist that they are infallible, they fail to understand that they must coexist in the same country with others who disagree with them. Political compromise is not a "sellout," as they often holler, but instead is the traditional way in which American politics has operated incrementally throughout history. In rejecting that tradition, Progressives and Tea Party libertarians threaten the ability of Washington to solve fundamental problems. Moderates of both parties are challenged to cooperate or else Washington will become irrelevant, but they may be defeated in primaries as the extremes become more numerous.

Barack Obama has shown good faith as an honest broker of compromise, steering the political debate to the center. On May 11, 2011, President Obama urged Democratic Senators not to "draw a line in the sand" that would make compromise on budget negotiations difficult. Moderate leaders in the Democratic Party do not want progressives to continually issue self-defeating ultimatums, such as Kucinich's frivolous lawsuit of June 15, 2011, to stop the American military role in Libya (see Chapter 13).

If Progressive Democrats are not very flexible, neither are Tea Party Republicans. Progressives want the national political dialog to move left, just as the Tea Party hopes for a permanent rightward tilt. To accomplish anything in Congress nowadays, therefore, moderate Democrats and moderate Republicans now hold the balance of power in Washington.

Progressive Democrats may be left out in the cold because they have repeatedly chosen to make President Obama's personality their number one issue. They want Obama, a fundamentally nonconfrontational person, to "fight," to use the bully pulpit, and to show "leadership." They want a person with a positive outlook to go on the attack, a calm person to show emotion, and a serene person to show anger. Having isolated themselves, they have alienated others in their party. But they constituted at least 10 percent of Obama's supporters in 2008, and they may not vote for him in 2012.

Despite nitpicking President Obama for two years and then failing to stem the Republican tide in the 2010 elections, progressives expect him to stand firm and not compromise without mobilizing to support him. In other words, they are living in fantasyland. When they emulate his personality and share his analysis about the tragedy of a fractured American polity, they may attract more support.

Meanwhile, America seems doomed to develop into a four-party system. The next chapter explains how.

Chapter 7
America's Nascent Four-Party System

The "Tea Party" may have done an amazing service to American politics by nearly institutionalizing a multiparty system. Some in the Tea Party movement do not consider themselves Republicans and are instead libertarians, dissatisfied by Republican Party triumphalists for overspending.

The "Tea Party," which emerged to national prominence in 2009 in opposition to major reforms being proposed by newly elected President Barack Obama, takes as its icon the Boston Tea Party of 1773. That event was a protest against taxes imposed to pay for the French and Indian War.

Tax protests are nothing new in American politics. Yet Zach Christensen's website *ChicagoTeaParty.com*, launched in August 2008, did not gain immediate momentum. Nor did Rick Santelli's rant on CNBC of February 19, 2009. But in early 2009 Keli Carender telephoned friends in Seattle to schedule a protest for February 16, 2009. Then, with the help of Fox News free publicity and a new *Facebook* page, Carender called for a second rally on February 27. Soon, the movement began to sprout local groups around the country without a national coordinating organization.

Meanwhile, democratic socialists who call themselves Progressive Democrats are increasingly emerging from the closet as a possible fourth political party. Both the Democratic and Republican parties have centrist elements, but the fervency of their extreme factions increasingly suggests that the United States is developing into a four-party system.

Ron Paul, a Republican member of the House of Representatives, has run as a presidential candidate of the Libertarian Party in the past (1988). Some Progressive Democrats, who have voted for the most famous Green Party candidate, Ralph Nader, once sought to form a movement similar to the Tea Party called the American Dream Movement. They were pleased when the Occupy Wall Street protest began in fall 2011.

Multiparty America in the Past

Most American national elections have involved two prominent political parties with inconsequential third parties. Yet three or four political parties have campaigned with some success in past presidential elections.

In 1824, no parties were on the ballot but several candidates considered themselves worthy successors of President James Monroe, whose two terms in office were coming to an end. The Federalist Party had collapsed after 1816, so the contest was within the dominant Democratic Party. Monroe's Secretary of the Treasury James Crawford and Secretary of State John Quincy Adams believed themselves to be heirs apparent. Henry Clay, Speaker of the House of Representatives, had distinguished himself by arranging the Missouri Compromise of 1820, which papered over the simmering North-South conflict over slavery. Senator Andrew Jackson, popular due to his victory in the Battle of New Orleans of 1815, felt that his time had come. When votes were counted, Jackson received more popular votes than the others. But nobody received a majority in the electoral college, leaving the choice of president up to the House of Representatives, where Clay threw the election to Adams.

By 1860, the Democrats were the dominant party. When they nominated Illinois Senator Stephen A. Douglas, those from Southern states walked out because of his support for the view that the territories (parts of the United States that had not been granted statehood) should vote whether to accept slavery rather than having Congress stipulate whether a new state would allow slavery. The Southern Democrats then nominated Vice President John C. Breckenridge. John Bell, a wealthy Tennessee slaveholder, was put forward by a group that formed the new Constitutional Union Party, which believed that he could hold the country together by finessing the slavery issue. The Republican Party, which had been formally organized in 1854 to oppose expanding slavery to the territories, even by popular vote prior to statehood, picked Abraham Lincoln, who won enough electoral votes to be declared the winner. Thereafter, Bell's party disappeared, and the Democratic Party was reconstituted.

In 1912, incumbent President William Howard Taft was re-nominated by the Republican Party for president to the chagrin of former President Theodore Roosevelt, who then formed the Progressive Party and ran again. The Democrats nominated Woodrow Wilson. But there was a fourth contender, Eugene Debs, of the Socialist Party, who received 6 percent of the votes (a little more than 900,000). Debs first ran for president in 1900 and continued to do so each year up to 1920. Nevertheless, Wilson won the election.

The Socialist Party decided to endorse another third party in 1924, when they threw their support to Robert M. La Follette's newly formed Progressive Party (unrelated to Roosevelt's effort in 1912), which won in Wisconsin and continued to run candidates until 1946. From 1928 to 1956, the Socialist Party continued to run candidates, electing nearly a thousand local legislators, but garnered fewer and fewer votes after peaking in 1912 and 1932.

In 1948, the Republican Party nominated Thomas E. Dewey. Even before the Democrats nominated incumbent President Harry Truman, Southern delegates stormed out of the Democratic National Convention in opposition to a civil rights plank in the party platform. Forming the Dixiecrat Party, their nominee Senator Strom Thurmond carried four states, but dissolved after the election, which Truman won.

A democratic socialist, Bernie Sanders of Vermont has been elected to Congress from 1990. He was elected to the Senate in 2006 on the Socialist Party ticket. He caucuses with the Democrats, as does Joe Lieberman, who was elected as an Independent Democrat after a defeat in the Connecticut Democratic primary to a progressive.

The election in 2000 is sometimes referred to in a third party context. Republican George W. Bush defeated Democrat Al Gore, thanks to a ruling by the Supreme Court of the United States. But Green Party candidate Ralph Nader received almost 3 percent of the votes, arguably enough to deprive Gore of victories in Florida and New Hampshire. Most Democrats who voted for Gore in 2000 returned to the fold in 2004, and the Green Party was not prominent during the 2008 election.

Electoral Fusion
New York State has long had a viable four-party system. After Democrats and Republicans pick their candidates for office, the Conservative Party (from 1962) and Liberal Party (from 1944) have had a choice. They can either run separate candidates under their own party labels or endorse candidates of the Republicans or Democrats—a practice known as "electoral fusion."

Actually, electoral fusion was not uncommon in the late nineteenth century. In some states, minor parties were permitted to run their own candidates or to endorse a candidate of one of the major parties. The Socialist Party, as noted above, endorsed the Progressive Party candidate in 1924. But states began to ban the practice in the early twentieth century.

Today, eight states still permit some form of electoral fusion—Connecticut, Delaware, Idaho, Mississippi, New York, Oregon, South Carolina, and Bernie Sander's Vermont. More states may adopt electoral fusion as the Tea Party and Progressive Democrats become disillusioned, respectively, with the Republicans and Democrats.

Libertarians and Progressive Democrats
In recent years, libertarians have struggled for control of the Republican Party in many counties if not entire states. Recently re-branding themselves as "Tea Party" Republicans, they knocked off traditional Republican incumbents in state conventions and primaries during 2010, and constitute a force in Congress that has made the Republican Congressional Party less monolithic. Many incumbent Republican triumphalists now fear that they may lose to libertarians in primary elections. Senator John McCain, known for moderate views throughout his career, began to endorse many right-wing views to ward off challengers in Republican primary elections in 2008 and 2010. More recently, he has characterized the Tea Party caucus as "isolationist."

Meanwhile, Progressive Democrats have quietly sought to wrest control of the Democratic Party in several states. During 2006 progressives failed to support the re-election of Senator Joe Lieberman in the Democratic Primary, who then won in the general election by starting a third party with en-dorsements from Republicans. He even supported John McCain for president in 2008. In California, left-wing Democrats successfully sponsored a "single payer" health plan, which was vetoed by former Republican Governor Arnold Schwartzenegger. They hope that his successor, Democratic Governor "Jerry" Brown, will sign the law into effect as a repudiation of centrist Obamacare.

Immobilism

One symptom of the incipient four-party system has been an inability to reach consensus in Congress. Such a problem afflicts Continental multiparty systems, particularly Belgium, which has been unable to form a government months after recent national elections.

Some immobilism, of course, is built into the American constitutional system, which allows "divided government," that is a Congress controlled by a party different from that of the president. Divided government has occurred many times over the years, most recently during 2007-2008 and today (2011-2012), with a Democrat in the White House and a Republican majority in the House of Representatives.

For Obama, the obvious solution has been for moderates in both parties to join forces. But Democratic and Republican leaders in Congress wanted to keep their parties internally united. Bipartisan cooperation in the context of intraparty divisions occurred when civil rights legislation passed in the 1960s. Fifty years later, that era was a distant memory.

During 2009 and 2010, Congress displayed immobilism in its inability to solve major problems because of the Senate filibuster and other chicanery that frustrated passage of legislation and approval of administration and judicial officials. Mitch McConnell, Republican minority leader in the Senate, announced that his number one priority was to ensure the defeat of Obama for re-election, thereby making the extraordinary schadenfreude declaration that the needs of the American people were secondary. Yet moderate Republicans complained that Democratic leaders in the House and Senate, Nancy Pelosi and Harry Reid, would not dialog with them in shaping legislation during the 111th Congress (2009-2011).

Cross-aisle compromise emerged astonishingly in the lame duck session of the 111th Congress. After Republicans insisted that Bush-era tax cuts must be extended or Congress would accomplish nothing after the 2010 election, Obama's advisers arranged a comprehensive deal—continuation of payroll tax cuts for the middle class, extension of unemployment insurance, repeal of the ban on gays in the military, and ratification of the renewed Strategic Arms Reduction Treaty with Russia.

Soon after the shooting of Congresswoman Gabrielle Giffords in January 2011, members of Congress sat together during the State of the Union Address. Thereby, they proved that they could rise above a spirit of division.

From 2011, however, a Republican majority in the House of Representatives has been unable to work smoothly with the Democratic-led Senate, resulting in a do-nothing 112nd Congress. Libertarians, who want very limited government, have been happy about that. To get anything passed, compromise across party lines has been imperative. And on 17 major votes in the House of Representatives, moderates of both parties have prevailed over the rest.

The scenario of compromise has been even more likely as long as President Barack Obama continues to play the role of Mr. Compromiser. Republicans now constitute a majority in the House of Representatives, so they have been on the spot to produce results. They may only be able to do so by spurning uncompromising members of the Tea Party. Thus, they may have to reach across the aisle, where party leaders have already found rigid Progressive Democrats to be an unhelpful drag on their efforts to solve serious problems. Potentially, Republicans who defeated Democrats in 2010 might lose their seats to Democrats in 2012.

But when a budget compromise was reached on April 14, 2011, Democratic leader Nancy Pelosi was not involved in the negotiations. In the House of Representatives, 59 Republicans voted against the deal, though only 27 of the new 87 Republicans were opposed. House Democrats voted against the budget 108-81. In the Senate, only 15 of the 47 Republicans voted No (along with 3 Democrats and 1 Socialist). Thus, moderation prevailed.

More signs of moderates voting together emerged in June 2011. Congress passed an extension of the Patriot Act 250-153, with 31 libertarian Republicans joining 122 leftist Democrats. Also in early June, a resolution in the House of Representatives urging early withdrawal of troops from Afghanistan and Libya failed 204-215, with 26 Republicans and 178 Democrats voting together. A separate vote for immediate withdrawal of combat troops also failed, but attracted 38 Republicans and 105 Democrats.

Later in June, moderate Democrats and Republicans again joined together to oppose libertarians and progressives. A vote to cut off some funding of the Libyan intervention was defeated 180-238, with only 144 Republicans and 36 Democrats in favor.

During the wrangling over raising the debt limit and reducing the federal deficit in mid-2011, libertarian Republicans insisted that they would vote against raising the debt limit unless Obama agreed to spending cuts that would bring the deficit under control. Progressive Democrats, meanwhile, wanted to raise taxes on the rich and close corporate tax loopholes to balance the budget. In a spirit of compromise, President Obama agreed in principle to spending cuts and increased taxes. But the libertarians would not accept any increased revenue, while the progressives insisted that revenues had to go up. Obama then criticized both extreme Democrats and extreme Republicans for being rigid. McConnell tried to advance a compromise, but his idea was nixed by libertarians in the House of Representatives.

Obama next negotiated with Speaker John Boehner directly. Boehner eventually pulled out of the talks theatrically, but Obama had in fact maneuvered him into a corner where his only escape was to work with moderate Democrats.

Then, on the eve of a government default, with millions of federal payments obligated to be sent out on August 2 in excess of the debt limit, Congress finally passed the Budget Control Act of 2011, authorizing Obama to raise the debt limit by $900 billion (by selling government bonds) while cutting $917 billion in spending projected over ten years. The law set up a bipartisan Congressional committee to identify specific spending cuts or else automatic cuts would be imposed.

Passage of the budget act of 2011 well illustrates both immobilism and the incipient four-party system. Immobilism was manifest while Congress dragged out negotiations for seven months primarily because Speaker Boehner was unable to get sufficient Republican votes for passage of any deal that could also pass the Democratic-controlled Senate. Tea Party Republicans refused compromise and would not vote with moderate Republicans. To get a majority in the House of Representatives, Boehner had to confront the reality of the four factions by forging a coalition between 174 moderate Republicans and 95 moderate Democrats, leaving 66 libertarians and 95 Progressive Democrats to oppose the budget deal. Majorities in both parties passed the measure in the Senate, where 7 Democrats and 19 Republicans opposed the measure.

Boehner, as the final vote indicates, could have passed the Grand Bargain much earlier: He wasted time appeasing Tea Party Republicans. Because of his dithering, the U.S. credit rating was downgraded for the first time in history.

A favorable prognosis for divided government and the burgeoning four-party system would be consensus building across party lines. Moderate leaders of both parties may gradually learn to work together, leaving inflexible factions on the far left (Progressive Democrats) and far right (Tea Party libertarians) in the cold.

Conclusion

If there is a shakedown cruise to build a consensus among moderates, the waters are still being tested. Formalizing splits within the two parties by adoption of a national four-party system is not in the immediate future. But when moderates cooperate consistently and successfully, leaving extremists dissatisfied, the latter may prefer to defect and retreat to the Green and Libertarian parties. Pressure then may build for more states to adopt electoral fusion, eventually resulting in a national four-party system.

Meanwhile, a third party movement plans to put a centrist presidential candidate on the ballot in all fifty states. Peter Ackerman, an independent-minded investor who tried to form a unity party in 2008, is now behind a movement known as Americans Elect. The plan is to hold a nationwide primary for possible presidential candidates on the Internet and to secure places on the ballots of all fifty states. As of mid-December 2011, eleven states already had accepted Americans Elect as a political party, and applications had been filed in twenty other states. Michael Bloomberg is the most discussed candidate. But the problem is that Congress is immobilist, so a president running under the Americans Elect label will not change the four-party reality in the legislative process. A better solution is to drain away extremes from both major parties so that moderates will continue to cooperate.

Because third- or four-party developments threaten the two major political parties, they will continue to sell the idea that there is a major political divide in the country. When the bipartisan Congressional debt committee failed in November 2011, that was their specious diagnosis of the dysfunction for which they were primarily responsible.

One might imagine that the solution would occur to those who now control both political parties. Ideally, moderate Democrats and Republicans would kick out their extremes and join together to solve problems. But that scenario is impossible as long as the extremes are determined to infiltrate, vilify the moderates, and seek to take over and dominate the two parties. If the extremes were to leave voluntarily, the political center would feel considerable relief, but the most enthusiastic voters appear to be on the extremes today.

What happens during 2012 may cast the die. Either a viable third centrist political party will emerge or the trend toward a four-party system will continue. Either way, the leader needed by America is a consensus builder, and that is precisely how Barack Obama sees his role.

The trend, if there is one, appeared much clearer in 2010. An analysis of that year's defeat for Democrats is provided in the following chapter along with a scenario for 2012.

Chapter 8
Why Democrats Lost in 2010
But May Win in 2012

A "shellacking" is how President Barack Obama described what the voters did to Democrats in the November 2010 election. Republicans picked up enough seats (63) in the House of Representatives to command a majority. Democrats lost 6 seats in the Senate but maintained a slim majority. Republicans won new governorships and obtained new majorities in several state legislatures.

Public Opinion in 2010
The most common explanation for the election results, based on voter turnout statistics, is an "enthusiasm gap." Many complacent or disillusioned Obama supporters stayed home, while Republicans were fired up and voted.

According to a *New York Times* summary of exit polls, the principal factor in the Democratic loss was that many who comprised the Obama majority of 2008 stayed home on election day 2010 (notably Hispanics, African Americans, union members, and younger voters). Republicans won majorities among Catholics, the elderly, independents, and women, groups that had predominantly voted for Obama in 2008. Those under 30 comprised the only age group supporting the Democrats with a majority, but only 11 percent of them took the trouble to vote in 2010.

Another explanation is that voters were misinformed. A poll conducted by researchers at the University of Maryland found that most voters incorrectly thought that the "economic stimulus" bill of 2009 (the American Recovery and Reinvestment Act) did not reduce unemployment. Only 8 percent were correct in believing that the bill created or saved 2-3 million of jobs. Similarly, most in the sample thought that Obamacare would increase the deficit; only 23 percent correctly thought that the law would not. In both cases, the level of education of respondents was unrelated to their assessments, but Republicans were more likely to be misinformed than Democrats, and Fox News viewers were more misinformed than others. Evidently left-wing MSNBC commentators were unable to counter misimpressions disseminated by Fox News.

According to a CBS exit poll, 55 percent of voters disapproved of how President Obama handled his job. Among those disapproving of the president, 86 percent voted for a Republican House candidate. Some 37 percent of voters overall, as well as 37 percent of independents, said that they voted Republican to express opposition to Obama. His disapproval was related to a belief that Republicans offered better solutions to economic problems than Democrats.

Strategic Explanation
My interpretation is that voters switched to Republicans because they campaigned with a vision of what they would do if elected. Democrats, evidently content to rest on their laurels, offered no specific plan for the future. Those with fears about the economy preferred the Republican focus on the deficit and jobs over Democrats, who claimed success in saving and creating jobs but had nothing new to offer if their majorities were to continue in 2011-2012.

The fundamental mistake of the Democrats was to run a rational campaign, citing facts, against Republicans who disseminated irrational fears. Having failed to appeal to the emotions of voters, wind went out of Democratic sails that had been unfurled in 2008.

Voters throughout the United States agreed on one thing: President Barack Obama was a disappointment. Many former supporters became adamantly opposed and voted Republican in 2010.

During the 2008 election, the Obama campaign facilitated meetings of supporters in communities throughout the United States. I attended three such meetings. Prior to the 2010 election, the call went out for similar meetings, so I volunteered as host, expecting to meet Obamacrats in my neighborhood again. But no person registered for the meeting, and nobody showed up. One of the previous hosts expressed chagrin that Obama had compromised on progressive stands. The president was not governing in accordance with progressive expectations.

Similar to critiques by leftist pundits (see Chapter 6), I heard complaints among those who supported Obama that he was hidden away in the White House rather than cajoling and leading the way toward fulfillment of his campaign promises. They did not understand his quiet personality and could not fathom his political philosophy. They did not appreciate that he was trying to govern from the center, bringing moderates of both parties together by incorporating good ideas from Republicans in his proposals.

Those displeased by Obama's performance, however, did not understand that the Constitution gives Congress the dominant role in American government. Constitutionally, presidents have limited powers. Obama deferred to Congress rather than making bold proposals that representatives were likely to ignore anyway, as President Ronald Reagan discovered when his budgets were declared "dead upon arrival." But Constitutional realities did not impress those who remembered bold actions by George W. Bush.

Firing up Obama's Supporters

Something unexpected happened in Los Angeles early in March 2011. At several diverse university forums, twice joined by former presidential candidate Michael Dukakis, I explained to some acclaim the puzzles about Barack Obama in connection with book launchings of my *Barack Obama, The Aloha Zen President*, which had been released two months earlier.

To the astonishment of my audiences, I indicated that his unusual personality can be traced to his background as a son of Hawai'i. His calm, consensus-building nonconfrontational demeanor, I explained, is typical of those who grow up in Honolulu (see Appendix A). Those who demanded that he should get angry and push hard, in other words, did not realize that they were asking him to betray basic values embedded in his personality.

I also explained Obama's political philosophy as a response to the culture shock that he experienced after he left Hawai'i for the Mainland United States. His view was that most Americans in the other forty-nine states were tired of culture wars and wanted government to play a more constructive role. I then explained how he wanted government to facilitate and support cooperative efforts at the corporate, local, and state levels rather than leaving solutions to bureaucrats in Washington (see Appendix B).

The repeated question from audiences was "Why didn't we know this earlier?" Those in attendance realized that the media had been giving them a totally false impression of Barack Obama as a person and as a thinker.

Nevertheless, when asked in various forums if President Obama would be re-elected in 2012, I expressed some pessimism. If the flawed strategy of 2010 were repeated, I answered, prospects were for a slim Obama victory at best. I conveyed the same caution on an Obama website without acknowledgement of my comment, a telling symbol of top-down campaign communications that may be turning off many Obamacrats for 2012. Things were different in 2008.

Voter Motivations
The basis of my comments on elections is rooted in my understanding of how voters make up their minds. Political scientists have identified at least three factors responsible for voter decisions—party preferences, positions on issues, and candidate assessments. Although political parties often oppose one another on issues, the three factors are separate in the minds of many voters.

Those who vote primarily for a particular political party do not need much new information during an election campaign. Their loyalty relieves them of the burden of evaluating candidates and studying issues. They constitute a candidate's solid base of support, sometimes sending in absentee ballots long before campaigns reach their peak. Incumbent legislators who stay in office over many years live in safe districts where party label is crucial.

Accordingly, most presidential campaigns focus on independents. As political party registration has declined, the percentage of swing voters has increased over the years. That's why issues and candidate assessments are so crucial.

One reason for the 2010 election outcome appears to be that the Republican issue narrative was more persuasive than the Democratic Party line. Republicans raised fears about the economy, attacking Obama's alleged "socialism," "government takeover of health care," failure to relieve unemployment, and government running up unsustainable deficits. Republicans promised to handle the problems, though without specific proposals. Democrats were unable to counter the Republican refrain by pointing out that most fears were completely unfounded, and they offered nothing new for the 112nd Congress.

For the 2012 election, prospects looked good for Republicans until Representative Paul Ryan proposed changing Medicare from a guaranteed government entitlement into a voucher system, and Republicans in the House of Representatives fell in line during May 2011 to vote for a budget with that proposal. Now Democrats can run a "fear" campaign, knowing that few voters want to torpedo Medicare and Social Security.

The Victory Plan for 2012
The Obama presidential re-election campaign plans a positive campaign. One proposed slogan is "Winning the Future," presumably referring to innovations that the country needs and which are denied or ignored by Republicans, but "We Can't Wait" appeared in fall 2011 as Congress became more intransigent. In contrast, "Yes We Can" was the slogan of 2008.

David Plouffe, an Obama campaign strategist, believes that victory is assured for the following reasons: (1) Obama will attract independent voters because he has worked with Republicans on a bipartisan basis. (2) Defections by Progressive Democrats are not a problem, as the president retains the loyalties of more than 77 percent of Democratic voters. (3) More Black, Latino, and younger voters are expected to vote in 2012, thanks to demographic trends. (4) Obama remains a superb campaigner. According to David Axelrod, another campaign strategist, polls in late summer 2011 appeared favorable to the president despite a hardening of Republican opposition throughout the year. But campaign advisers and managers who flunked the job in 2010 have been rehired for 2012!

Plouffe's prescription leaves out a campaign on issues. The 111st Congress put what Obama called a "down payment" on many of his goals for change, but thus far the 2012 campaign lacks a PowerPoint-type reminder of exactly what was accomplished during Obama's first years in office (see Chapter 15). In September 2011, I wrote his close adviser David Axelrod to propose a nationwide on-line "Obamaquiz" that could inform voters by posing questions about the president's record and then rewarding those who score high in each Congressional district. I received no reply to my letter.

The voters need better explanations of complex domestic reforms—from economic initiatives to Obamacare (see Chapters 9-11). President Obama has often failed to directly answer false criticism and has admitted that he has not taken time to construct a positive narrative of his many accomplishments, as outlined in Chapter 15.

The Republican Alternative
During most of 2011, Obama conscientiously tried to work with Republicans, treating them with more dignity than was reciprocated. The aim was to change the culture in Washington by proving that bipartisanship could work. On more than a dozen pieces of major legislation, moderates of both parties joined together to reach a majority vote, but only after Republican rhetoric became extremely heated. The resulting compromises displeased progressives, who believed that Obama capitulated. Plouffe's strategy was to depict the Republicans as unreasonable while Obama appeared to be the only adult in town. But approval ratings for both Congress and Obama dropped, so the strategy appears to have boomeranged.

For example, Republicans promised that immigration reform would follow increased deportations of illegals. Deportations skyrocketed under Obama, but Republicans refused to act. The Hispanic community's support for Obama was halved, but not because of lack of reform: About 25 percent of all Hispanics knew of someone who had been picked up on minor offenses, detained without legal representation, and sent home; they had knowledge of children, American citizens, remaining in the country without one or both parents.

In September 2011, Barack Obama's two speeches on jobs and on debt reduction appeared to be the opening salvo in the 2012 campaign. The first proposal was merely a half-priced "stimulus" bill to lower the unemployment rate by one percent at most. The second unveiled a debt reduction plan that the Republicans had already rejected. But when the Republicans countenanced bringing the United States to the brink of default, Obama noticeably changed his demeanor. They had crossed a line, and the twelfth principle of Hawai'i's multicultural ethos became evident: His samurai instincts emerged. Soon, he sounded an unexpected "Give 'em hell, Barry" campaign theme to expose Republicans nearly as racketeers, putting "party before country." He now considers himself a "warrior" for the middle class.

Republicans often attack Democrats for being "weak" on national security, but that charge will not stick in 2012. Having expanded military action in Afghanistan, killed Osama Bin Laden, and risen to the defense of besieged Libyans, President Obama hardly appears to be a "peacenik." Although progressives may not go along because his most important national security decisions have raised serious if unanswered legal questions (Chapters 12-14), nobody disputes Barack Obama's competence to serve as commander-in-chief for another term.

Republican candidates, meanwhile, face a fundamental dilemma. To win in the Republican primaries, a candidate must appeal to Tea Party extremists. Then in general elections, they may appear too far from the mainstream to win. For example, shortly after Newt Gingrich announced his candidacy, he opposed tampering with Medicare. Mainstream Republicans then forced him to retract, leaving him branded as a two-faced politician with little credibility.

Then came the elections of 2011, where voters repudiated extreme positions of newly elected Republicans in a few states. The rise of the Occupy Wall Street movement, in other words, resonated with moderate voters.

Republicans have another problem. Throughout the debates leading up to the primaries of 2012, they were saddled

71

with unappealing candidates. Some denied science and offered nothing to solve the problems of the country. Many appeared to be in the race so that they could eventually get the nomination for vice president.

During spring 2011 Donald Trump appeared to test the waters with a lot of bombast. But he attacked libertarians, displayed ignorance of basic political knowledge, and joined the birthers. When Obama's original birth certificate was published, Trump was left with egg on his face, and he soon ended his candidacy exploration after being satirized at the annual dinner of the White House Press Corps on the eve of the death of Osama Bin Laden.

Many reasonable Republican candidates have declined to run, believing that their chances are slim. Obama's campaign strategists believe that he will win re-election by default, since the Republican candidate will be unappealing. And President Obama is certain to win a debate with any of those now seeking the nomination. But Republicans may pull a rabbit out of the hat: If none of the contenders gets a majority vote at the 2012 Republican National Convention, a consensus may develop behind a much stronger candidate, who will emerge from a freshly united party.

The Challenge
An incumbent president is difficult to defeat unless he either is judged incompetent or displays personal flaws. Rather than having a disagreeable personality, Obama is portrayed by columnists as cerebral, detached, remote, and unenthusiastic. Pundits refuse to dispel that impression. They might revise their views after reading my book, *Barack Obama, The Aloha Zen President*, which explains how Obama represents a culture very different from that of East Coast journalists, who remain fundamentally monocultural and ignorant of Hawai'i. Meanwhile, Republican hammering at Obama, leading to compromises, may have infuriated Obama's 2008 supporters, who seem less likely to support the president's re-election because he has been perceived as anything but a hard bargainer. But when Speaker Boehner backed out of a deal over the debt ceiling in August 2011, Obama began to appeal directly to the people rather than ever being left at the altar again.

More Democratic Senate seats face contests than Republican seats in 2012. And the fate of elections to the House of Representatives may depend upon how well the economy recovers in several dozen Congressional districts. Because of the considerations presented above, Obama's coattails are likely to be very thin in 2012.

Meanwhile, no role for Vice President Joe Biden in the campaign plans has been revealed. Some vice presidents in the past have been "attack dogs," answering critics so that the president can play a positive role. The disappearance of Biden from prominence during Obama administration battles has deprived the president of someone who could have countered irrational charges and statements before the 2010 election. Biden's foot-in-the-mouth infirmity doubtless explains why.

The challenge for 2012, thus, is for Barack Obama to rekindle the message of transformation that he brought from Hawai'i to Washington. That can best happen when his ethical views, philosophical principles, and accomplishments are better known. But how can they be translated into easily understood epigrams and electrifying empathetic experiences? One model is the kind of "fireside chats" that endeared Franklin Delano Roosevelt to his supporters during periods of crisis. Obama's preference is for town hall meetings, where he feels closer to the people.

Central to the Obama message is his overall perspective on economic and social issues. Republicans had a winning argument by stressing the fact that the economy did not return to normal under Obama's policies. Accordingly, the next two chapters examine what I call Obamanomics and Obamacare. Hitherto, his record on both subjects has not been comprehensively analyzed.

Chapter 9
Obamanomics

Two basic principles of Obamanomics have quietly guided the 44th president of the United States in reforming how the government spends the taxpayer's money. They locate him in the center, almost equally attuned to moderate Republicans and moderate Democrats. And, thanks in part to the advice of economist Austan Goolsbee (chair of Obama's Council of Economic Advisers until mid-2011), away from rigid ideological views that "government is the answer" or "government is the problem."

Humanistic Capitalism
The first principle of Obamanomics is ethical—that Americans should be more responsible for one another. Rather than individualism and winner-takes-all Social Darwinism, Barack Obama's number one priority has been to steer the culture in Washington toward a more communal sense that people must band together, rising above political party, to solve common problems for the good of the country. Greater economic equality has been a common theme of Barack Obama.

Perhaps the most frequently word used word in Obama's remarks about the economy is "responsibility." For example, he criticized "fat cats" on Wall Street for being irresponsible when they refused to use bailout funds for loans to regenerate the economy, and instead doled out enormous bonuses (taxpayers' money!) for themselves. He also expressed disapproval of the way in which banks made money by duping individuals into making risky loans and then made profits by bundling the loans and betting against them. After all, the insolvent banks caused the crisis by making bad loans, and the solution to restoring credit was bailouts to those "too big to fail," that is, banks with so many assets that a long, drawn-out bankruptcy process would imperil the entire financial system. To curtail future scams, Obama signed the Wall Street Reform and Consumer Protection Act of 2010, though Congressional compromises put some false teeth into the bill.

The term "social market capitalism," as used in Western Europe, is closest to describing the cultural and moral basis of Obamanomics. But Obama puts people before ideology. His principle of humanistic capitalism, is similar to the social philosophy of the kibbutz system of early Israel and the communal economy that existed in pre-capitalist Hawai'i. He believes in a welfare state but opposes socialism.

For Obama, the loss of 'ohana (community) in the United States is tragic. He wants to develop a shared perspective throughout American society, with government's role as "catalyst." In issue after issue, Obama's solutions have provided a framework for cooperation among diverse interests, whether in education, the economy, or in other sectors, to bring America into the more competitive 21st century.

Early in his presidency, some advisers urged that he let Chrysler go bankrupt. What clinched his decision to give the automaker a new lease on life was the realization that he would be laying off 300,000 workers, many in their mid-50s who would likely never be employed again.

The trust-busting capitalism of Theodore Roosevelt, William Howard, Taft, and Woodrow Wilson was humanistic. They saw how the richest and most ruthless corporations were driving out competitors in an unregulated free market, so they established anti-trust legislation. And from Andrew Carnegie to Bill Gates, public-minded philanthropists have long set the tone for an American humanistic capitalism.

But faceless chief executives on Wall Street are nowadays beholden to global investments, not to America. Accordingly, Obama has been trying to encourage American-based businesses to return to humanistic capitalism—to become economic patriots of the United States.

Pragmatic Social Investment
Obama's humanistic capitalism is the antithesis of Social Darwinism. But to be a practical basis for a different vision of how to design budgets, the second plank of Obamanomics needs to be appreciated—pragmatic social investment.

Pragmatism originated in the 1870s with the writings of Charles Pierce, William James, and John Dewey, who wanted science to replace ideology as a guide for public policy. They argued that answers to public problems must be found in experience. Local governments, following pragmatism, should design pilot projects to solve problems, and then those that work should be adopted as national policy.

Barack Obama's Inaugural Address immediately identified him as a pragmatist. He said, "The question we ask today is not whether our government is too big or too small, but whether it works."

Ever since, the president has agreed to several compromises. Although some have called him "pragmatic" for brokering deals to get legislation passed, what they really should have said is that he is often just plain "expedient."

His pragmatism is not about deal-making, but instead involves choosing social investment programs that work. His adopted hometown Chicago, after all, enjoys calling itself "The city that works."

Barack Obama's **Race to the Top** (RTT) program, which was included in the "stimulus bill" (the American Recovery and Reinvestment Act of 2009), is a prime example of pragmatic social investment. Race to the Top invites school districts to develop innovative programs to receive seed money at first and more funding if the programs prove to promote educational outcomes. As a result, more than forty states quickly developed innovative programs in education and received funding during 2009.

In rewarding innovative professionals for designing new programs that achieve better outcomes, Obama seeks to replace "formula funding," that is, doling out block grants to educational institutions solely based on the number of students in school districts and regardless of student outcomes. RTT is a way to achieve a "bigger bang for the buck" in allocating federal funding to cities as well.

At the same time, Obama wants to reward excellence in teaching with extra pay, and he believes that families are the most crucial institutions for promoting better educational outcomes. In his address to Congress on February 24, 2009, he said:

> In the end, there is no program or policy that
> can substitute for a mother or father who will

> attend those parent/teacher conferences, or
> help with homework after dinner, or turn off
> the TV, put away the video games, and read
> to their child.

In other words, Obama counts on parents to be responsible—
to encourage their children to do well in school.

RTT-type programs exist outside public education. Under
Obamacare, a program called Communities Putting Prevention to Work funds projects that promise to encourage better
health. In Obama's 2012 budget, similar programs were
planned for electric vehicle infrastructure, removal of regulatory barriers, public safety, juvenile justice, early learning
(Head Start), higher education, and job training. One could
imagine RTTs across the full range of discretional spending.

Another Obama proposal, **Social Impact Bonds** (SIBs),
would encourage private sector financing for new programs.
If invested in public education, they would pay off only if
they improve educational outcomes. SIBs in the future might
include one aimed at curbing recidivism, that is, preventing
released prisoners from re-offending. Indeed, a recidivism pilot program that already exists in Hawai'i may be embraced
nationally if found workable.

Social investment economics has operated elsewhere
throughout the Obama administration. In the economic crisis
in 2009, with the automobile industry on the verge of insolvency, President Obama asked Chrysler and General Motors to design their own restructuring plans *before* providing
them with needed government capital to survive. Ford Motor
Company's president then congratulated the president for res-
cuing self-restructured Chrysler and General Motors. Both
companies have paid back most of their government loans in
the form of stock purchases—and at a profit to taxpayers.
Otherwise, Ford would have collapsed, since otherwise domestic parts suppliers would have gone out of business.

Similarly, President Obama took a different approach to
the Troubled Assets Relief Program from the no-questions-
asked approach under President George W. Bush. Obama instead employed "stress tests" to determine whether certain
banks had the capacity to rebound. After they appeared to

pass the tests, he established rules for the financial institutions to operate so that they would eventually pay back their loans to the U.S. Treasury. His description of the reforms was phrased in humanistic social investment terms:

> It's not about helping banks—it's about helping people. Because when credit is available again, that young family can finally buy a new home. And then some company will hire workers to build it. And then those workers will have money to spend, and if they can get a loan, too, maybe they'll finally buy that car, or open their own business. Investors will return to the market, and American families will see their retirement secured once more.

Alas, banks did not do their part to extend immediate credit, sticking to their own priorities. But most paid back their loans to avoid having their bonus payments to top employees placed under governmental scrutiny.

In mid-February 2009 Congress passed a $787 billion "stimulus" bill, the American Recovery and Reinvestment Act. The spending could have bloated the federal bureaucracy. Instead, the federal government served as a conduit for funds to private sector contractors, to state and local governments, and to middle-class pocketbooks.

The Wall Street and Consumer Protection Act of 2010 limits bank size, bans risky investments, gives authority for regulators to dismantle a failing firm, and gives shareholders a say on executive salaries. Yes, Wall Street was unhappy.

When a British Petroleum (BP) platform caught fire, releasing oil into the Gulf of México, fishing and tourism were seriously threatened. Obama encouraged BP to set up a compensation fund establishing a neutral party, Kenneth Feinberg, who could make payments without government interference.

Obama's top domestic priority, health insurance reform, is yet another example of humanistic social investment. Employers are to match contributions of employees, thereby ensuring that they will pay much more attention to occupational safety. Employers then may collectively bargain with insurance companies to lower premiums, while insurance firms ensure cost containment by reining in overcharges by physicians and hospitals, similar to Medicare. (For more information on Obamacare, see Chapter 10).

Obama has proposed another innovation in pragmatic social investment—the **Impact Investment Fund** (IIF) to promote domestic entrepreneurship. Government-backed bonds would match private finance on a 2:1 basis to organizations that fund companies in economically distressed areas and in such emerging sectors as clean energy. Pledges were sought to capitalize IIF at $1 billion, but without success.

A major proposal is for a **National Infrastructure Reinvestment Bank**, with $60 billion in government funds to be matched by $500 billion in private funds. The bank, designed to create construction jobs, was originally proposed by Senators Christopher Dodd, a Democrat, and Chuck Hagel, a Republican, in 2007. If adopted, there would be a multiplier effect for the economy through projects in bridges, energy, high-speed trains, and roads. Legislation has been introduced for the bank, but Congress has not adopted the proposal.

Economic Recovery and the Deficit
Obama became president when the economy was in dire straits, close to a depression. The federal deficit (shortfall between expenditures and revenues) was about $10 trillion. The main reason was that President George W. Bush pushed appropriations for national security and the prescription drug addition to Medicare without proposing corresponding taxes to pay for the innovations.

In 1993, when President Bill Clinton took office at the end of a recession, he secured approval from Congress for more taxes on the wealthy and tax cuts for those with middle incomes. The result was a booming economy and a budget surplus rather than a deficit. Republicans went along with his proposals. But Obama has not enjoyed much cooperation from Republicans ever since he took office, and his advisers have clashed with one another on what to do.

Obama's economic "stimulus" bill of February 2009 prevented a depression by pumping money into the economy in the form of investment in infrastructure and tax cuts aimed at the middle class, consistent with Obamanomics, but at a cost of adding $787 billion to the deficit. At the end of 2010, to extend unemployment benefits and middle class tax cuts, the president agreed to continue Bush-era tax cuts for the rich. With a continued gap between revenues and expendi-tures, the deficit rose to around $15 trillion by late 2011.

The "stimulus" infrastructure money was forwarded to the states, which promised "shovel-ready" jobs, but in fact few such jobs existed. The states even failed to utilize some of the money because they could not design appropriate pro-jects before their allocation ran out two years later. When Democrats later realized that the economic stimulus had been too little, they could not interest Republicans in more govern-ment spending, such as a bill to create infrastructure jobs in light of higher unemployment in the construction industry (20 percent). Obama never proposed a federal jobs program in light of adamant opposition by Republicans.

During 2011, the economic recovery was sluggish, and unemployment remained high (about 9 percent). The Re-publican solution was to continue tax cuts for the rich; that is, the very Social Darwinist trickle-down economics that was partly responsible for Bush's $10 trillion deficit legacy. Yet those with higher incomes invest rather than spend money lavishly. Increased investment creates permanent jobs only when investments pay off and demand for consumer goods is high. But not all investments succeed, and consumer demand falls in a recession.

Compared to millionaires, the middle class spends a higher percentage of income on necessities, so tax cuts for the middle class can best create demand to spur production, re-sulting in job creation. But in a recession even the middle class can barely afford necessities. What little extra income they may have will be more likely to be spent on cheap goods made in China rather than high-quality manufactured pro-ducts made in the United States.

Upon entering office, President Obama called attention to the need to reduce the government deficit before the issue was taken up by Republicans. Although he urged passage of the Task Force for Responsible Fiscal Action Act of 2009 to set up a Congressional body to tackle the deficit on a bipartisan basis, Republicans blocked the proposal. He then set up a bipartisan commission by executive order. When the Commission reported recommendations in December 2010, House Democrats flatly refused to consider them, leaving Obama with no core of support in Congress to make them a centerpiece of debt reduction planning.

Had he embraced the recommendations, there might have been smoother sailing in 2011. What happened instead is that in January 2011 newly elected Tea Party Republicans, also ignoring the commission's recommendations, hatched a plot to demand spending cuts before agreeing to an upward adjustment of the federal debt limit, which had been routinely increased from 1917. For seven months, negotiations focused on particulars. When the Budget Control Act of 2011 finally passed in August, nobody was elated. Rating agency Standard & Poors then downgraded the credit rating of the United States primarily because Congress had proved itself to be dysfunctional. The stock market plunged, threatening to bring about a new recession. Obama strongly objected that the downgrade decision was not based on solid economic criteria.

The same division between Republicans opposing serious tax cuts and Democrats wanting to raise taxes continued throughout 2011. The "supercommittee" created by the Budget Control Act was doomed to fail because both party leaders chose panel members who were opponents of a bipartisan deal. As a result, $0.6 trillion in defense spending cuts and another $0.6 trillion for nondefense cuts are now mandated. But the required across-the-board cuts are not to be made until after the 2012 election, and the new Congress might repudiate the massive cuts. Any budget slashing would adversely affect the economic recovery, so the failure of the "supercommittee" was welcomed in some quarters.

What Congress obscured in the mid-2011 debt debate, perhaps intentionally, was the need for job creation. After signing the Budget Control Act to raise the federal debt limit, Obama pushed a $447 billion mini-stimulus bill paid for by increasing taxes for the rich. He also proposed to extend middle-class-oriented payroll tax cuts and to allocate funds for infrastructure and other jobs. When the $447 bill did not receive a hearing in the House of Representatives, he began to split the bill into individual components, such as funding for firefighters, police, schoolteachers, and veterans. Republicans wanted to neuter his presidency and some even objected to the measure about job assistance for veterans, which passed, as a political stunt.

Ignored has been the main cause of the deficit—fighting terrorist threats. Under President Bush, the budgets for defense and civilian counterterrorism skyrocketed. Discretionary spending nearly doubled. Few Republicans have come clean on how to cut nondefense programs significantly because they would have to slash popular programs. The Democratic proposal to impose more taxes on millionaires might ease the deficit by $3 trillion over the next decade but Republicans have resorted to unsubstantiated claims that higher taxes on millionaires would kill jobs. Accordingly, a group known as Patriotic Millionaires for Fiscal Strength arose to ask Congress to increase taxes, noting that Republi-cans were making phony arguments yet supported the bigger government that President Bush created. Republicans in Congress, ignoring the need for revenue to pay for the new national security needs since 9/11, were unwilling to cut that funding. Accordingly, the deficit increased.

The economy, meanwhile, was in focus while Republicans refused to do anything to help those most hurt by the recession. In response, President Obama used executive orders to ease loan repayment terms for government college student loans and home loans. His efforts were calculated to have some economic stimulus, but they were not enough to catapult much beyond a slow but steady economic recovery.

For economist Robert Samuelson, there is very little that a president or even a Congress can do to impact the economy, particularly in a downturn. Although Republicans claim that excessive government regulations slow the economic recovery, a poll of employers cites regulations as a reason for layoffs in only 0.2 percent of the cases, and economists assess their impact as minimal. Instead, lack of demand is cited much more often. In October 2011 about half of businesses reported that they were having difficulty filling jobs because applicants lacked prior experience. For students graduating from college and high school, too many American businesses had give up on hiring those with potential and then offering on-the-job training.

To improve the economy today, President Obama has few options. His repeated stress on having the ultra-rich pay more taxes is justified as "shared sacrifice," a concept deeply rooted in Zen Buddhism and Native Hawaiian communal economics. Yet the Republican-controlled House of Representatives, consistent with Social Darwinism, exhibited no responsibility to do anything concrete for millions of unemployed Americans.

Conclusion

There are many more examples of President Obama's pragmatic social investment economics (see Appendix B), a concept that could revolutionize how government spends taxes. Rather than throwing money at failed programs, he wants disparate interests to get together in order to find common ground for more innovative approaches.

It will be a daunting task to transform the federal government budget process that is now based on programmatic formula funding, into a diligent pursuit of pragmatic social investment programming. It will take time and agreement among moderates in both political parties.

Obamanomics offers a long-term vision of how to change the way government operates financially. Better outcomes can be achieved with less spending if programs are designed to be effective and only supported when they are. Meanwhile, Obama draws a line at proposals to gut Medicare, Medicaid, and Social Security, which did not cause the deficit. His humanistic economics measures policies by their impact on people.

Nevertheless, Obamanomics requires government action. More prudent spending does not reduce the alarming deficit between revenues from taxes and expenditures by government. And Obamanomics largely leaves job creation up to the private sector, which has failed to be revitalized by tax cuts for the affluent, contrary to Republican claims.

Republicans are determined to preserve tax cuts for the rich while cutting government spending that would choke off assistance to those in need—the disabled, the elderly, the poor, and the unemployed. One intended result is to pinkslip hundreds of thousands of public sector workers. As long as Republicans espouse Social Darwinism, economic recovery will lag behind voter expectations.

Republicans, thus, seem determined to wreck the economy and then pin the blame on Obama to defeat him in 2012. Republicans disavow responsibility for reducing the cause of the $10 trillion deficit created in part by tax cuts to the rich. Instead, they have focused on $4-5 trillions run up by Obama, a Democratic president, in a time of national economic emergency while again ignoring the obvious need for additional revenue. Instead, Obama's approach is to preserve the American Dream by insisting on pragmatic social investment and tax breaks for the middle class to keep capitalism humane.

But Obama holds the trumps in regard to extending tax cuts for the rich: If defeated for re-election, he will have no reason to extend them. If re-elected, he will have a mandate to let them expire. Either way, he can singlehandedly cut the deficit more than Congress—but after the 2012 election.

Some Republicans have accused President Obama of having a "socialist agenda." However, "socialism" exists only when the government controls, owns, and operates businesses. Although for a time the Obama administration had a controlling interest in some businesses (auto companies and banks) by buying stock in them, that was a temporary expedient to recapitalize those companies so that they would not become bankrupt. Today, that emergency period has ended, the government has sold its stock at a profit to taxpayers, and those firms are back on their feet.

Republican leaders worry that government accounts for 35 percent of the gross domestic product, up from 30 percent under Bush. But that is primarily because of the contraction of the economy, which has yielded fewer revenues (26 percent of the gross domestic product under Obama compared to 33 percent under Bush).

Meanwhile, too much inequality remains. Economic researchers report that economic growth increases in times of economic equality and stagnates when the gap between rich and poor is as great as what Republicans want. Obama bases his policies on sound economic scholarship while Republicans espouse Social Darwinist dogma.

At his speech in Osawatomie, Kansas, on December 6, 2011, Obama cited statistics to prove that inequality is "the defining issue of our times. . . . [W]hat's at stake is whether this will be a country where working people can earn enough to raise a family, build a modest savings, own a home, secure their retirement." Promoting the idea of a humanistic capitalism, he sounded the alarm that the American middle class might be abolished by trickle-down economics. The Republican response was to call the speech "class warfare" rhetoric, whereas Obama was talking about Republicans hell bent on class homicide. The middle class has shrunk in part due to home foreclosures and massive layoffs of white-collar and skilled blue-collar workers.

The public may know little about Barack Obama's pragmatic social investment economics, which sees government as a vital watchdog of economic and social health. The application of Obamanomics has not corrected the unemployment problem because the "stimulus" was too small and the Republican majority in the House of Representatives from 2011 has focused more on cutting federal spending than on job creation. There has been steady if slow economic growth in the last two years, but not enough to constitute full recovery from the Great Recession.

Obama's rigorous cost-benefit analysis of government spending through Race to the Top programs and his pruning of $1 billion from the federal budget may make him the most frugal president in modern political history. Obamanomics marries his ethical principles and his sense of practicality to bring people together in order to restore the long-term vision known as the American Dream by humanizing and reinvigorating the country's capitalistic economy. One element of Obamanomics is his health care plan, often called Obamacare, which is analyzed in the next chapter.

Chapter 10
Obamacare

During the early part of the 2008 presidential campaign, candidate Barack Obama favored a limited national health care plan featuring an "employer mandate," that is, a requirement that every employer should match health insurance contributions of employees. Some would not be covered by his plan, as rival candidate Hillary Clinton pointed out. Her plan would have covered everybody.

In 2010, after much debate and negotiation, Congress passed a health care plan, the Patient Protection and Affordable Health Care Act, establishing a program colloquially known as Obamacare. Congress adopted not only an employer mandate but also an individual mandate, so everyone will be required to buy health insurance by 2014. Some 32 million uninsured will get health insurance anew.

Objections to Obamacare have come from the left and the right, and there is confusion over the origins of the plan itself. But facts can clear up misunderstandings.

Origins
The country instituting the earliest government health care legislation was Germany, which adopted measures in 1883, 1884, and 1889. Britain took the first steps in 1911.

Theodore Roosevelt proposed national health care in his unsuccessful bid for the presidency during 1912. In 1917, proposals for health insurance were debated in four American states, but the success of the Bolshevik Revolution, which adopted universal government health care, provided an excuse to label the idea "communist."

President Franklin Delano Roosevelt tried to include universal health care in the Social Security Act of 1935, the Wagner Act of 1937, a plan just for medical care of the needy in 1938, and the revised Wagner Act of 1939. FDR's plans suffered the same fate as the Wagner-Murray-Dingell Bill, which in 1943 called for compulsory national health insurance to be funded by a payroll tax. The latter bill, re-introduced for fourteen straight years, never passed.

In 1945 and again in 1948, when Britain adopted a universal health care plan, President Harry Truman proposed a national health care plan. But Republicans in Congress turned him down, calling the idea "socialist." They also dissuaded Dwight Eisenhower, who felt that the neediest should receive assistance, from a similar reform. Nevertheless, many businesses and governments have offered health care plans for employees, sometimes under pressure from unions.

When I joined the faculty at the University of Hawai'i in 1964, I was immediately covered by a state government health care plan that had been adopted in 1961. Funds were deducted from my paycheck and matched by the state government. I had a choice of two private-sector plans—Hawaii Medical Services Association (the Blue Shield affiliate) or Kaiser Permanente. My coverage expanded over the years, including medical, hospital, dental, vision, and prescription drugs, all with modest copayment requirements. I am still covered by that plan as a secondary carrier to supplement Medicare. Federal and other state governments have similar plans.

In 1965, Medicare and Medicaid were adopted, though only for the elderly and the poor, respectively. President Lyndon Johnson deserves credit for marshalling votes for passage after Congress turned down a proposal from John Kennedy, who campaigned to provide a national health care plan but had too narrow a margin in Congress to gain support.

On February 6, 1974, President Richard Nixon proposed a plan with an employer mandate and drug coverage. But Congress was more interested in his impeachment than in his proposal.

Nevertheless, later in 1974, union pressure in Hawai'i succeeded in having the state legislature adopt the Prepaid Health Care Act, a plan similar to that proposed by Nixon with an employer mandate for employees working more than halftime. The law more than 95 percent of those who were not already covered by Medicare, Medicaid, or other government programs. Then in 1986 the governor proposed to cover nearly all the remaining 5 percent in the State Health

Insurance Program Act, which finally passed in 1989. Thus, Hawai'i was the first state to adopt government-mandated health insurance for most of its residents, including Obama's grandparents.

In 1985, meanwhile, Congress adopted the Consolidated Omnibus Budget Reconciliation Act (COBRA), which applied to companies with at least twenty employees that offer health insurance for employees and their dependents. COBRA requires employers to continue coverage for a period of time after their employees lose their insurance due to job loss, reduction in hours worked, or divorce.

In 1988, presidential candidate Michael Dukakis promised if elected to establish the Hawai'i health plan as the basis for the nation's health care plan. However, he lost.

Also in 1988, the final year of Ronald Reagan's presidency, Congress passed the Medicare Catastrophic Health Care Act to provide coverage for seniors that would cap hospital costs as well as provide payments for nursing home care and prescription drugs. But the law was repealed in 1989 because seniors strongly objected to the surtax imposed on Medicare recipients to defray coverage under the 1988 law.

After his defeat in 1988, Dukakis decided to find out more about the Hawai'i health care plan. Appointed to the political science faculty at the main campus of University of Hawai'i for a semester from January 1991, he prepared a detailed study and took his publication back to Massachusetts to gain local support.

In 1992, when Bill Clinton was running for president, Dukakis tried to interest the Clintons in the Hawai'i plan. But they were not interested. As president, Clinton reportedly asked John Waihe'e, the governor of Hawai'i, to be his first Secretary of Health and Human Services so that he could sell a plan for universal health care. However, Waihe'e declined. Although a bipartisan group of members of Congress developed a plan for universal health care and asked Hillary Clinton for an endorsement, she refused to go along. Instead, she developed a plan of her own. Then she tried in vain to get Congress to back her plan.

While the Clinton plan was being defeated in 1994, Hawai'i adopted a program to cover children under age 19 with family incomes of up to 200 percent of the federal poverty level. In 1997, Congress followed the Aloha State's model by passing the State Children's Health Insurance Program, known as SCHIP.

After taking office, President George W. Bush advocated a prescription drug plan (Part D of Medicare) without providing a trust fund or any other way to pay for the costs. He signed the law in 2003, and Part D went into force in 2006, thereby raising the deficit.

In 2006, Dukakis's efforts to have Massachusetts adopt universal health care paid off. Governor Mitt Romney signed into law a bill modeled on the Hawai'i plan's employer mandate. The bill also contained an individual mandate, requiring everyone in the state to buy health insurance.

In 2008, President Bush vetoed a law passed by Congress to continue and expand SCHIP. When Congress passed SCHIP again in 2009, President Barack Obama signed the law. He also secured funds for health care computerization within the economic "stimulus" legislation passed soon afterward.

Obama's Health Care Reform
As an employee of Bank of Hawaii, Barack Obama's grandmother was covered by the Hawai'i health care plan from 1975, when the law went into effect, until her death in 2008. So was Obama's grandfather.

Obama's mother, however, had a frustrating experience with her health care. After being diagnosed with cancer, she flew back to Hawai'i. But she did so as a new resident. Not covered by her mother's plan, she utilized her employer's insurance company, Signa, while in the hospital. Her application for disability coverage, however, was turned down because her cancer was considered a pre-existing condition. In the end, she could not pay for the full cost of her hospitalization, a fact that was impressed upon her son Barack, who flew to be with her in the hospital before her death but was unable, acting as her lawyer, to resolve her insurance problems.

Today, Obama's half-sister and brother-in-law are both covered by the Hawai'i plan. Barack Obama, thus, is intimately familiar with the Hawai'i health plan, though he has never said so.

Although the cost of living in Hawai'i is very high, the average cost of health care for individuals in the Aloha State is the lowest in the nation because of the employer mandate provision, a key provision that Obama originally proposed on the campaign trail. With employers required to fund half of the cost, employees purchase health insurance at half price.

After President Barack Obama took the oath of office, he left most details of the health care plan to Congress. He wanted to avoid the mistake committed sixteen years earlier, when Hillary Clinton preferred the plan that she drew up in the White House and rejected a compromise plan.

When calculations determined that a health care bill based solely on an employer mandate would not reduce health care costs in the country, a major change in Obama's plan was required. That's why an individual mandate was incorporated—to set up a larger pool that would pay for itself because the majority who are well would pay for the few who would be sick. Another cost-saving proposal was to modify Medicare Advantage, a plan that enables seniors to obtain more benefits than with Medicare alone.

Members of Congress tend to want their footprints on major legislation. The proposed legislation went through additions and revisions for months, reaching more than one thousand pages with so many provisions that few in Congress knew the full particulars.

One such modification was a proposal dear to the heart of Georgia Republican Senator Johnny Isakson—end-of-life counseling. He wanted those covered by the law to learn about advanced directives, living wills, and trust arrangements. But Alaska's Sarah Palin then fulminated that Obama and the Democrats were sponsoring "death panels."

Other Republicans spread the word that there would be cuts in Medicare under the proposal, which of course was true—though they did not specify that they were referring to changes in Medicare Advantage. Members of Congress were unable to agree on a bill on a bipartisan basis by the summer recess of 2009, so they went home to obtain feedback from their constituents.

Many "town hall" meetings on the health care proposal proved chaotic. Democratic members of Congress were besieged by an onslaught of disturbed constituents, while Republicans closed ranks to say that they were firmly opposed to the proposal. South Carolina Senator Jim DeMint even said that defeat of the proposal would ensure that Obama would not be re-elected, a goal around which Republicans decided to unite.

A timid president would have ditched the idea as a lost cause. But President Obama insisted that passage of universal health care legislation was his number one legislative priority. When Republican Senator Chuck Grassley indicated that he would not vote for the bill even if all his suggested changes were incorporated into the text, Congressional Democrats stopped approaching the subject on a bipartisan basis.

But Democrats still had to gain support within their own party. Conservative Democrats in the House of Representatives decided to oppose the bill after visits with their constituents. They presciently feared defeat for re-election in 2010.

Conservative Democratic Senators from Louisiana and Nebraska voted in favor, but only after they received special deals—more Medicaid money for their states. The Senate vote on the Patient Protection and Affordable Care Act on December 24, 2009, was 60-39.

Progressive Democrats in the Senate provided no strong obstacle to passage. Bernie Sanders, elected as a member of the Socialist Party of Vermont, would have preferred a "public option," that is, an opportunity for individuals to buy a government health care plan in case private insurance premiums were too high. But he went along with Democrats to comprise part of the 60 votes required for passage in order to overcome a Republican filibuster threat.

In the House of Representatives, however, Progressive Democrats held out for the "public option" and would not compromise. Then President Obama had a talk with Dennis Kucinich, a leader of the progressives. When the matter came up for a vote on March 21, 2010, Kucinich voted in favor. The vote was 219-212, with 34 Democrats voting No.

Key Provisions

When legislation occupies more than a thousand pages of text, few know the details. Certain provisions have already taken effect:

- No person can be turned down for health insurance because of pre-existing conditions.
- No person can be terminated from a health insurance policy because of an adverse health condition.
- Lifetime and annual insurance coverage caps are prohibited.
- Insurance companies are limited to 20 percent for overhead and profit for individual policies; 15 percent for group policies.
- A parent's insurance plan covers children past 18 up to the age of 26.
- Based on Medicare information, "report cards" are issued on doctor effectiveness.

The following major provisions take effect in 2014:

- Every individual must have a health care insurance policy or pay a fine.
- Every employer must contribute to health care insurance policies for their employees or pay a $2,000 fine.
- Employers with fewer than fifty workers can obtain a government subsidy to help to pay their share of premiums for their employees.
- Insurance seekers will be able to buy policies through government-established exchanges (similar to high-risk pools offered to motor vehicle drivers under the age of 26 in some states).

- Medicaid eligibility will expand to those 1/3 above the poverty level.

Less well known are the following important provisions:

- Minimum standards are to be established for health insurance policies by the new Independent Payments Advisory Board.
- Subsidies to pay health insurance premiums will be provided to low income persons and families not on Medicaid up to 400 percent of the poverty level.
- Medicare prescription drug coverage will eventually expand to cover everyone, eliminating the "donut hole."
- Medicare hospital reimbursements will change from "fee-for-service" to "bundled payments" so that all aspects of care will be placed on a single bill rather than separate bills from each provider.
- "Essential coverage," that is, annual physical "wellness" exams, will be free.
- More funding will be allocated to medical research.
- Co-payments will gradually be reduced, and physicians will receive smaller percentages of authorized Medicare costs.
- To attract more physicians to practice primary care, their fees will be raised to 80 percent of that paid to specialists.

Obamacare stresses "integrated care," that is a coordination among all those who provide health care so that patients are assured that the various specialists they visit do not prescribe contradictory regimens. Computerization of records is supposed to facilitate coordination. However, during the long debate in Congress the initial goal on improved health care and health safety in hospitals morphed into debates about health insurance costs.

Cost Analysis

A principal reason why President Obama pushed for a national health care plan is that costs of health care in both Medicaid and Medicare have been skyrocketing, eating up a larger share of the federal budget. There are several reasons: (1) Insurance companies charge high rates because healthy people do not apply. (2) As the "baby boomer" generation has come of age for Medicare, utilization has been rising beyond the amount in its trust fund. Similarly, the Bush-era pre-scription drug plan never allowed for cost savings for consumers. (3) Costly tests have been ordered by physicians in some parts of the country with no discernible impact on health improvement. (4) Before Obamacare, uninsured indi-viduals have waited until their health deteriorated from a chronic to an acute condition, whereupon treatment has been very costly. Large medical bills, in turn, bankrupt individuals and fami-lies. Lacking financial means, they have been treated gratis in hospital emergency rooms. The hospitals, then, have had to raise their rates for everyone else, including charges to Medicaid and Medicare beneficiaries billed to the govern-ment. Citizens without health insurance, in other words, have imposed costs on those prudent enough to buy health in-surance.

The overall aim of Obamacare is to save the government millions if not billions. Accordingly in October 2011, the Obama administration stopped implementing the Community Living Assistance Services and Support program because of recalculations; the program proved to be too expensive. Otherwise, cost savings will emerge from the following four innovations:

(1) Insurance rates will come down under Obamacare because everyone must buy health insurance, creating a larger pool including healthy individuals who do not immediately need health care. Since some may still decline coverage, raising the cost of health insurance for everyone else, the fine for opting out will serve to defray the increased cost for those covered.

(2) Obamacare reduces benefits to those covered by Medicare Advantage and taxes so-called Cadillac health care plans that offer much more than Medicare. Because the baby

boomers are now qualifying for Medicare, adjusting the minimum age for Medicare and means testing might be considered but is not included in Obamacare. During debate about raising the debt limit, President Obama offered some cuts in Medicare in private negotiations with Speaker John Boehner, who turned him down. The following month, Obama made his proposal public in an effort to pay for legislation to create jobs. He proposed a 4 percent cut in Medicare ($248 billion) over the next decade, of which 90 percent involved reducing payments to drug companies and health care providers. The remaining cuts, to begin in 2017, would initially come from higher co-pays from those earning more than $85,000. Each year thereafter, the co-pays would increase down the income scale until they reached the middle class. Also in 2017, those on Medigap plans (secondary insurance to Medicare) would pay surcharges. New enrollees would also pay higher deductibles. Obama's proposal is the first serious effort to stave off Medicare insolvency since the Reagan administration, when the present fixed-price billing was established so that medical providers would not impose exorbitant costs.

(3) Reduction of costs from over-testing will have to rely on regulations under Obamacare adopted by an Independent Payments Advisory Board, which will seek to reduce abuse, fraud, and waste. Below I discuss one possibility about tests.

(4) Under Obamacare "essential coverage," the insured are encouraged to take routine annual tests. If problems are detected early, incipient or chronic problems may be avoided and treated at a modest cost without hospitalization. Another cost savings provision is provided by the Minimum Loss Ratio (MLR). From January 1, 2011, insurance companies must spend at least 80 percent of premiums on direct health care to the insured. The MLR provision moves the United States closer to the universal care operating in France and Germany, where health insurance companies are nonprofits.

Obamacare also has some special programs. Communities Putting Prevention to Work funds efforts to encourage the use of community gardens and farmer's markets so that residents in low-income areas, where fast food is more available than supermarkets, will get in the habit of eating healthily.

The Partnership Program under Obamacare pays for the cost of home care for those on Medicaid. The alternative, nursing home care, is much more costly. By mid-2011, forty-three states had adopted the plan.

Meanwhile, doctors and their employees have been either milking the system for everything they can get or they have not attended cost containment seminars. I can provide some personal examples of how physicians today inflate Medicare costs.

On one occasion, I arranged for surgery to relieve carpal tunnel syndrome. On the day of my surgery, I informed the surgeon that I had a hangnail. Instead of applying an ointment to the finger, my usual home treatment, the surgeon performed a lance at an additional cost of $1,000. I only found out what he did after bandages were removed. By then, mold developed around the nail, needing dermatological treatment.

On another occasion, I sought a routine annual checkup for a chronic condition involving a lab test. When I called to make the appointment for the test, the receptionist insisted that I must see the doctor first. I then wrote a letter to the physician to plead for the test instead of an unnecessary doctor visit. But the letter was placed in my file and never delivered to the physician. When I went to the appointment, the physician agreed that the visit was unnecessary. I then made a second appointment for the routine annual test. Medicare, thus, was billed $300 for an unnecessary doctor visit because of a stubborn receptionist and a nurse who refused to direct mail to the physician.

Similarly, HIV patients usually have quarterly blood tests. If the tests cannot be performed without prior physician visits, the unnecessary medical cost is $1,200 annually. Some physicians will not telephone the results, requiring an appointment instead, thus extorting an additional $1,200 from patients, Medicaid, or Medicare each year.

Elderly patients often have several chronic conditions requiring yearly or even quarterly re-testing. Under a broad interpretation of the "essential coverage" provision in Obamacare, tests for chronic conditions could be performed without ever seeing a physician, who in turn could simply evaluate the results at a desk before reauthorizing medications to a pharmacy without ever having to see the patient. One of my physicians did so nine months after I took a test!

Multiplying my examples by millions of persons in similar situations, billions could be saved. Such savings could be put into effect even if Obamacare did not exist. But mechanisms to do so were obviously not in place before Obamacare passed.

Reactions to Obamacare

Republicans have been adamantly opposed to Obamacare, which they characterize as "government takeover of health care." But the government under Obamacare is largely uninvolved in health care, which is left as before to health care professionals, insurance companies, and patients. What Obamacare does is to ensure that everyone has health insurance (or pays a fine), and that insurance companies operate responsibly. The government under Obamacare will not make health decisions for patients or physicians.

Another absurd objection to Obamacare is that the impact is to kill jobs. The specious argument is that nearly 800,000 jobs would be lost by Obamacare. Instead, the nonpartisan Congressional Budget Office predicts that 800,000 persons will quit their jobs to take advantage of Obamacare, thereby opening 800,000 positions for new workers. Moreover, insurance companies will have to hire thousands of new employees to handle millions of new health care policyholders.

Some court cases, with contradictory results, have been filed to challenge individual provisions or the entire law. The initial effect of the controversy was to provide a campaign issue for the 2010 election, when Republicans defeated more than sixty Democrats to gain control of the House of Representatives.

The provision that voters most dislike is the individual mandate, that is, the requirement that everyone must buy health insurance or pay a fine. Ironically, Obama never campaigned for an individual mandate. The requirement, added to effect cost savings for those covered by the employer mandate, is similar to required motor vehicle insurance. In both cases, the incentive to purchase is to avoid a fine. Similarly, tax credits to buy houses and many other products are also government incentives to purchase something.

What is uncertain is whether employers will decide to discontinue their own insurance coverage for employees to cut business costs, thereby transferring costs to individuals in the insurance exchanges to be set up by the fifty states. If the choice is between a fine of $2,000 and an employer contribution of $10,000 for each employee, the employer may decide to opt out of Obamacare. But the most productive workers may then migrate to employers who do participate.

One of the first acts of House Republicans in 2011 was to vote to abolish Obamacare. The Senate Democratic leadership, however, did not schedule a debate or a vote on the repeal measure.

Later, House Republicans voted to change Medicare into a program in which the government provides vouchers for seniors to buy their own private insurance. The proposal, as advanced by Representative Paul Ryan, was defeated in the Senate. Five Republicans joined all the Democrats in opposition to Ryan's proposal to gut Medicare.

More interesting perhaps is the effect of Obamacare's passage on Progressive Democrats of California. Before Obamacare, the California legislature passed a "single payer" plan, which was vetoed by Governor Arnold Schwartzenegger. After Obamacare passed in 2010, Progressives continued to push for a "single payer" health plan for the state, in effect repudiating Obamacare. They had made up their minds about "single payer" long before Obamacare passed and had no interest in reviewing its provisions with care, including the fact that costs would be halved for individuals under Obamacare because of the employer mandate (see Chapter 6).

One reason for the adamant stand of Progressive Democrats may be that some of them are employers and do not want to pay their fair share for their workers. They would rather put the full burden on employees through increased taxes. The claim of some Progressive Democrats that "single payer" would save millions is true, but the savings would accrue only to employers. Another claim, that millions of jobs will be created by "single payer," may be true, but the same functions of health care are performed, whether workers are covered by the government or, under Obamacare, in the private sector.

Accordingly, I decided to contact the national Progressive Democrats of America (PDA) organization to ascertain if the parent organization agreed with Progressive Democrats of California in opposing Obamacare. What I learned was that PDA's website advocates a government health care plan with no co-payments—Medicaid (not Medicare) for all. But when I emailed the headquarters of PDA, National Director Tim Carpenter replied on December 28, 2010, they he did not want to abolish Obamacare. Instead, he was for amendments to improve the law and wondered why California progressives were not in sync with PDA—and who they were.

Nevertheless, Progressive Democrats have a point that will not be fully realized until Obamacare is implemented: Employers are the most vigorous opponents of Obamacare. Currently, through their membership in the U.S. Chamber of Commerce, employers prefer no government-mandated health plan at all. When all provisions of Obamacare become a reality, they may band together to pressure insurance companies to lower their rates, as in Hawaiʻi. Or they might prefer to pay a small fine rather than matching employee contributions, thereby forcing their workers to qualify for expensive government subsidies. Individuals also may opt out, preferring a fine at lower cost than the premium for a health insurance policy.

After Obamacare fully goes into effect in 2014, employers may once again seek to abolish the plan. But if there are insufficient votes in Congress to do so, they may indeed opt for "single payer" to reduce the requirement to match contributions of their employees. If so, Obamacare will have served as a transitional plan to "single payer," something that current Republican opponents fear.

Meanwhile, Vermont voted to adopt a "single payer" health plan in May 2011. The state wants Congress to allow their scheme to operate before 2017, the date set in the law for states to opt out of Obamacare for their own universal health care plans.

Conclusion

Lost in most of the debate are statistics on the lower health status of Americans compared with other advanced industrial democracies. The ultimate objective of Obamacare is to improve the health and life expectancy for millions of Americans. Early treatment of contagious diseases will save many from avoidable sickness. And employers, mindful that working conditions can produce illness, will be encouraged to improve occupational safety. For Obama and many others, health care appears to be a right.

Republican opposition to Obamacare galvanized many voters to defeat Democrats in the 2010 elections. Republicans oppose both the employer and individual mandates, believing that costs will be kept down by competition between competing private health insurance plans. But that was the system before Obamacare, when health insurance was not affordable for many. The difference between Republican market-oriented optional health insurance and Democrats who want to require health insurance, in short, is based on ideologies that separate the two parties.

Meanwhile, individuals will continue to seek affordable health insurance. The main practical difference between the political parties is that government-mandated insurance will lower costs for individuals, especially employees. Today, without a government mandate, costs have been soaring for years. Thus, the Republican market-driven plan indulges in fantasy in expecting insurance premiums to drop some day.

There the matter rests as various provisions of Obamacare gradually go into effect. The Supreme Court of the United States, which will finally rule on the constitutionality of Obamacare, will have to decide whether Congress has the authority to pass such a law. If major portions of the law pass constitutional muster, and the Supreme Court rules that the law is valid because the scope is included in the constitutional provision that Congress can regulate interstate commerce, all provisions of Obamacare will be in effect from 2014. However, a Republican landslide for Congress in 2012 could mean repeal of the law in 2013.

What Obamacare promises is a new spirit of cooperation between employers and employees, consistent with Obama's desire to bring people together to solve common problems.

Employers, in turn, will seek to provide the lowest cost health insurance programs for their employees. Individuals who now resist mandatory health insurance may ultimately realize that they will no longer have to face bankruptcy in the event of a medical emergency. Only selfishness explains why some oppose the individual mandate, which will lower costs for all and raise America's public health to a level comparable with other industrial democracies.

For all Americans, Obamacare brings a sense of social consciousness and responsibility toward others. President Barack Obama has tried to foster such a transformation in all his policymaking. Although his domestic policies have many critics, his transformative approach to foreign policy has been judged more favorably. The elements of an Obama Doctrine are the subject of the following chapter.

Chapter 11
The Obama Doctrine in Foreign Policy

Presidents differ in their approaches to foreign policy. George Washington, in his Farewell Address of September 19, 1796, warned of the adverse consequences of "entangling alliances." One of the assumptions of the modern system of nation-states, as established in 1648 by the Peace of Westphalia, is that every country is supposed to avoid meddling in the affairs of other states yet has a right to respond when its own people are under attack.

Yet for nearly 200 years, American presidents have been willing to use military action in foreign lands. President Barack Obama has done so, largely in the context of previous foreign policy justifications, known as "doctrines," but he has contributed a new doctrine that has created controversy.

Foreign Policy Doctrines from Monroe to Bush
No doctrine was thought necessary in the War of 1812, when the official American reasons were that Britain was blocking American trade with France during its war with Napoléon, forcing Americans on commercial ships to serve in the British navy, and was also supporting raids by various Indian Nations into the United States. A less honorable reason was to settle boundary disputes with Canada by force.

In 1823, more than two decades after Washington's warning, President James Monroe declared that it was the responsibility of the United States to protect the Americas from European colonization. His concern was that Russia was claiming territory in the Pacific Northwest and Spain was emerging from the Napoleonic Wars eager to reassert control over former colonies in Latin America that had declared independence. Known as the Monroe Doctrine, his policy was the first to justify an American foreign policy that might involve the United States in using the military abroad despite a lack of direct attack on the United States. He did so in coordination with George Canning, Britain's Prime Minister, who also hoped to stop European rivals from controlling territory in the Americas.

In 1842, President John Tyler extended the Monroe Doctrine to protect the Kingdom of Hawai'i from potential imperial designs. Britain and France accepted Tyler's declaration in 1843.

But in 1845, the United States annexed Texas, which had once been governed by México, and sent troops to occupy the Río Grande. When Mexican forces attacked in 1846, believing that the correct border was the Nueces River, the Mexican War began, at first as an act of "self-defense" over a disputed border. But American troops clearly engaged in aggression without a doctrine when they marched past the Río Grande until they occupied México City and achieved victories in California by the end of 1847.

The Monroe Doctrine was implicitly invoked to justify the Spanish-American War of 1898 regarding Cuba. But the annexation of the sovereign state of Hawai'i and military conquests of the Philippines and Puerto Rico occurred that same year without a justifying doctrine.

In 1904, the "Roosevelt Corollary" was enunciated. President Theodore Roosevelt declared that the American military had the right to enforce the Monroe Doctrine by sending troops to block any possible foreign intervention in the Western Hemisphere. But he really considered the Caribbean as an American lake, that is, as an arena wherein the United States could operate with relative impunity. Woodrow Wilson acted on that "corollary" when he became president, but the Clark Memorandum of 1928, issued secretly by Calvin Coolidge's Undersecretary of State J. Reuben Clark, repudiated Roosevelt's corollary to reassure Latin America that the United States had peaceful intentions. The memo was made public in 1930, when Herbert Hoover was president.

President Wilson's reason for entering World War I, "to make the world safe for democracy," has been called the Wilson Doctrine. But his "Fourteen Points" went beyond justifying the use of American military forces abroad. He advocated self-determination of peoples and pacific settlement of international disputes, and he opposed secret treaties. Although he

104

sent American troops to Europe, they did not stay after the war to enforce the "Fourteen Points."

There was no need for a special doctrine after the attack on Pearl Harbor on December 7, 1941, and when Germany declared war on the United States soon afterward. The United States engaged in a war of self-defense during World War II.

With the advent of the Cold War, the Truman Doctrine justified American involvement in backing the Greek and Turkish governments from possible Communist takeovers: "The policy of the United States [is] to support free peoples who are resisting attempted subjugation by armed minorities or by outside pressures." Articulated in 1947, the form of support that President Harry Truman had in mind was economic and military assistance. The Marshall Plan of 1948 provided aid to countries pressured from inside and outside—Western European democracies, which needed capital to rebuild their economies. Then in 1950 Truman responded to aggression by North Korea by sending troops to defend South Korea, an action approved by the United Nations Security Council in accordance with the UN Charter.

The North Atlantic Treaty Organization (NATO), formed in 1949 while Truman was president, established a treaty obligation to defend any member country under attack. Thereafter, presidents could refer to treaty requirements to justify military intervention abroad.

In 1954, after Dwight Eisenhower became president, the Truman Doctrine might have been viewed as justification for using covert military action to topple the democratic government of Guatemala, which had adopted land reform and wanted to nationalize American businesses. Administration officials feared that the government was "communist" and would become a beachhead for the Soviet Union. But Eisenhower never cited the Truman Doctrine.

In 1957, President Eisenhower proclaimed a policy "to secure and protect the territorial integrity and political independence of such nations, requesting such aid against overt armed aggression from any nation controlled by international communism." Known as the Eisenhower Doctrine, the immediate aim was to isolate Egypt's Gamal Abdel Nasser from support in the rest of the Middle East.

Nasser, who had been accepting aid from the Soviet Union, nevertheless survived until 1967, when Israeli armed forces launched an attack and defeated Egypt in the Six Day War. Nasser then resigned, having lost the confidence of his Egyptian supporters.

The Kennedy Doctrine, in response to Fidel Castro's successful revolution in Cuba in 1959, extended the Truman Doctrine to Latin America. President John Kennedy feared that Cuban communism would be exported. Subsequent support for Latin American dictators was one element of that policy.

President Lyndon Johnson did more than offer aid to counter the spread of communism. The Johnson Doctrine, at first applied to the Dominican Republic in 1965 and later applied to Vietnam, was that American troops would be sent whenever Communists were likely to overthrow a "free" government.

The Nixon Doctrine, announced in mid-1969, qualified the Johnson Doctrine to require any country requesting American aid to bear primary responsibility for its own defense. President Richard Nixon, of course, wanted to withdraw American troops from Vietnam, so he hoped that the fighting would gradually be "Vietnamized." A lesser known element of the Nixon Doctrine was the promise to provide a "shield" if a nuclear power threatened an ally or a country that an American president decided was vital to its own national security.

In 1976, President Gerald Ford declared that the United States would take "appropriate action" if Cuba intervened any place in the Western Hemisphere. Known as the Ford Doctrine, his speech was a response to the dispatch of Cuban troops to Angola.

Not until 1980, in the final year of his presidency, did President Jimmy Carter enunciate a policy known as the Carter Doctrine: "An attempt by any outside force to gain control of the Persian Gulf region will be regarded as an assault on the vital interests of the United States of America, and such an assault will be repelled by any means necessary, including military force." Carter was reacting to the Soviet invasion of Afghanistan that year and was concerned that its aggression might serve as a stepping stone toward control of oil in the states bordering the Persian Gulf.

In 1985, President Ronald Reagan gave a speech on foreign policy to justify American support for rebels in Honduras who were trying to topple the Nicaraguan government. Known as the Reagan Doctrine, he argued that the United States had the right to aid in the overthrow of Communist-inspired left-leaning governments.

But communism became irrelevant with the fall of the Berlin Wall in 1989, the year when George Herbert Walker Bush became president. Nevertheless, later that year Bush suddenly invaded Panamá to arrest its president, Manuel Noriega, without proclaiming a doctrine. Bush gave four reasons: (1) to protect the Panamá Canal, (2) to safeguard potential threats against American citizens, (3) to defend democracy and human rights in Panamá, (4) to eradicate a major center of drug trafficking.

Then in 1991 Bush mobilized a coalition of countries to defend Kuwait against a war of annexation by Iraq as a violation of the UN Charter. The UN Security Council authorized the intervention, and Bush forged a coalition of countries to expel Iraqi forces from Kuwait. Bush got Congressional authorization as well.

President Bill Clinton was primarily interested in domestic affairs. Under this presidency, the United States did nothing to stop the Rwanda genocide of 1994, ethnic cleansing in Bosnia by ethnic Serbs in 1992-1995, or in Krajina by Croatians during 1995.

But in 1994 Clinton sent American troops to Haïti in order to stop unrest due to repression that was provoking an outpouring of refugees. And in 1999 Clinton ordered the bombing of Serbia to stop a potential genocide in Kosovo by Serbian armed forces. The Clinton Doctrine, formulated with knowledge that the United States was the world's only superpower, implied that Washington had a responsibility to intervene militarily to prevent gross human rights abuses, even without the approval of the UN Security Council, which did not authorize the Kosovo War.

Perhaps more notorious today is the doctrine of George W. Bush. Soon after the attacks on 9/11, Bush declared that

107

the United States had the right to root out terrorist groups as well as to attack countries that harbor or give aid to terrorist groups. However, the Bush Doctrine soon expanded to justify a war in Afghanistan to root out terrorists as well as to round up alleged terrorists for interrogation and later incarceration. To pretend that aggression against Iraq was self-defense, President Bush claimed that Iraq's Saddam Hussein possessed weapons of mass destruction that could somehow be used against the United States. The Bush Doctrine, in other words, argued for preemptive war to avoid eventual massive loss of life. And he obtained vague Congressional authorization.

When objections were raised that the Bush Doctrine was allowing the sweeping use of force to go to war or to arrest anyone anywhere on the pretext of stopping terrorism, Bush tempered his policy in his State of the Union address in 2006 by taking a leaf out of the Wilson Doctrine, arguing that the United States had a special responsibility to spread democracy.

The Obama Doctrine

Because of his upbringing in Honolulu and Jakarta, with relatives in Kenya and other countries, President Barack Obama would inevitably adopt a different foreign policy from his predecessor. His assimilation to Hawai'i's multicultural ethos meant that he would be friendly to other peoples and respectful of differing value systems. Instead of bullying other leaders in meetings, he would listen to them with a humble, non-confrontational, serene composure. He would not try to advance American interests to the detriment of other friendly countries, preferring to find common ground in policies that would put the interests of peoples and responsibilities of governments above ideological principles.

In his first major speech on foreign policy, delivered on April 23, 2007, to the Chicago Council on Global Affairs, candidate Barack Obama identified problems caused by the administration of George W. Bush as well as how the United States might lead again, focused on "common security", "common humanity," and serving as "a beacon of freedom and justice for the world":

- Bring a responsible end to the war in Iraq and refocus on the broader region.
- Build the first truly 21st century military (add 65,000 to the Army and 27,000 more Marines) and show wisdom in how they are deployed.
- Marshal a global effort to secure, destroy, and stop the spread of weapons of mass destruction.
- Rebuild and construct alliances and partnerships necessary to meet common challenges and confront common threats, including global warming.
- Invest in "our common humanity" through foreign aid and supporting the "pillars" of a sustainable democracy—a strong legislature, an independent judiciary, the rule of law, a vibrant civil society, a free press, and an honest police force.

In a campaign speech on July 15, 2008, he dropped expansion of the military and the foreign aid investment goal but added the following:

- Finish the fight against Al-Qaeda and the Taliban.
- Achieve true energy security.

But goals do not make a doctrine, which involves a principled statement about means, in most cases military means. And upon taking office President Obama was more interested in establishing a new presidential style that would break American foreign policy out of the isolated, unilateralist box of the previous administration.

Nevertheless, he inherited an ongoing war in Afghanistan and many other commitments. Rather than making a single speech to declare a new approach, incremental, case-by-case bits of an Obama Doctrine have emerged from individual decisions. They are described next.

The first occasion to send a new signal to the world came two days after his inauguration, when he signed executive orders requiring compliance with the Geneva Conventions at Guantánamo and a closure of the facility within a year "in the interest of justice." But no such closure occurred, in part because Congress tied his hands by banning the use of funds to do so (see Chapter 12). Nevertheless, he arranged for the United States to join the UN Human Rights Council, which the previous administration had boycotted.

In ordering compliance with the Geneva Conventions at Guantánamo, Obama indicated that he wanted to follow international law. But he also asked the Central Intelligence Agency to increase unpiloted aerial vehicle (drone) attacks on Al-Qaeda operatives living in Pakistan. Although drone attacks clearly involve extrajudicial executions of terrorists, the Obama administration claimed that the raids were justified as acts of self-defense under international law because in the context of a "War on Al-Qaeda." Since Guantánamo did not close as he had hoped, indefinite detention, contrary to the International Covenant on Civil and Political Rights, still remains a tool in the presidential arsenal.

Obama refrained from describing his military policy as opposition to "Islamic extremism" or "jihadism." In effect, he declared an end to Bush's "war on terror," preferring to focus on a more limited set of enemies: "Our enemy is not terror because terror is a state of mind." After all, National Security Adviser John Brennan affirmed in 2010, "Terrorism is but a tactic." Instead, Obama clarified, the "enemy is Al-Qaeda and its terrorists affiliates."

On February 24, 2009, he addressed Congress in what appeared to be an opportunity to announce a new foreign policy doctrine. After declaring that "a new era of engagement has begun," he said:

> For we know that America cannot meet the threats of this century alone, but the world cannot meet them without America. We cannot shun the negotiating table, nor ignore the

foes or forces that could do us harm. We are
instead called to move forward with the sense
of confidence and candor that serious times
demand.

In other words, Obama declared an end to George W. Bush's
unilateralism and the beginning of multilateral engagement.
The subtext appeared to be that the United States was em-
barking on a post-imperialist foreign policy, mindful that the
country had limited resources.

He began an outreach to the Muslim world by giving his
first press interview to Al-Arabiya television on January 26,
2009. Then he went to give a major speech in Cairo on June
4, 2009, to assure Muslims that the United States was not engaged in a war against Islam. Eleven days later, protesters
crowded the streets of Tehran, soon to be arrested and gunned
down.

Subsequently, he gave speeches in Ankara, Prague, and
Strasbourg. He made clear that he first wanted to listen to the
leaders of the world before he would make decisions on matters of foreign policy. He infuriated conservatives in the United States by admitting that America had "shown arrogance
and been dismissive, even derisive," but he also criticized
some Europeans for "casual" if "insidious . . . anti-Americanism."

Obama's outreach went to leaders whom Bush eschewed
as enemies. He dispatched two letters to Iran's supreme cleric
Ayatollah Ali Khamenei; sent special representatives to Burma, North Korea, and Sudan; lifted a ban on travel of relatives to Cuba; and, after receiving Venezuelan President Hugo
Chávez's anti-American book, sent an ambassador to Cara-
cas. He also pushed the "reset button" with Russian President
Dmitry Medvedev and Prime Minister Vladimir Putin by
scrapping Bush's proposed missile defense installations in the
Czech Republic and Poland. He urged the Israeli government
to freeze construction within settlements, although they ignored him.

Reactions to unexpected developments often serve to de-
fine a president's foreign policy approach. The earliest example of his toughness came on April 12, 2009, when he dis-

patched Navy SEALs to intercept Somali pirates in order to rescue an American captain held prisoner. He was clearly not reluctant to use military options.

At international conferences during 2009, Obama scored some successes. He persuaded the richest countries to support a $1.1 trillion bailout of developing economies, an almost unparalleled example of successful inclusiveness. In Copenhagen, representatives of 183 countries agreed to reduce more greenhouse gasses than at the Kyoto Accord of 1997, and pledges were affirmed at Cancun (2010) and Durban (2011).

Obama traveled to several other countries during his first year in office, including the People's Republic of China. When asked about his policy toward Taiwan during in a Shanghai "town hall meeting" in mid-November 2009, he replied that the issue required "dialog and negotiations." Criticized at home for apparently abandoning Taiwan (the Republic of China), he responded two months later by proposing a new $6.4 billion arms sale to the Taipei government.

The next big test came during mid-2009, while he deliberated on whether to send more troops to fight in Afghanistan, something that he had promised to do as a candidate. During a speech in West Point on December 1, he announced that he would send an additional 30,000 troops to reverse the momentum of the Taliban insurgency. Although he authorized fewer than the amount requested by some in the military, he cited Eisenhower's frugality about deploying military means as justification (which later applied to the Libyan intervention). Obama also planned to withdraw an unspecified number of troops from Afghanistan by July 2011, presuming that the mission would be nearing completion and that Afghan forces could be trained to handle the job, reminiscent of the Nixon Doctrine of Vietnamization. His overall justification was to bring a better life to the Afghan people by freeing them from the threat of oppression by the Taliban, who had provided safe haven to Al-Qaeda in the past and might be expected to do so in the future.

His Afghan policy thereby apparently married American national interest with the Clinton Doctrine of humanitarian intervention, but he again avoided stating an ideological justification, preferring to reiterate the following as overall goals of his foreign policy (without bullets) in his West Point text:

- countering violent extremism and insurgency
- stopping the spread of nuclear weapons and securing nuclear materials
- combating a changing climate and sustaining global growth
- helping countries feed themselves and care for their sick.

Earlier, during October 2009, Obama was surprised to learn that he had been awarded the Nobel Peace Prize. He then had to deliver an acceptable speech nine days after the West Point address. What could he say after arguing for military means to advance his country's national interest? Press coverage of the speech focused on that fundamental contradiction, and he indeed defended American wars on the same basis as at West Point—to bring freedom and stability to other countries in time of need.

What the press did not emphasize from his Oslo speech was that he added a significant element to the evolving Obama Doctrine by being the first president to endorse the concept of "just peace," namely, that peace should not be considered merely the absence of war but the absence of structural violence. As developed by Norwegian sociologist Johan Galtung, "structural violence" exists when elites deprive masses of basic human rights, such as when some in a country are overfed while others starve. Obama was implying that the world would continue in turmoil as long as some governments failed to grant basic civil and economic rights to their people. That, he suggested, was why the United States had gone to war in the past.

For Obama, the next challenge came on January 12, 2010, when a massive earthquake hit Haïti. Obama immediately sent aid, including military troops to keep order, noting that in times of tragedy, the United States of America steps forward and helps. That is who we are. That is what we do. For decades, America's leadership has been founded in part on the fact that we do not use our power to subjugate others, we use it to lift them up—whether it was rebuilding our former adversaries after World War II, dropping food and water to the people of Berlin, or helping the people of Bosnia and Kosovo rebuild their lives and their nations. . . . When we show not just our power, but also our compassion, the world looks to us with a mixture of awe and admiration. That ad-vances our leadership. That shows [that] the character of our country . . . is acting on behalf of our common humanity.

Obama, thus, again stressed a key element to his incrementally developing foreign policy—the "just peace" idea that America has the responsibility of providing material support to those around the world who suffer in times of emergency, including the use of military forces to produce order from chaotic conditions.

On April 8, 2010, his quiet (behind-the-scenes) diplomacy with Russia bore fruit. In Prague he signed a nuclear arms reduction treaty with his counterpart, Prime Minister Medvedev. In fulfillment of a term paper written while he was a student at Columbia University, he was committed to making the world safer by seeking a total elimination of nuclear weapons. Russia, in turn, obtained a commitment from North Korea in mid-2011 to stop nuclear weapons tests.

Later in April 2010, heads of states and governments from forty-seven countries agreed in a conference at Washington to secure weapons-grade materials from falling into the hands of terrorists. The latter meeting was the largest assembly of world leaders since 1944, when government heads met in San Francisco to adopt the United Nations Charter.

Harold Koh, State Department legal adviser, has stressed that Obama's foreign policy has been realigned to be consistent with international law. According to Koh, there are four components:

- principled engagement
- diplomacy as a critical element of smart power
- strategic multilateralism
- living our values.

None of the four provide a specific justification for the use of force abroad, but Koh's speech refers to the right of self-defense as the legal basis for drone attacks, a matter discussed in more detail in Chapter 14.

During early 2011, peaceful demonstrations in Tunisia brought an end to a dictatorship and the prospect for a more democratic regime. Following that, Egyptians went into the streets with similar demands. At first, President Obama's foreign policy team was divided on how to respond—whether to back a longtime ally in Cairo or to side with the demonstrators. He urged the Egyptian government of President Hosni Mubarak to avoid violence and begin a dialog with those in the streets, but that did not happen. In the end, Obama left Egyptians to handle the situation themselves.

Then Obama's foreign policy took a new turn. On March 28, 2011, he announced that the United States had a "responsibility to act" by enforcing a no-fly zone over Libya, where rebels had been mobilizing support over the past month. He did so after a UN Security Council resolution authorized the use of a no-fly zone to protect the population, in particular to save the populous city of Benghazi from a bloody massacre threatened by Libya's leader Muammar Al-Qadhafi. His announcement followed behind-the-scenes efforts to gain support among Arab League nations, the UN Security Council, and the North Atlantic Treaty Organization. Quiet diplomacy had worked again, though his critics characterized his tendency to announce new policies after mobilizing support from allies as "leading from behind."

President Obama's justification for his policy on Libya was humanitarian intervention, that is, R2P—the Responsibility to Protect Resolution adopted by the UN Security Council in 2006 and the UN General Assembly in 2009. The R2P principle is that the international community is collectively responsible to stop or prevent genocides and widespread massacres, a justification that Clinton implicitly used in the Kosovo War. Obama's means, however, were quite limited—first establishing a no-fly zone and then allowing other NATO countries to enforce the zone. No American ground troops were to be involved. But the actual goal in the Libyan operation increasingly changed from R2P to regime change (see Chapter 13).

In addition, antigovernmental demonstrations erupted in Bahrain, Syria, and Yemen. Once again, Obama urged the governments to avoid violence and engage in dialog with the dissidents. His major speech on the uprisings in the Middle East and North Africa on May 19, 2011, called for democratic solutions and economic aid to new democracies, but he did not call for more military intervention, evidently because there was no single rebel group to back and no support by the Arab League or any other international body.

July 2011 marked the deadline for President Obama to determine how exactly many American troops to withdraw from Afghanistan, as promised in his West Point speech during 2009. Rather than following advice from anti-war advocates or from military officers, he chose a middle course between the two extremes. One phrase in his speech underscored his eclectic foreign policy:

> We must chart a more centered course. Like generations before, we must embrace America's singular role in the course of human events. But we must be as pragmatic as we are passionate; as strategic as we are resolute. When threatened, we must respond with force—but when that force can be targeted, we need not deploy large armies overseas.

His frugality harkened back to the Eisenhower and Nixon Doctrines. His desire for results underscored his pragmatic philosophy of governance.

Then the most celebrated accomplishment of his foreign policy was announced on May 1, 2011: Osama Bin Laden had been shot and killed within a compound in Pakistan (see Chapter 14). President Obama announced the event as a significant development in the "War on Al-Qaeda." Although no doctrine was cited, the right of self-defense against those plotting against America was clearly implied.

Meanwhile, China has posed a military threat in Asia. The claim over small islands in the South China by Malaysia, the Philippines, and Vietnam seems weaker every time Chinese naval vessels ply the area. And the launching of China's first aircraft carrier suggests preparation for an invasion of Taiwan. Obama's symbolic response in 2011 was to send a contingent of 2,500 Marines to Australia's northernmost port, Darwin, while approving more sales of military aircraft to Taiwan and lecturing Beijing on the need to observe international standards of fair trade (that is, to stop allowing pirate copies of American films).

Conclusion
Barack Obama eschews ideology in both domestic and foreign affairs. No White House wants to proclaim a "doctrine," preferring to deal on a case-by-case basis. The president rejects both a purely idealist foreign policy that enforces American goals on the world as well as a triumphalist unilateralism that advances national interest regardless of consequences to other countries. Similar to his domestic policies, he seeks to build consensus in the world polity. But he is mindful that the American economy can only provide finite resources on behalf of any major policy.

Still, the components of an Obama Doctrine remain elusive. To be a "doctrine" parallel to doctrines of previous presidents, there must be a coherent justification to threaten or use military force abroad.

The following points summarize what Barack Obama has said to defend his use of American military force:

1) Limit military action to the least costly options.
2) Rescue Americans in harm's way abroad.

117

3) Support the military needs of allied countries.
4) Relieve chaotic conditions in countries where the people desperately need humanitarian aid.
5) Act preemptively, using force in self-defense, so that an enemy will never obtain a safe haven in a host country or carry out a violent plot in the United States.
6) Use force only if supported multilaterally with real burden sharing by allies.
7) Protect large civilian populations from threats of massacre.
8) Bring about a "just peace" by stopping elite regime deprivation of the people.
9) Support local groups of freedom fighters.

To be a unique "Obama Doctrine," he should go beyond the previous presidents. Except for George W. Bush, most presidents have agreed with (1), (2), and (3). Clinton adopted (4) when he sent troops to Haïti. Obama's immediate predecessor advanced (5). Clinton implicitly favored (6) and (7) in relation to Kosovo, and Obama also made burden sharing and regional support as conditions for the use of force.

Having backed seven previous justifications for using American military forces abroad, President Barack Obama's unique contribution, therefore, is twofold—the advancement of the concept of "just peace" and the stipulation that there must be a local group worthy of support. The Obama Doctrine can be inferred from his Nobel Prize speech, his justification for the no-fly zone over Libya, and the dispatching of troops to Uganda to stop Joseph Kony.

Obama's foreign policy has been unsuccessful in solving many problems, including China's currency undervaluation as well as the desirability of a new Palestinian state. The Obama Doctrine provides little guidance regarding China but doubtless shapes his view that an independent Palestinian state should emerge from Israeli occupation.

Aloha Diplomacy

But there is another way to assess Obama's foreign policy. As Senator Daniel Akaka has often said, those from Hawai'i have a special responsibility of "extending Aloha to the world." Through his idealistic speeches, which always refer to "values," Barack Obama, once considered the third Senator from the Aloha State, clearly seeks to project Aloha in order to win hearts and minds for America around the world. He said so explicitly at the Asia-Pacific Economic Cooperation forum in November 2011, quoting the Hawaiian proverb, *'A 'ohe hana nui ke alu ia.* (No task is too big when done together by all.)

Many have questioned why Obama, who is so enthusiastic about the Afghan War and the War on Al-Qaeda, received the Nobel Peace Prize. For members of the committee in Norway that determines the recipients, Obama's "extraordinary efforts to strengthen international diplomacy and cooperation between people" was apparently enough. More eloquently, University of Hawai'i anthropologist Alice Dewey believes that his award was for "ending policies that pitted America in a death match with other cultures."

According to columnist David Ignatius, "Alliances are stronger, the United States is (somewhat) less bogged down in foreign wars, Iran is weaker, the Arab world is less hostile and Al-Qaeda is on the run." Polling around the world concurs. In a word, Barack Obama's diplomacy has worked.

But the Obama Doctrine has not helped him in trying to close the detention facility at the naval base in Guantánamo Bay. As described in the next chapter, recalcitrant members of Congress have not accepted the Obama Doctrine.

Chapter 12
The Guantánamo Quagmire

Perhaps Barack Obama's biggest blunder relates to Guantánamo, which remains a blight on his presidency and the nation. His inability to clean up a problem left by his predecessor means that he has been unable to fulfill a major campaign promise. And the annual cost for each prisoner on Gitmo is $800,000, approximately $140 billion per year; therefore, more than $1.4 trillion since the facility opened in 2002.

Guantánamo, Then and Now
After 9/11, President George W. Bush put out an order to capture terrorists. With the aid of bounty hunters in Afghanistan and Pakistan, more than one thousand were rounded up and screened. Of those, 774 were initially shipped to Guantánamo (Gitmo for short) in the belief that they were the "worst of the worst." From the day they first arrived, they were mistreated.

The Third Geneva Convention of 1949 governs the treatment of prisoners held in time of war, and the International Covenant on Civil and Political Rights of 1967 establishes standards on how prisoners captured out of combat are to be treated. The mistreatment of those at Guantánamo soon became evident after the first photographs of twenty prisoners in orange jumpsuits was made public on January 11, 2002, a "public display" that was banned as early as the Geneva Convention of 1929 relating to prisoners of war.

Guantánamo immediately became a symbol of American barbarism throughout the world. Al-Qaeda was able to recruit more terrorists on the basis of accounts of the cruel and unusual treatment of prisoners at Gitmo as well as later at Abu Ghraib in Iraq. George W. Bush later sent many home from Gitmo and even expressed a desire to close the facility.

In my recent book *George W. Bush, War Criminal?* (2009), more than 100 war crimes are documented in the treatment of prisoners, mostly at Guantánamo. I sent a copy of the book to Barack Obama just before his inauguration.

121

During the 2008 presidential campaign, Barack Obama promised to close Guantánamo. So did John McCain, who proposed to send all the prisoners to Fort Leavenworth, Kansas, to the chagrin of Republican senators from that state.

Two days after President Obama took the oath of office, on January 22, 2009, he signed an executive order to close the detention facility within a year. His cautious approach, however, backfired on May 20, 2009, when a wide bipartisan majority in Congress voted to block funds for the transfer of those held to any of the fifty states.

Obama's executive order also required compliance with the Geneva Conventions at Guantánamo and a report on the situation within a month. The resulting report, however, dealt only with one article of the Geneva Conventions and made a recommendation that those held in solitary confinement should be allowed to socialize during two hours of daily exercise. But the Third Geneva Convention bans separating prisoners into classes as well as solitary confinement, so the military was clearly defying Obama.

Subsequently, there have been reports of improvements in treatment of Gitmo prisoners. Most issues in dispute now relate to their legal status, as noted in more detail below.

Thanks to quiet diplomacy during 2009, some 68 prisoners were transferred from Guantánamo to host countries abroad. A plan to send a few to Virginia was aborted due to objections from a member of Congress from that Congressional district. Two Obama appointees, Greg Craig and Phillip Carter, worked to close the facility, but they resigned after their efforts had been undermined.

Obama has expressed chagrin over the unresolved problem. On January 7, 2011, when he signed the National Defense Authorization Act for Fiscal Year 2011, his signing statement objected to the Congressional requirement that the prisoners could only be transferred to a prison in the United States with specific Congressional approval. Funding was banned not only for the transfer or release of the prisoners but also for assistance in transfer or release, thereby hampering any further planning on lowering the number of those held at Gitmo. On January 2, 2012, he penned a similar signing statement for the 2012 National Defense Authorization Act.

Classification of Currently Held Prisoners

Today, there are about 174 prisoners at Guantánamo, which has become a penitentiary, contrary to Article 22 of the Third Geneva Convention. In October 2011, Attorney General Eric Holder told the European Parliament that he would try to close the facility by the end of 2012. Those held today fall into the following five categories:

- **Temporary detainees.** Exactly 5 Uighurs from China are approved for immediate transfer if a country volun-teers to receive them and the Uighurs agree. Opposed to China's repression in their province, they were picked up in Afghanistan and mistakenly classified as terrorists. Another 27 prisoners from oth-er countries are cleared for release and await foreign host sponsorship.
- **Conditional detainees.** Some 84 are designated for "conditional detention." Of those, 30 are Yemenis held due to the precariousness of Yemen's current security environment, including Adrian Al-Shar'abi, who was acquitted of all charges in a 2010 trial.
- **Confessed or convicted prisoners.** Currently, 3 persons are being held at Gitmo in connection with prosecutions. Ali Hamza Ahmad Suliman Al-Bahlul, convicted in 2008, is serving a life sentence. Omar Khadr, who pled guilty in 2010, is serving an eight-year sentence and may then be repatriated to Canada. Noor Uthman Mohammed pled guilty but is to be released in 2014 if he testifies against some of the other prisoners at their trials.
- **Prosecutable prisoners.** About 36 persons are the subject of active cases or in-

vestigations. After prosecution, they are still likely to be held, as then they might be re-classified into the next cate-gory.

- **Dangerous prisoners**. The rest, 46 in all, are considered "too dangerous to transfer but not feasible for prosecution" because evidence against them was derived from torture or other illegal means. According to Attorney General Eric Holder, they are held in indefinite detention under unspecified "laws of war," presumably because they have declared the intention of harming the United States.

Creative Approaches to Closing Guantánamo

By default, there is only way to close Gitmo under present conditions: All those not transferred out would have to die there. Eight already have.

Accordingly, creative solutions need to be explored. Some of the following suggestions were enclosed in a letter placed inside the copy of *George W. Bush, War Criminal?*, which went to Obama just before his inauguration:

Resettlement in the United States. Seventeen dissidents from Western China, the Uighurs held at Gitmo, could easily be accommodated with their brethren in Virginia. They were wrongly imprisoned, as they have no animosity toward the United States and instead oppose repression of Uighurs inside China. Yet in 2009 President Obama refused to accept a court order for their release to the Mainland United States, deferring to Congressional opposition.

Transfer to foreign countries. Congress currently allows transfer of prisoners cleared for release to settle abroad, provided that the Secretaries of Defense and State stipulate that the host countries meet specific strategic requirements.

Swapping prisoners. Whenever an American is imprisoned or held hostage, they might be released by trading a Gitmo prisoner. Presidential candidate Herman Cain offered that idea and then backtracked on the same day. The problem is that there is a longstanding American policy of not negotiating with terrorists. A rash of American hostages would be taken by various terrorist organizations if they thought that they could get comrades back.

Transfer to the UN refugee authority. Part of Guantánamo now could be considered a refugee camp, as was the case with Haitians in the early 1990s. Prisoners already approved for transfer are technically "refugees," as they reside neither in their home country nor in a country accepting them as residents, and they hope to leave soon. The UN High Commissioner for Refugees could handle those already cleared for release, as the agency agreed to do so for at least 3,000 Iranian refugees held by Americans in Iraq until 2011. If reassigned to the Geneva agency, Congressional strategic requirements could be met at existing UN refugee camps.

Join the International Criminal Court. If the United States joins the International Criminal Court (ICC), those with prosecutable offenses might be sent to The Hague for trial. However, the Senate must first be persuaded to ratify the ICC treaty, which seems unlikely at present, as that would open the door to prosecution of George W. Bush and company. However, a country that has ratified the ICC treaty might bring such a case.

Return prisoners to Afghanistan. Those held at Guantánamo who were engaged in active combat when captured could have remained under military detention in that country. In conformity with Geneva Convention requirements, some have already been sent back. The UN Security Council, which annually approves of the Afghan War, aiming to stabilize the country, might address their resettlement. The United States is building a new prison facility in Afghanistan today, possibly to accommodate those now at Guantanamo.

Trials in civilian courts. Some prosecutable prisoners at Guantánamo are accused of various crimes related and unrelated to air piracy and murder on 9/11, offenses that are appropriate for civilian courts, as they are criminal offenses. The International Covenant on Civil and Political Rights requires a civilian trial for them. Federal courts have already successfully prosecuted some 400 similar cases, including one transferred from Guantánamo, Ahmed Ghailani. On May 21, 2009, President Barack Obama declared that civilian trials were appropriate in these cases, echoed by Attorney General

125

Eric Holder on June 16, 2011. But political leaders in New York objected to the cost of providing security for a high-profile trial in Manhattan, so there must be a change of venue. Security can be handled more economically around federal courts in Fargo, Grand Forks, or Minot, North Dakota, and elsewhere. Jury trials could even have defendants present through videoconference if necessary. If prosecution witnesses are called upon to confront defendants directly, they can be flown to Gitmo for that purpose.

Trials by military courts. "Dangerous prisoners," who might be exonerated if put on trial because of tainted evidence could, nevertheless be put on trial anyway. Juries are unpredictable. If they are found guilty, they would be locked up. If they are found not guilty, they can be released, subject to current Congressional restrictions. And if they subsequently become terrorists, they can be tracked down, arrested, and tried in a manner similar to criminals released from American prisons who re-offend by committing arson, murder, or rape. Given the vast American counterterrorism network that has been erected since 9/11, only cowards would fear a few more potential terrorists on the loose today.

Plea bargains. Some prisoners may have committed minor offenses. They would jump at the chance to plead guilty to minor offenses if they could be sent home sooner. One already convicted at Gitmo, Salim Hamdan, is now home in Yemen on that basis.

Confinement in federal prisons. Whether convicted in civilian or military trials, the prisoners could be sent to prisons in Terre Haute, Indiana, or the Supermax prison in southern Colorado, which respectively incarcerate suspected or convicted terrorists. For that matter, all prisoners could be sent to either place or scattered among many federal prisons.

Reassignment to other territories. Gitmo is not the only possible venue. Prisoners could be split up and sent to military bases elsewhere in the United States or its territories, such as Guam, Midway Island, St. Thomas, Virgin Islands, or Wake Island. Although such transfers might be perceived as a shellgame, at least Guantánamo would be closed, once and for all.

Assertion of executive authority. President Barack Obama declared in a signing statement on December 23, 2011, that he would ignore Congressional meddling in the executive branch operations regarding Guantánamo. The constitutional separation of powers gives the executive branch full responsibility over the disposition of prisoners under the control of the national government. Congress, which did not arrest them, has tried to set administrative rules for handling them, thereby pretending to exercise a legislative veto over acts of the executive branch, in effect making those at Gitmo prisoners of Congress. Congressional laws on the subject, including the defense appropriation act signed on that date, nearly amount to passage of a Bill of Attainder, that is, an attempt to impose a sentence on prisoners by legislative means. According to former Chief Justice William Rehnquist, those who wrote the Constitution had experience with the English practice of "a legislative act that singled out one or more persons and imposed punishment on them, without benefit of trial." That's why the Constitution prohibits bills of attainder.

However, a Republican House of Representatives might draw up an article of impeachment if Obama were to appear to be defying Congress. Although there would be insufficient votes to remove him from office, the spectacle of impeachment should be avoided, so some of the creative suggestions presented above may have to await election of a Democratic majority in the House of Representatives to overturn current Congressional restrictions.

Problems of Military Commissions
Some prisoners are slated to be prosecuted before military commissions and will not have civilian trials. Although Senator Barack Obama voted against the Military Commissions Act of 2006 as contrary to basic American values, he urged Congress to pass a revised Military Commissions Act in 2009, which is now the basis for trials at Guantánamo.

Since the trial of civilians in military courts contravenes international law, the question remains whether revamped military commissions under Obama will comply with either domestic or international law. For example, the Supreme

127

Court ruled in *ex parte Milligan* (1866) that civilians committing acts of war must be tried in federal criminal courts.

The Bush-era phrase "unlawful enemy combatant" has been replaced cosmetically under Obama with "unprivileged enemy belligerent." Three grounds qualify for prosecution under the latter designation:

- having engaged in hostilities against the United States
- purposeful and substantial material support for hostilities against the United States
- membership in Al-Qaeda.

There is little dispute about the first basis for prosecution, but the second is vague. The third infringes on the right of association. Only the first is a truly military offense. The other two, if truly offenses under the law, are civilian actions.

Whereas the Military Commissions Act of 2009 states that only aliens can be tried before military commissions, that requirement violates the Fourteenth Amendment to the Constitution of the United States. American legal precedent disallows aliens from being treated differently in judicial proceedings from non-aliens.

Nevertheless, the following features of Gitmo's Expeditionary Legal Center, in accordance with the Military Commissions Act of 2009, make fair trials somewhat more likely:

- The defendant is notified of charges against him and is provided with legal counsel to assist in his defense.
- The prosecution must prove guilt beyond a reasonable doubt.
- The defendant is entitled to be present at his trial, to cross-examine witnesses against him, to compel the attendance of witnesses (if they are within the U.S. jurisdiction), and to testify on his own behalf.

- The prosecution is required to turn over to the defense all exculpatory and mitigating evidence.
- The government may not appeal a verdict of not guilty.
- A defendant may challenge a guilty verdict through a habeas corpus petition or a direct appeal to civilian courts.
- The decision to impose the death penalty must be unanimous.

In addition, the following are available to the defense:

- in capital cases, a minimum of two defense attorneys
- in capital cases, one of the defense attorneys must be "learned" in such cases.
- "reasonable" opportunity to obtain expert and other witnesses.

But the "reasonable" standard does not mean that prosecution and defense will enjoy parity in securing evidence, as some prosecution evidence might be from secret sources.

Most objections to the military commissions focus on standards of evidence. Although statements obtained through illegal means (that is, while subjected to cruel, degrading, or inhumane treatment, including torture) are not allowed, the following are permitted, subject to a judge's discretion:

- voluntary statements by the accused or witnesses
- hearsay
- involuntary statements from the accused if public safety appears to be in immediate danger
- involuntary statements derived from persons other than the accused.

The main problem with "voluntary" statements is the "poisoned tree" argument—that those once been questioned illegally might volunteer information during subsequent legal interrogation out of a reasonable fear that that further questioning will be a prelude to being severely roughed up if they do not volunteer answers that interrogators appear to demand. And involuntary statements are questionable as evidence.

Military judges are employees of the Department of Defense and located on the chain of command, therefore subject to potential political pressure in deciding what evidence to allow and what verdicts to rule. In the past, several Guantánamo judges resigned when pressured. In other words, military commissions are fundamentally flawed because judicial personnel are members of the executive branch.

In short, there are ample grounds for a defense attorney to appeal adverse rulings by a military commission judge. Appeals based on individual cases could travel through the court system for years, possibly keeping Gitmo open for a decade or more. There is no sunset clause in the Military Commissions Act of 2009. Guantánamo may become a permanent facility for detaining alleged terrorists caught in the future, as some members of Congress prefer. If prisoners are kept at Gitmo even after found innocent, the proceedings will be mocked as "show trials."

Guantánamo as a Symbol

When word about the mistreatment of Guantánamo spread around the world, Muslims in Arabic-speaking countries may have wondered whether they would also be suddenly kidnapped, transported to torture sites, and dumped into the island prison for life. Later, they learned that most of those initially at Gitmo were innocent, as a few hundred were released while Bush was still president, so America's pursuit of terrorists appeared irrational. The perception of the United States as a rogue country has lingered.

Even if all prisoners are transferred out of Guantánamo soon, issues related to past illegality will remain. Torture, abuse, and possibly murder were committed at Gitmo, and their perpetrators have not been brought to justice. Until then, Guantánamo will remain an indelible stain on America, a recruiting symbol for Al-Qaeda. Meanwhile, justice is being denied, since major offenders remain unprosecuted.

130

Although compliance with the Geneva Conventions at Guantánamo has improved since Barack Obama took the oath of office, prisoners are still separated into classes. Some remain in solitary confinement without a speedy trial, fair or even unfair.

American and international law (the Convention Against Torture and Other Cruel, Inhuman or Degrading Treatment or Punishment of 1987) authorizes compensation for victims of torture and similar offenses. The U.S. Army routinely pays compensation to victims of collateral damage and prosecutes American military perpetrators of war crimes in court-martial trials. Civilian contractors have been convicted of war crimes offenses (for example, for murdering Afghan civilians) in domestic criminal courts. Of about one hundred cases referred by the Central Intelligence Agency (CIA) to the U.S. Department of Justice, two are now being readied for prosecution.

But many former prisoners at Guantánamo have been denied compensation. Although Australia, Britain, and Canada awarded compensation payments for their role in torture of their own citizens held by American authorities, federal courts have dismissed such cases, citing "national security" and "state secrets" justifications. In so doing, the judiciary is leaving "political" matters to the discretion of the executive branch.

One important court case, however, is now before a federal court in Chicago. The defendant is former Defense Secretary Donald Rumsfeld. He is being sued by two Americans who were wrongly held at Camp Cropper in Iraq, the same facility that held Saddam Hussein and other members of the "deck of cards." The suit is based on Bill of Rights violations, including cruel and unusual punishment. The case, *Vance v Rumsfeld*, has met preliminary requirements for trial, though no trial date has yet been set. Similar cases (*Doe v Rumsfeld* and *Ameur v Rumsfeld*) are being pursued in other federal courts.

Several compensation cases against the United States have been filed abroad. According to the Geneva and Torture conventions, victims of torture can file claims in the courts of any country that has ratified the treaties and has provided a legal basis within its jurisprudence.

Since 1991, the UN High Commissioner for Human Rights has maintained a voluntary torture compensation fund. An Australian has recently filed a claim based on his detention at Gitmo.

One related case has been successful. In 2007, Italy charged twenty-two CIA officials and five Italian collaborators with capturing Osama Moustafa Hassan Nasr on the streets of Milan during 2003 for "extraordinary rendition" to Egypt, where he was tortured. In 2009, the court convicted the CIA officials in absentia. Now international fugitives, they have been ordered to pay compensation to the victim and his wife and will be sent to prison if extradited to Italy. Meanwhile, two of the Italians are serving three-year sentences.

Cases have been dismissed in Belgium, Britain, Denmark, Germany, and Lithuania due to American pressure or noncooperation in supplying evidence. As of mid-2011, nevertheless, active cases for compensation by torture victims have been pursued in Australia, France, Lithuania, Macedonia, Pakistan, Poland, Spain, and Switzerland. Two cases have been referred to the Inter-American Commission on Human Rights, one to the UN Human Rights Committee, and two to the European Court of Human Rights.

The Polish case involves CIA torture inside a secret prison in Poland. The claimant, Abu Zubaydah, has been granted "victim status" by a Polish court. He is still held at Guantánamo.

Two former Gitmo prisoners filed the Swiss case in February 2011. A few days later, George W. Bush canceled a planned trip to Geneva. He could have been arrested upon arrival. Similarly, Ronald Rumsfeld had to sneak out of France in 2007 to avoid arrest after he landed in Paris to give a talk.

Conclusion

President Barack Obama has been modestly successful in matters of domestic and foreign policy. The Guantánamo quagmire, however, is a millstone around his neck, a potential cloud over his legacy. The detention of American Muslims at

Terre Haute only on suspicion continues as a domestic Guantánamo.

But Congress is primarily responsible for the mess, not Obama. Those who implore Obama to "fight" to correct problems at Guantánamo should realize that he is opposed by a wide bipartisan consensus in Congress. Until members of Congress relent and creative solutions are tried, the problem of Gitmo will remain for successive presidents, continuing to allow America's detractors to depict the world's first representative democracy as an unworthy country, violating the law of nations with impunity.

In the end, domestic political considerations prevail over court decisions in the United States. Judges apparently view lawsuits against high-ranking officials as more political than juridical. American public opinion has been supportive of extreme measures to ensure national security. The media has refrained from any hint that war crimes might have occurred.

A trial of George W. Bush for torture might resemble what happened in France after Alfred Dreyfus was tried for treason during 1894: The entire nation was bitterly divided and immobilized for fifteen years thereafter.

Barack Obama's preference for nonconfrontational politics and his desire to unite the country suggest that no prosecution of Bush-era officials for torture or other crimes at Guantánamo or elsewhere will occur. And now Obama is implicated in some of the same Geneva Convention violations. Although American government compensation may never be paid to victims of torture, Donald Rumsfeld might be held personally liable.

Al-Qaeda, pointing to war crimes under the Bush administration that are not being prosecuted under the Obama administration, will continue to have a basis for recruiting more terrorists to attack the United States. Although Attorney General Eric Holder is determined to close Gitmo before the end of 2012, Congress will have to be persuaded to give President Obama more latitude to deal with the problem.

Yet Congress has not universally approved of his conduct of the wars that he inherited from President George W. Bush or his new military adventures. The next chapter explains Obama's use of military power.

Chapter 13
Protecting Afghanistan, Iraq, and Libya

When Barack Obama assumed the duties and powers of the president, he was immediately commander-in-chief of two wars. A wartime president always has detractors, so he has had to provide appropriate reasons for the American military presence abroad, thereby applying the Obama Doctrine.

Iraq
Although President George W. Bush justified the Iraq War in part to prevent Saddam Hussein from developing weapons of mass destruction, Barack Obama referred to the Iraq conflict as a "dumb war" even before he decided to run for president. As president, he sought to end the American military presence in that country. Iraq in 2009 had a government of its own, albeit a fragile one due to ethno-sectarian rivalries, personality conflicts, and continuing terrorist attacks.

Obama made his only Oval Office speech to announce that he would stick to the Bush-negotiated timetable for withdrawal of all 100,000 combat forces by August 31, 2010, leaving a 24,000 residual force for emergencies, and complete withdrawal by December 31, 2011. And he did. Because Iraq wanted military training personnel to continue their work, about 200 army personnel will now be located at ten Iraqi bases, and the staff at the American embassy in Baghdad, including various contractors, numbers about 16,000.

Afghanistan
President Bush pursued the Afghan War as the best way to eliminate the power of Al-Qaeda, based on the Authorization for the Use of Military Force resolution of September 18, 2001. Candidate Obama promised to finish the job of denying Al-Qaeda any possibility of a safe haven in Afghanistan.

Since late 2001, North Atlantic Treaty Organization forces have been annually approved by the UN Security Council to stabilize the country and restore human rights.

135

Obama, however, has said nothing about UN approval as a legal basis for the continuation of the war in Afghanistan.

On February 17, 2009, less than one month after his inauguration, he authorized an increase of 21,000 American forces to Afghanistan. During much of the rest of 2009, Obama deliberated on what to do about a situation in which the Kabul government's corruption was driving Afghans into the arms of the insurgent Taliban. On December 1, 2009, he announced an increase of 30,000 troops with the aim of reversing the momentum of the Taliban. An Afghan army was to be trained to replace American forces, with a partial withdrawal beginning in July 2011.

On June 22, 2011, Obama announced that 5,000 troops would be pulled out the following month, as scheduled. An additional 5,000 would leave by the end of 2011, and 23,000 more by autumn 2012. That would leave 68,000 troops, which Obama predicted would finally depart in 2014.

The situation remains unsettled because serious negotiations with the Taliban have not even begun, though its leader Mullah Mohammed Omar often appears to invite them. The Taliban has never declared war on the United States. Only a political settlement will end the struggle, now a civil war.

Shortly after his inauguration, Obama authorized a significant increase of drones inside Pakistan to kill Al-Qaeda operatives who might ultimately set up camp in Afghanistan again. The drones often flew from Pakistani air bases.

But drone attacks on innocent Afghan and Pakistani civilians have been unwelcome, occasioning public demonstrations and government protests. Attacks inside Pakistan include the killing of Osama Bin Laden on May 1, 2011 (see Chapter 14), whereupon increasing calls for ending the Afghan operation were heard.

Libya

On March 28, 2011, President Obama announced that American forces were being deployed to a mission in Libya that would last "days, not weeks." And he obtained UN Security Council approval. But the intervention raised so many questions that some perspective is needed to understand the full implications, as discussed below.

136

According to the Convention on Duties and Rights of States in the Event of Civil Strife of 1928, countries must be neutral in civil wars similar to Libya. However, Article 42 of the UN Charter empowers the Security Council to authorize "action by air, sea, or land forces as may be necessary to maintain or restore international peace and security."

Vietnam's intervention in Cambodia, which began in 1978 to drive the Khmer Rouge from power, was justified by Hanoi as "humanitarian intervention." Legal scholar Gary Klintworth agreed in an official Australian government publication. Although the UN and the United States did not agree, Cambodia's Prince Sihanouk concurred that Hanoi's aims were humanitarian.

Then in *Nicaragua v United States* (1986), the International Court of Justice ruled that humanitarian intervention in a civil war was justified "to protect life and health and to ensure the respect of persons." In so doing, the court declared that the mining of a Nicaraguan harbor in 1984 by the United States was unjustifiable. In other words, that action was identified as a war crime. But the ruling implicitly accepted Vietnam's claim.

In 1994, the world community failed to stop genocide in Rwanda. Accordingly, Australia's Gareth Evans and others began to develop the concept of "responsibility to protect" (R2P) as a clearer basis for military intervention in internal conflicts within the corpus of international law. R2P was finally endorsed by UN Security Council Resolution 1674 in 2006 and UN General Assembly Resolution 63/308 in 2009.

In 1999, meanwhile, Serbia threatened to engage in ethnic cleansing in Kosovo. President Bill Clinton then invoked the concept of humanitarian intervention to justify bombing Serbia until Belgrade agreed to leave Kosovo alone. With no UN Security Council authorization, American attacks on Serbian military targets also killed civilians, and the legality of the operation was questioned.

The concepts of "international humanitarian intervention" and "responsibility to protect" are not settled in international law. The former relies on the abovementioned court decision and the latter on UN resolutions. Although neither are ratified treaties, the UN Charter authorizes the Security

Council to codify international legal obligations that are binding on all states. R2P is one of those codifications.

Libya, thus, became a test case of R2P. After riots broke out, they were brutally suppressed by the Libyan government. Muammar Al-Qadhafi, the country's head of state, soon threatened to massacre insurgents in Benghazi.

The UN Security Council then adopted Resolution 1973 on March 17, 2011, by a majority with abstentions, authorizing a no-fly zone over the country. But the resolution did not state specifically that the situation in Libya was a threat to international peace and security. Instead, civil strife in Libya was implied in the resolution to have been internationalized because (1) refugees were fleeing to neighboring countries, (2) Libyan military actions placed civilian Libyans and non-Libyans in jeopardy, and (3) Al-Qadhafi's actions were deemed to violate international humanitarian law.

President Obama then called upon Al-Qadhafi to comply with Resolution 1973 by agreeing to a ceasefire and to move his troops away from Benghazi. When Al-Qadhafi refused, Obama announced on March 28 that the United States was setting up the infrastructure for a no-fly zone, leaving some of its partners in the North Atlantic Treaty Organization, with Britain, France, and Italy in the lead, to enforce the no-fly zone. Invoking R2P, he stated that the aim was to prevent a massacre in Benghazi, a city of 700,000.

But after military operations began, questions arose whether aerial attacks on the command-and-control system of the Libyan military far from Benghazi exceeded the UNSC mandate. After all, the Responsibility to Protect mantra was being used to kill Libyans in Tripoli.

China and Russia, having abstained from Resolution 1973, now objected that regime change appeared to be the hidden agenda. Although Obama earlier called for Al-Qadhafi to resign so a democratic government could emerge, he specifically assured on March 28 that "broadening our military mission to include regime change would be a mistake."

Although President Obama consulted some top leaders of Congress before the American operation in Libya began, full Congressional approval was not sought. In a note to Congress on March 21, Obama stated that he authorized the humanitarian intervention in Libya consistent with the War Powers Resolution.

By May 20, that law presumably required Congressional approval on the disposition of American combat forces involved or withdrawal of the military contingent within thirty days. When that day arrived, however, Obama wrote a letter to Congress arguing that the American role by then was too "intermittent" for the War Powers requirement to apply. Instead, he asked Congress for a resolution of support.

European NATO members were then involved in the airstrikes, though U.S. forces appeared to be flying most missions related to reconnaissance, surveillance, and refuel-ing. One estimate was that American aircraft accounted for 35 of 150 NATO missions flown daily. But none were for "combat" (an exchange of gunfire), so some but not all law-yers in the Obama administration argued that the War Powers Resolution of 1973 did not apply.

Several members of Congress then challenged the legality of the operation, which was dragging beyond "days, not weeks." They objected that Obama was defying the War Powers Resolution, especially when they learned from the Pentagon that American aircraft were engaged in strike sorties on Libyan defense capabilities, though the Libyan military never returned fire. Clearly, American aircraft were "ready for combat," a crucial requirement that would require compliance with the War Powers Resolution, which no president has ever conceded was binding, lacking as it does the force of a legal statute.

On June 3, in a 268-145 vote (with 223 Republicans joining 45 Progressive Democrats), the House of Representatives asked the president to provide a "compelling rationale" for the operation within two weeks. When that deadline was not met, the House on June 13 voted 248-163 (110 Democrats joining 138 Republicans) to withhold funding from the operation, though the Senate did not agree.

On June 15, Representative Dennis Kucinich, two other Democrats, and seven Republicans went to court to ask for an injunction to demand a pullout from Libya. Later that day, Obama sent a comprehensive statement to Congress, noting that American forces were not engaged in "hostilities" in Libya and therefore the operation was legal. The court dismissed the lawsuit in October; as members of Congress, the ten were judged to have no standing to sue.

On June 24, the House again defied Obama. Support for the Libyan operation failed 123-295. However, the vote to cut off funding also was defeated 180-238. Once again, the leadership in the Senate ignored the vote.

Then on July 7, several more House votes were taken on Libya. A total cutoff of funds was rejected 199-229, but stopping aid to Libyan rebels passed with support of 48 Democrats and 177 Republicans.

Meanwhile, Al-Qadhafi hired mercenaries, mobilized support in Tripoli, refused to resign, and thanked Congress. And the U.S. military soon acknowledged that one goal was to target him for extrajudicial execution, contrary to Obama's stated opposition to the goal of regime change. A stalemate ensued for several months, annoying everyone, until the rebels achieved victory in Tripoli during mid-August and killed Al-Qadhafi in mid-October 2011.

Somalia, Uganda, and Yemen

Consistent with the Authorization for the Use of Military Force Resolution of 2001, American military drone attacks have been launched in Somalia and Yemen from time to time. The aim has been to kill terrorists linked to Al-Qaeda.

Drones were stepped up in Yemen during 2011, when President Ali Abdullah Saleh went to Saudi Arabia for medical treatment after an insurgent attack on his residence seriously burned much of his body. One major strike, approved by the Yemen government, was to kill Anwar Al-Awlaki, who inspired several terrorist attacks inside the United States (see Chapter 14 for more on the latter assassination).

In October 2011, President Barack Obama sent some 100 Special Forces to Uganda, implementing a unanimous joint Congressional resolution of 2010 to deal with the notorious Lords Resistance Army of Joseph Kony. The military is instructed to assist local authorities in defeating Kony but not to engage in combat, as his army consists of children whom he has forcibly recruited.

Implications

Obama, who regularly watched *Star Trek* while growing up in Honolulu, has proved to be a dynamic commander-in-chief, a samurai warrior of sorts. He does not want to appear "soft on terrorism," as many Republicans would like to claim.

But war is popular only when there is a clear enemy and a quick, victorious end. From 2001, the cost of military adventures has contributed at least $4 trillion to the American government's deficit. By 2011, public opinion in the United States was increasingly opposed to involvement in the various wars.

In December 2010, President Obama set July 2011 as the month to begin a phased withdrawal from Afghanistan, and he kept his promise. Continuing war in Afghanistan seemed less urgent after Osama Bin Laden's death. By the end of 2011, American military forces left Iraq despite its fragile government. The intervention in Libya without American ground troops ended when Tripoli, the capital of Libya, fell into rebel hands.

For the international system, the action in Libya may serve as a precedent that the UN's Responsibility to Protect resolutions empower the Security Council to act in a manner similar to Resolution 1973 in future situations. For example, the Burmese government might slaughter peaceful protests by monks, joined by foreigners in the street, with refugees pouring out of the country. That the UN Security Council did not vote later in 2011 to intervene in Syria, where thousands were being gunned down and refugees were escaping to Turkey, suggests limits to R2P.

Thus, the Libyan intervention has much significance for the future of the world polity. A precedent has been established without a formula or a metric to determine how far R2P might apply in a future crisis, though Obama indicated that a massacre of 700,000 would be intolerable.

But drone attacks that kill innocent civilians, in Pakistan or elsewhere, are clearly unwelcome if not counterproductive. According to former National Intelligence Director Dennis Blair, CIA drone attacks have had less value since the killing of Osama Bin Laden. Although justified as actions in "self-defense," they stopped in November and December 2011.

141

Presumably, President Barack Obama will only under-take major future military operations after getting approval from a coalition of countries, consistent with his desire to have the United States facilitate world reconciliation similar to his domestic agenda of bringing people together to solve problems. Better relations with Congress appear to be a pre-requisite to any new adventure.

R2P, now also interpreted as ending structural violence (socioeconomic tyranny), remains the crown jewel of the Obama Doctrine. But targeted assassinations of Al-Qaeda leaders, as analyzed in the following chapter, seem more dif-ficult to justify.

Chapter 14
Killing Osama Bin Laden

Al-Qaeda's dissatisfaction with the United States, as informed observers know, has been based on foreign policy differences. A major source of contention has been over the existence of Israel and the presence of American military forces in countries with Muslim majorities.

Although the iconic Osama Bin Laden (OBL) is now dead, as announced by President Barack Obama on May 1, 2011, terrorist attacks are expected to continue. Clearly, Al-Qaeda's cause remains. American foreign policy is changing, thanks to President Barack Obama, but not enough to please jihadists.

The manner in which Operation Neptune Spear killed Osama Bin Laden has been questioned. Two aspects of the raid that produced his death are crucial. What really happened? What are the legal grounds for the operation? Answers to both questions may serve to predict the next stage in the battle against terrorists inspired by OBL.

What Happened?
Details of the raid remain incomplete. Did the Americans ask for the surrender of the inhabitants of the compound before opening fire? Could the operation have been conducted without any deaths? Exactly who died and who survived? Were innocent civilians killed? Was an unarmed Osama Bin Laden killed?

Reports state that about two dozen persons were in OBL's compound, but there was no advance assurance that Osama Bin Laden was inside. Most in the main residence stood out of the way or surrendered when the U.S. contingent arrived in the compound. Three women and thirteen children had zip ties applied to their wrists. The raid lasted about 30 minutes. Aside from OBL, four others were killed.

Obama evidently preferred to capture OBL alive. Although he vowed never to be taken alive, he was sighted unarmed and did not put up a fight. The raiding party, mostly

SEALs, was ordered to capture him alive only if there was evidence that he did not carry hidden ordnance on his body—in other words, if he were naked and threw up his hands to surrender. Since he did neither, he was shot dead.

(The SEALs had acted contrary to Obama's order to capture someone alive once before. That happened in 2009, when they shot Somali pirates while liberating an American whom they held prisoner.)

Subsequently, OBL was dumped into the waters near Yemen, where the *U.S.S. Cole* was attacked in 2000. The military has assured that he was given a decent Muslim burial, but independent observers were not present to provide confirmation.

Legal Questions

What is the legal basis for a foreign military force to enter a civilian home? Was the raid an example of extrajudicial execution or the exercise of the right of reprisal? What was Osama Bin Laden's crime?

In 1998, OBL was secretly indicted in New York for conspiracy in the 1993 attack on the American defense installation in Mogadishu, Somalia. Now those charges have been dismissed.

There has been no official identification of the crime that warranted a raid on OBL's compound beyond that 1998 criminal indictment, now declared moot. Clearly, he was the leader of a criminal conspiracy to murder Americans on 9/11. But that is a domestic offense for which criminal laws and extradition would apply.

Under customary international law, the right of reprisal gives every country a license to respond to another country's unprovoked attack. The United States, for example, responded militarily to interference in shipping by the Barbary States in the early nineteenth century. But no country and no army attacked America on 9/11; a criminal gang was instead responsible.

The unprovoked attack on 9/11 violated the Convention for the Suppression of Unlawful Seizure of Aircraft of 1970 and an American law with provisions implementing the treaty. Afghanistan, Pakistan, and the United States have ratified the treaty. In addition to the 1998 charge of conspiracy to attack American military forces, OBL could also have been charged with conspiracy to engage in air piracy on 9/11.

The 1970 treaty obligated the Taliban government to take action to arrest OBL and any others responsible for the 9/11 attacks when Al-Qaeda was inside Afghanistan. Although the Afghan government offered to capture OBL and turn him over to the United States, the Taliban authorities attached one condition—proof implicating OBL with 9/11. Bush refused to supply proof and insisted that all members of Al-Qaeda should be arrested and surrendered to the United States. But OBL did not admit culpability for 9/11 until a tape released in October 2004. By then, he had escaped to Pakistan.

Pakistan did indeed capture some of those responsible for 9/11 and turned them over to the United States, which in turn imprisoned some at the Guantánamo Bay facility. But the Islamabad government never took OBL into custody.

When a country refuses extradition, the 1970 treaty against air piracy suggests that the complaining party should seek arbitration or file a case with the International Court of Justice. The Bush administration took no such action, thereby failing to follow procedural requirements in the treaty before attacking Afghanistan. The Obama administration, similarly, did not go to third parties to require accountability from Pakistan, where OBL's presence somewhere was long assumed.

Action under the 1970 treaty and the related American law does not include a right of military reprisal for air piracy. That may be one reason why the 9/11 attack was elevated by President George W. Bush into a "war on terror," since he interpreted 9/11 as an unprovoked military attack that could justify military retaliation against Afghanistan for harboring Al-Qaeda. Yet in 2001 Congress voted down any official recognition of a "war on terror."

President Bush may have believed that the Afghan War was an exercise of the right of reprisal. However, any reprisal under customary international law must be proportionate to the initial attack, so the war waged against the entire country of Afghanistan went too far. Bush instead supported one side in what became a civil war.

(More proportionate was a limited American aerial strike on Libya during 1988 in response to Muammar Al-Qadhafi's complicity in the bombing of a discotheque in Berlin during 1986. His refusal to surrender those responsible inside Libya's East German embassy for the attack was the basis for the reprisal.)

Thus, the American war in Afghanistan was initially contrary to international legal requirements. On December 20, 2001, however, the UN Security Council approved of the presence of North Atlantic Treaty Organization forces to stabilize the new Afghan government. Ever since, the UN Security Council has approved the presence of foreign military forces to support the government in Afghanistan, though the NATO occupation of Afghanistan is limited by international human rights guidelines.

When President Barack Obama took office, he avoided Bush's term "war on terror." During the early period of his administration, he defined his policy as a more limited "War on Al-Qaeda."

The 1970 treaty authorizes trial after capture of those involved in plotting and carrying out air piracy. Obama's raid against Osama Bin Laden's residence, thus, might be seen as a proportionate form of reprisal for the 9/11 attack or as consistent with the terms of the 1970 treaty. But there is no legal precedent for an armed military unit of country #1 to enter country #2 to murder those associated with conspirators in an air piracy plot carried out in country #1.

In 1989, American military forces captured President Manuel Noriega in the midst of an invasion of Panamá and flew him back to Miami for trial. Although treated as a prisoner of war because he was apprehended in the context of ongoing battle, he was charged with money laundering and other offenses unrelated to the war. Noriega was the first head of state to be put on trial in an American court.

The capture of Adolf Eichmann in Argentina during 1960 involved a raid by Israeli citizens that might have been similar to the events of May 1, 2011, but only if Osama Bin Laden had been rounded up for trial. Instead, the leader of Al-Qaeda and some of his relatives were executed during the raid. Although both clandestine raids might be deemed to

146

have violated the sovereignty of the host countries, only the 2011 raid was by government military forces.

Accordingly, was Osama Bin Laden a victim of extra-judicial execution, contrary to Articles 6 and 14(2) of the International Covenant on Civil and Political Rights? That's why more details of the raid within the compound in Pakistan are important in vindicating the American unilateral action.

Assessment

Accounts of the incident are in conflict over exactly how OBL was killed. There were two raiding parties, consisting of about 25 SEALs, CIA officers, and possibly Delta Force personnel. They arrived at OBL's compound at about 1 A.M.

The first group entered the guesthouse, where a courier was present. He opened fire, whereupon both he and an unidentified woman, presumably his wife, were shot and killed.

The second group approached the main house. As they sought to ascend from the first floor, they encountered one of OBL's brothers, who had one hand behind his back. Believing that he was about to fire, he was immediately shot dead. Proceeding up to a higher floor, two of OBL's wives rushed toward an armed American soldier, provoking him, but they were pushed away. Outfitted with special goggles, as the night was moonless, the SEALs first encountered a man who resembled OBL, fired at him, but he retreated to his bedroom. When the soldiers entered the bedroom area, another wife was present, got in the way, and was shot in the leg. Osama Bin Laden, still in his bedclothes, was then shot dead though unarmed.

The raiding party apparently did not ask anyone to identify themselves or to surrender, either in English or Arabic, though a translator was part of the group. OBL was not given the order to surrender or strip naked, to prove that he did not have a bomb or other lethal device on his person. He was therefore killed on suspicion that he routinely slept in an armed vest or had access to a weapon as he retreated to his bed chamber. Inside the bedroom, there were two weapons, but OBL did not reach them before he was shot dead. His identity was determined definitively only after his death.

Al-Qaeda, hence, can claim that his death was an instance of extrajudicial execution. Only one of those living in the compound evidently opened fire, so some may claim that all five deaths were murder.

Poorly reasoned arguments that the killing was legal have appeared in the American media. More telling is the fact that Harold Koh, the State Department's international law adviser, has been curiously silent on the matter. The action, however, could be justified as self-defense—to protect America.

Under the military mindset OBL was an enemy in a war. OBL could be considered a common criminal under domestic law. After all, the administration was originally committed to a civilian trial of Khalid Sheikh Mohammed, the alleged mastermind of the 9/11 plot. Obama obviously changed his mind, since both have been deemed enemies of the United States.

Consequences of the Raid
Calls for an investigation to determine the legality of OBL's killing have come from the UN High Commissioner for Human Rights. Two experts that report to the UN Human Rights Council have asked for more information about the killing—Christof Heyns, an expert dealing with extrajudicial, summary or arbitrary executions, and Martin Scheinin, whose expertise is human rights and counterterrorism. But such an inquiry would ultimately require disclosing the names of the SEALs, and the American government will doubtless refuse to disclose their identity as confidential information.

With martyred Osama Bin Laden out of the picture, Al-Qaeda may now justify terror attacks on the United States on the grounds that the raid was illegal. Previously, Al-Qaeda leaders threatened a nuclear attack if OBL were arrested or killed. That American authorities redoubled efforts in expectation of retaliation from Al-Qaeda suggests that they are aware of the possibility of reprisal, though of course Al-Qaeda may not claim that right under international law because it is not a sovereign state. Nevertheless, statistics collected in Baghdad reveal that terrorist attacks tended to increase in Iraq after targeted assassinations by the United States.

Pakistan has decreased cooperation with the United States due to Islamabad's unhappiness that its sovereignty was violated by a secret raid. Drones are now banned from Pakistan.

The death of Osama Bin Laden has resulted in much rejoicing within the United States and around the world. But the continuation of policies by the United States to which OBL objected, including civilian deaths on Afghan battlefields, American military forces in Muslim-majority countries, as well as continued detention without trial of prisoners at Guantánamo, ensures that militant opposition will continue.

To forestall retaliation by jihadists, withdrawal of American troops from Afghanistan and the closure of Guantánamo might serve as condign signals that illegal excesses are ending. President Barack Obama has claimed that war on the Taliban is necessary to prevent Al-Qaeda from returning to a safe haven in Afghanistan. Now, with Al-Qaeda's leader dead, that justification rings hollow to those who see little strategic value in the Afghan War.

The Al-Awlaki Killing

Although Pakistan now cooperates less with the United States, Yemen has increased cooperation. On September 30, 2011, a drone strike killed Anwar Al-Awlaki, the American-born Muslim cleric who inspired the Fort Dix attack of 2007, the Fort Hood shooting of 2009, the underpants bomber of 2009, and the Times Square bomber of 2010.

Similar to the assassination of OBL, Al-Awlaki was a victim of extrajudicial execution, though the Obama administration evidently justified the action once again as consistent with the Authorization of Military Force resolution passed by Congress soon after September 11, 2001. A secret memo prepared by the Obama administration has declared that killing Al-Awlaki (and presumably OBL as well), an American citizen who could be tried for treason, was an act of "self-defense." The Obama administration's apparent argument is that those who plot against the United States are belligerents who have made the ground on which they think and walk into a battlefield. Belligerents on a battlefield are presumably shot on sight whether in or out of uniform if they fail to surrender.

The self-defense justification, according to interpretations of the secret memo, has three components: (1) Al-Awlaki's plotting posed an immediate threat to the United States. (2) Similar to the Taliban, he was an ally of Al-Qaeda. (3) Capturing him alive was infeasible. But there is a fourth implicit rationale: (4) Al-Awlaki, having embarked on treasonous acts against the United States, had renounced his American citizenship and thereby any protections under the Bill of Rights.

An American citizen, thus, can be executed in another country without due process of law. Obama, thus, has lost respect from civil libertarians for his targeted assassinations. His acceptance of indefinite detention has also drawn fire.

Conclusion

Obama's "War on Al-Qaeda" is considered a military matter, a view similar to that of the Bush administration. But the precedent that an American citizen could be gunned down in a friendly country, where he could have been arrested and subsequently placed on trial, suggests that domestic police may have open season to gun down anyone they suspect, at any place and any time, rather than following constitutionally-accepted principles of criminal justice. The precedent is very troubling, especially to Attorney General Eric Holder, who would prefer to try all terrorists in federal courts but has lost the turf battle with the Department of Defense.

Today, there is widespread agreement that a weakening of Al-Qaeda required an OBL dead rather than alive. Al-Awlaki's death, retaliation for his plotting, sends a signal that those who plan attacks against the United States could be murdered. President Obama may ultimately be confronted with a resurgent Al-Qaeda, but he was willing to take risks despite advisers who urged caution and progressives who have been disappointed.

For Obama, world harmony is a major goal, but his samurai approach to Afghanistan and Libya contrasts with ninja exercises in regard to Osama Bin Laden and Anwar Al-Awlaki. To the chagrin of civil libertarians, Obama has not dismantled the intrusive and expensive counterterrorism apparatus erected by his predecessor.

Will the world be safer, now that Osama Bin Laden and other Al-Qaeda leaders are dead and at most only 5,000 anti-American terrorists are being tracked? Time alone will tell.

Is Obama to be judged as a commander-in-chief who is firm on matters of national security? Definitely yes.

Chapter 15
Mr. Calm and Effective's Accomplishments

When Barack Obama was 17, incumbent Governor George Ariyoshi was running for re-election. The Japanese American's slogan in that race was "quiet but effective." President Obama appears to have been emulating that unforgettable role model, who epitomized the multicultural ethos of Hawai'i that Obama now represents before the nation and the world.

When health care legislation was languishing in Congress, a reporter asked Obama on January 25, 2010, whether he was considering moving on to other issues. In response, he said "I would rather be a really good one-term president than a mediocre two-term president."

Then in early 2011 Obama dispelled rumors that he was too cautious and indecisive by first ordering American troops to intervene in the Libyan civil war and later announcing the killing of Osama Bin Laden as the penultimate result of a quiet decision shortly after taking office to make the latter objective the number one priority of the Central Intelligence Agency. The effort to gain coalition support for the no-fly zone over Libya, he revealed, was a result of quiet diplomacy, that is, unpublicized negotiations.

Observers then revised their views about President Barack Obama. They newly assessed him as a bold president with undisputed national security credentials. And, once again, commentators displayed their ignorance of his basic personality—particularly the influence of Japanese culture on him as he was growing up in Honolulu: Instead of announcing a policy with arrogance and bluster, as did his immediate predecessor, his speech on May 1, 2011, about the death of Osama Bin Laden was delivered with modesty, that is, without an arrogant or pretentious "mission accomplished" neonlike backdrop.

Checkmating Obama
Prior to May 1, 2011, critics on the right and left have often charged that Barack Obama has accomplished little as presi-

dent. But most accusations assume that the president has more power than Congress.

In fact, Congress is the dominant institution in the American Constitution, which in Article 2 assigns to the president only the powers to pardon, make treaties, nominate high officials and judges, veto legislation, serve as military commander-in-chief, and to convene Congress. And if Congress cannot agree when to adjourn, the president can pick the day.

The chief executive also has certain responsibilities—to provide information to Congress on the "state of the union," organize the common defense, and to implement laws passed by Congress. However, Congress can refuse to ratify treaties, block appointments, override vetoes, and remove a president from office.

President Obama has indeed learned of many limitations on his power since his inauguration:

- Congress has prevented him from closing Guantánamo.
- Congress has rejected some of his legislative proposals, for example refusing to empower judges to renegotiate mortgage loans in order to avoid foreclosure.
- Republicans in the Senate have blocked confirmation of many administrative and judicial appointments.
- Innocent civilians have been repeatedly killed by the military.
- The Supreme Court ruled against his administration's legal argument that corporations should not have an unlimited right to contribute funds to political campaigns or candidates.
- Voters in 2010 defeated members of his own party in the House of Representatives, ending control by his Democratic Party allies.
- Other countries have defied him, from an Iran apparently continuing to support ter-

rorism to an Israel defiantly expanding settlements on the West Bank.

The Problem of Mass Society

The theory of mass society perceives three layers in politics—elites, masses, and intermediate institutions that could intervene between elites and masses. The intermediate institutions, also known as "civil society," are interest groups and political parties. In a democratic society, all three layers exist, and the masses are able to utilize intermediate institutions to press their demands on government. In undemocratic regimes, intermediate institutions are either banned or severely limited, making the public helpless in relation to all-powerful government.

Yet people in the United States no longer find political parties responsive to their needs, and corporate interest groups appear to be the most successful in influencing legislation. The isolation of Americans from organizations that influence governmental institutions on their behalf accounts for mass uprisings in recent American society, both the Tea Party and the Occupy Wall Street/99 Percent movements.

Communitarian philosophy, as developed by sociologist Amitai Etzioni and others, offers an antidote to mass society trends in the United States. Barack Obama clearly subscribes to mass society theory, in part because he was shocked by what he saw in Chicago when he was a community organizer—African Americans separated from the levers of power. His experience in Hawai'i was just the opposite—communities that were interconnected and trade unions pressuring government for people-oriented reforms, such as universal health care. That's one reason why he wants America to become more like Hawai'i.

Obama's 2008 campaign encouraged grassroots members of communities to meet together in order to inform him of their policy priorities. In his economic policies, he has worked to strengthen institutions closer to the people than Washington's bureaucracy (see Chapter 9).

In foreign affairs, consistent with his opposition to structural violence, President Obama has viewed popular uprisings in Middle Eastern and North African countries as rumblings that were inevitable because the people want intermediate institutions and free elections to gain prosperity. He also sees a global mass society, that is, a world in which countries rarely cooperate to solve problems together.

Accomplishments

Barack Obama's efforts to change America from a politics of mass society to a genuine community of responsible citizens involves bringing people together, such as through Obamanomics and Obamacare. On the international stage, Obama seeks to move from an imperial, unilateral America that threatens other countries into a world of cooperating nations with a decent modicum of leadership and support from Washington.

Although cultural and political change takes time, the Obama administration has been unusually effective in carrying out his campaign promise for change. But he has not fulfilled all his promises, and he has disappointed Progressive Democrats who supported him in 2008.

Both as an executive and in working with Congress, major accomplishments are to his credit. Some, though mentioned in the preceding chapters, are reiterated below, with the most prominent in boldface. The following are executive orders that he adopted on his own:

- compliance with the Geneva Conventions at Guantánamo (2009)
- closure of all "black sites" formerly used to interrogate and torture suspected terrorists (2009)
- **decision to close Guantánamo** (2009)
- adoption of the Making Home Affordable plan, aimed at helping homeowners to avoid foreclosure (2009)
- rescue of an American captain kidnapped by Somali pirates (2009)
- **bailout of financial firms, Chrysler, and General Motors** (2009); **subsequent re-sale at profit to taxpayers of**

stock in both companies held temporarily by the government (2010-2011)

- G-20 agreement to provide a $1.1 trillion bailout of developing economies (2009)
- agreement to reduce greenhouse gasses at the UN Conference on Climate Change at Copenhagen (2009)
- joining the UN Human Rights Council (2009)
- imposition of a 35 percent tariff on Chinese-made tires, which were being dumped on the American market (2009)
- first national limit on automobile emission standards (2009)
- decision to place coal-burning power plants, industrial complexes, and refineries under Environmental Protection Agency regulation
- cut salaries for 65 bailout executives (2009)
- hosted Nuclear Nonproliferation Treaty Review Conference (2009), involving 47 heads of state
- launched *recovery.org* to show how tax dollars are spent (2009)
- rescinded restrictions on stem cell research (2009)
- ended the stop-loss program, which made soldiers serve as many as four combat tours (2009)
- **decision to send 51,000 more troops to Afghanistan** (2009)
- decision to increase drone attacks on Al-Qaeda leaders in Pakistan (2009)
- establishment of the bipartisan National Commission on Fiscal Responsibility and Reform (2009)
- ban on discrimination based on sexual orientation in federal employment, hospi-

tals, mortgage loan approvals, passport and visa issuance, and spousal benefits to federal employees (2009-2010)

- **signed an extension of the Strategic Arms Reduction Treaty with Russia** (2010)
- **end of combat operations in Iraq** (2010)
- **required British Petroleum to compensate victims of the oil spill** (2010)
- set up the National Commission on the DP Deepwater Horizon Oil Spill and Offshore Drilling (2010)
- hastened the establishment of the new Republic of South Sudan (2010-2011)
- **prevention of a massacre in Benghazi, Libya** and **end of the reign of Muammar Al-Qadhafi** (2011)
- **killing of Osama Bin Laden** (2011)
- **partial withdrawal of troops from Afghanistan** (2011)
- waivers to states, exempting them from compliance with the No Child Left Behind Act if they find new ways to improve educational outcomes (2011).
- renegotiate free trade agreements with Colombia, Panamá, South Korea with environmental, labor safeguards (2011)
- sent 100 troops to advise and train the central African armies to defeat the Lords Resistance Army (2011)
- **withdrawal of all troops from Iraq** (2011)
- **relaxed government college loan repayment terms** (2011)
- **refinancing: removal of the limit on Fannie Mae/Freddie Mac borrowers owing more than 125 percent of their homes; cut some refinancing fees**

- dispatched 2,500 soldiers to a base in Darwin, Australia, as a signal to provocations by China.

President Obama has specifically adopted some of the most recent executive orders because of frustration that Congress refuses to act on reasonable reforms with bipartisan support, either because House Republicans refuse to schedule hearings and call for votes on proposals or due to Senate Republican use of the filibuster to block voting on reforms.

In conjunction with Congress, President Obama can point to the following results in legislation that he signed (again, with the most prominent accomplishments highlighted):

- Children's Health Insurance Program Reauthorization Act (2009)
- Family Smoking Prevention and Tobacco Control Act (2009)
- Lilly Ledbetter Fair Pay Act (2009)
- **American Recovery and Reinvestment Act** (2009), creating and saving 2-3 million jobs, providing tax cuts, and giving subsidies to alternative energy projects
- Medicare Physician Payment Reform Act (2009)
- Veterans Health Care Budget Reform and Transparency Act (2009)
- Foreign Account Tax Compliance Act (2009), requiring information about offshore tax havens
- Veterans' Compensation Cost-of-Living Adjustment Act (2009)
- Weapons Systems Acquisition Reform Act (2009), aimed at stopping fraud and wasteful spending
- Fraud Enforcement and Recovery Act (2009) to facilitate prosecution of lending fraud

- Helping Families Save Their Homes Act (2009), designed to stop foreclosures
- Worker, Homeownership and Business Assistance Act (2009), with tax credits for first-time homebuyers
- Military Spouses Residency Relief Act (2009)
- Omnibus Public Land Management Act (2009), adding 2 million acres to wilderness status
- North American Wetlands Conservation Act (2009)
- **Credit Card Accountability, Responsibility, and Disclosure Act** (2009), requiring credit card companies to make fuller disclosures
- Credit Card Technical Corrections Act (2009)
- Improper Payments Elimination and Recovery Act (2009) to root out government fraud and waste
- Cash for Clunkers Act (2009)
- Matthew Shepard and James Byrd, Jr., Hate Crimes Prevention Act (2009)
- Small Business Financing and Investment Act (2009)
- Military Commissions Act (2009)
- **successful nomination of two females, including one Hispanic, to the Supreme Court** (2009, 2010)
- Satellite Television Extension Act (2010)
- Caregivers and Veterans Omnibus Health Services Act (2010)
- Haiti Economic Lift Program Act (2010)
- Haiti Debt Relief and Earthquake Recovery Act (2010)
- Emergency Aid to Survivors of the Haiti Earthquake Act of 2010

- **Patient Protection and Affordable Health Care Act** (2010)
- **Wall Street Reform and Consumer Protection Act** (2010)
- Jobs for Main Street Act (2010)
- Health Care and Education Affordability Reconciliation Act (2010)
- **Restoring American Financial Stability Act** (2010)
- Lord's Resistance Army Disarmament and Northern Uganda Recovery Act (2010)
- Preservation of Access to Care for Medicare Beneficiaries and Pension Relief Act (2010)
- **ratification of the Strategic Arms Reduction Treaty extension** (2010)
- **Don't Ask, Don't Tell Repeal Act** (2010)
- Tax Relief, Unemployment Insurance Reauthorization, and Job Creation Act (2010)
- extension of the Patriot Act (2011)
- **Budget Control Act** (2011)
- America Invents Act (2011), streamlining the patent approval process
- ratification of free trade agreements with Colombia, South Korea, Panamá (2011)
- **passage of the Veterans Employment Transition Act** (2011)
- extension of the payroll tax cuts and unemployment insurance to Leap Year Day (2011).

Without the support of Congress, President Obama has had a less impressive record on civil liberties, having urged an extension of the Patriot Act, and on immigration issues, wherein abuses of illegals have increased. And although he sought to advance an environmental agenda through the 2009

161

"stimulus" bill, in 2011 he rescinded pollution rules for corporations as impediments to economic growth. Due to Republican opposition, he has otherwise had to rely on executive orders to advance environmental goals.

A $500,000 loan guarantee was approved in 2009 for Solyndra, a maker of photovoltaic cells that went bankrupt two years later. Although the company was already high on the list for a loan guarantee during the waning years of the Bush administration, Energy Secretary Steven Chu assumed responsibility for rushing the deal to meet a deadline. The Bush administration appointee with prior responsibility for screening the loan volunteered that he would have also approved the deal and that Chu evidently did nothing illegal or improper, but the Obama administration official who signed off on the loan guarantee soon resigned.

Conclusion

Some of the results identified above may be interpreted favorably or unfavorably, depending on one's policy predilections. Most legislative accomplishments can be credited to support from Democratic Party leaders Nancy Pelosi and Harry Reid. With 60 solidly loyal Democrats in the Senate, he could have accomplished more by avoiding Republican filibuster threats. And the Republican majority in the House of Representatives in 2011-2012 has deprived the country of more legislative accomplishments.

The most serious failure has been to gain cooperation from Congress in getting the economy back on track. Republicans whittled down the "stimulus" bill of 2009 so that job creation would not be adequate for the problem, and in 2011 they spent seven months debating ways to cut the federal budget so that even more jobs would be lost. Speaker John Boehner even relished the thought of laying off 300,000 federal employees.

For Barack Obama to win re-election, a favorable rating of the results of his four years in office is necessary. Promises that he has not accomplished thus far might be fulfilled if he is re-elected with Democratic majorities in both houses of Congress. But the most important campaign theme will ultimately be his vision of what he will do in a second term.

President Obama has demonstrated effectiveness, piling up accomplishments humbly and modestly. He has operated quietly, thereby ensuring that bargaining positions will not be prematurely frozen. His public addresses, whether before audiences at universities or during grassroots campaign encounters, have been extraordinarily visionary. He had hoped to accomplish more, but Congress blocked or neutered many reforms in regard to the economy.

Yet even his detractors will honestly have to agree that on an overall basis Barack Obama deserves to be called the "Calm and Effective President."

Appendix A
Monoculturalism Versus Multiculturalism

On the following pages, I contrast the multicultural ethos of Hawai'i with a somewhat stereotypic characterization of less desirable traits of the culture operating on the U.S. Mainland. Most of those in Hawai'i appreciate Mainlanders who are amiable, hardworking, industrious, orderly, sincere, and well-intentioned, but monocultural behavioral traits do not work in the Aloha State.

Most of the Island multicultural ethos flows from Native Hawaiian culture. Several traits are typically Japanese. Those who are puzzled by Barack Obama's personality should become familiar with the chart to better understand why he does not match Mainland expectations:

Hawai‘i Multiculturalism	Mainland Monoculturalism
1. *Seductive friendliness* Obama's mannerisms and voice have been described as "loose and inviting" and "Mesmerizing." According to the president, "No place else . . . could have provided me with the environment, the climate, in which I could not only grow but also get a sense of being loved." Aloha is something very deep inside Islanders, who often smile.	**1. *Suspiciousness*** People from Hawai‘i are unaccustomed to the Mainland habit of talking without smiling and withholding a sense of acceptance of other persons. Brusque, frowning, impersonal treatment indicates a distrust of all outside the "mainstream." Mainlanders rely on such aphorisms as "Beware of Greeks bearing gifts."
2. *Inclusiveness* Everyone is invited and welcome. No group is left out. Although various ethnic groups have their own societies to organize cultural events, they are open to everyone. For Obama, "the multicultural nature of Hawai‘i helped teach me how to appreciate different cultures and navigate different cultures, out of necessity."	**2. *Exclusiveness*** Various ethnic groups have their own societies to organize cultural events, which are often closed to outsiders. Within each group, members maintain privacy to avoid being overwhelmed by those who do not belong. As a result, there is little opportunity to learn about the culture of others. One's own group serves as a refuge from those who differ.

Hawai'i Multiculturalism	Mainland Monoculturalism
3. Charismatic humility Arrogance, pretentiousness, and claims of superiority are disapproved in Hawai'i; Island unpretentiousness is truly awe-inspiring. Obama, the self-styled "unlikely" president, repeatedly admits his mistakes as endemic to being human, believing that "It is hard to find your individual potential or sense of self-worth unless you are also concerned about the collective potential and self-worth of others."	**3. Arrogance** Arrogance, condescension, and pretentiousness are used to maintain hierarchies between people. Mistakes are rarely admitted. Self-esteem is often achieved by berating, even lecturing, others. Some Mainlanders feel good if they can put others "in their place." Those who differ are picked on by members of cliques, yet insecure people form cliques to provide support groups that may collapse due to power plays.
4. Joviality For some, President Obama is too prone to amusement. What they do not fathom is that his tendency to smile when asked leading questions during interviews demonstrates that he takes mischaracterizations lightly. Self-deprecating Island humor is hard to describe to Mainlanders, as everyone is gently ribbed for their flaws and thereby learns to laugh at themselves and at the human condition.	**4. Overseriousness** Mainlanders often withhold laughter from simple jokes, making nasal sounds in disapproval rather than just remaining silent. The aim is to be judgmental, proving that they are not frivolous and will only laugh at the "best" jokes. When jokes are on them, they take offense and may even fire back a nasty remark in defense, unable to laugh at themselves.

Hawai'i Multiculturalism	Mainland Monoculturalism
5. Respectfulness	**5. Disrespectfulness**
As Obama describes his personality and political style, "People in Hawai'i generally don't spend a lot of time, you now, yelling and screaming at each other. I think that there is just a cultural bias toward courtesy and trying to work through problems in a way that makes everybody feel like they're being listened to."	During discussions, Mainlanders are prone to say "I disagree" and state a point of view that criticizes what someone else has said. Then the discussion becomes an argument in which each side tries to score points, leaving one or all with bruised egos. What they lack is the desire to find common areas of agreement amid diversity; instead, they often rely on namecalling.
6. Nonconfrontationalism	**6. Confrontationalism**
Conflicts in Hawai'i are rarely expressed openly. There is a preference for quiet dialog involving neutral intermediaries. Those who wonder why President Obama will not "fight" for his principles should realize that he refuses to get in the gutter: "We must talk and reach for common understandings precisely because all of us are imperfect and can never act with the certainty that God is on our side."	Conflicts are expressed openly. Nobody objected when the administration of George W. Bush used bluster, scolding, and threats. Ill-mannered confrontational politics has now become the norm in Mainland politics. But standing up for principles with fiery rhetoric has produced chasms between ethnic groups, people, and political parties, resulting in an inability of different people to solve problems together.

168

Hawaiʻi Multiculturalism	Mainland Monoculturalism
7. Communitarianism	**7. Individualism**
Caring for others and generosity without expectation of reciprocity are valued interpersonal norms that operate beyond one's family and ethnic group in Hawaiʻi. For Obama, "We have a sense that beneath the surface of things, all of us share a common set of hopes, a common set of dreams and a common set of values. That's what the Islands have always been about." People in Hawaiʻi recognize that they have a responsibility to the larger society.	A sense of self-interest dominates concerns about what happens to the larger society. Groups push their own interests without regard to the consequences for other groups. A desire to be free from governmental interference collides with very real collective needs, such as reducing pollution. Free speech is upheld as a value in itself, even when the content is abrasive, inaccurate, or even vulgar. Drivers cut one another off while changing lanes. "My way or the highway" is the political credo.
8. Harmony	**8. Negativism**
Islanders avoid negative news, people, and situations (bad karma). For Obama, "Hawaiʻi is a fabulous model for the kind of America I hope this campaign will bring about, a place where different cultures can come together in harmony, and a place that rises above the barriers that divide us."	Journalists tend to focus on the latest difficulties, leaving listeners tired of "bad news." Yet that kind of coverage produces the highest ratings. Negative people and situations lie like a heavy burden on many Mainlanders. Looking for the bright side or for solutions is lost in coping with problems thought to come from "outsiders."

Hawai'i Multiculturalism	Mainland Monoculturalism
9. Serenity	**9. Irritability**
Obama's most puzzling characteristic is his calm, unflappable demeanor and unexcitable steadiness—his self-described "serenity." Signs in saunas and on public busses in Honolulu warn not to make loud sounds to upset others. Without meditation and "downtime," according to Obama, "you start making mistakes or you lose the big picture." Showing anger in Hawai'i is viewed as a sign of immaturity and weakness.	Mainlanders readily show anger when frustrated. Anger can be used to assert one's power, to deter further frustration, or simply to let off steam. In the venting of anger, aggression and snap decisions might be made. Regaining composure may then occur too late to rectify an even more difficult situation. As a result, Mainlanders often keep some distance from one another to avoid unpleasant scenes and then explode when they occur.
10. Humanism	**10. Dogmatism**
People come before principles. Universalistic approaches that ignore individual cases enjoy little favor in the Islands. One size will not fit all in a diverse society. Obama's view of the bank bailouts was: "It's not about helping banks—it's about helping people." He nominated a Supreme Court justice with "empathy."	Universalistic approaches often ride roughshod over individuals who differ from the mainstream. For candidate Obama, what was wrong about Jeremiah Wright was that he was "divisive." Ideological rigidity inhibits compromise, leaving real problems to fester. Some avoid practical solutions lest they are accused of betraying "principles," which are basically excuses for selfishness.

170

Hawai'i Multiculturalism	Mainland Monoculturalism
11. *Piety*	**11. *Irreverence***
Many people in Hawai'i are intensely spiritual, but live their beliefs without pontification. For Obama, "It's faith that gives me peace." Those in Hawai'i of all religions practice the Christian Second Commandment ("Love thy neighbor").	People in the United States are very religious, but they are sometimes stirred up to trample on the views of others, exhibiting religious intolerance that belies the very basic principles of their own faith.
12. *Preserving multiculturalism*	**12. *Preserving monoculturalism***
Hawai'i is a "special place" seeking to be preserved against inroads from the chaotic Mainland. The principal way to enforce the culture is social ostracism. Those who move to Hawai'i but resist assimilation to the multicultural ethos generally leave friendless in a few years. But, as Obama has noted, the culture of Hawai'i is more forgiving of cultural clumsiness. He is annoyed by those who deliberately spread lies, refuse to learn, and sew division. He wants the United States to regain a sense of community to solve problems together.	To maintain monoculturalism, many Mainlanders view the country in absolutistic terms. Rather than trying to find solutions to problems, discussions often focus on assigning blame to someone or some group. Despite an agricultural labor shortage, for example, some want all undocumented workers deported. Some Supreme Court justices adhere to the "original" meaning of the constitution rather than adapting the text to modern times. Despite evidence of the ill effects of global warming, some resist laws that would require changes in overconsumption lifestyles.

Appendix B
Communitarian Solutions

Communitarianism stresses individual responsibility to the community and thus differs from left-wing policy proposals, which would leave solutions to social problems for bureaucrats in government, and the right-wing view that most problems should be solved by individuals within the private sector.

For example, all agree that indigents charged with a crime should be given a proper defense in court. Left-wingers would beef up the public defender budgets to do so, whereas right-wingers would cut those budgets to the bare minimum. Communitarians, in contrast, would assist local Bar Association in setting up a panel of pro bono attorneys, particularly for the most difficult cases. The communitarian approach would increase quality while cutting costs.

Many of Barack Obama's policies may appear on the left because he wants change, whereas conservatives resist change. But when one examines how Obama wants changes to be implemented, what emerges is a focus on bringing businesses, government, and people together in issue after issue in a communitarian manner, as indicated on the following pages:

PROBLEM	LEFT-WING SOLUTIONS (leave to bureaucrats in government)	COMMUNITARIAN SOLUTIONS (increase individual responsibility to the community)	RIGHT-WING SOLUTIONS (leave to the individual & private sector)
bank insolvency	Nationalization	Stress tests to determine viability. → Government buys stock in banks. → Government later sells stock at a profit for taxpayers.	Let them fail when insolvent. (Force them to file for bankruptcy.)
prevent future bank failures	Government requires larger reserve fund.	Require the bank industry to set up its own reserve fund.	Let them fail when insolvent.
predatory lending	Comprehensive regulations and strict enforcement	Consumer protection agency to investigate and stop abuse	Do nothing: Expect those who take out loans to buy only what they can afford.
auto industry insolvency	Nationalization	Government requires industry to develop restructure plans. → Government buys stock. → Government later sells stock.	Let them file for bankruptcy.

174

PROBLEM	LEFT-WING SOLUTIONS	COMMUNITARIAN SOLUTIONS	RIGHT-WING SOLUTIONS
credit card debt	Comprehensive regulations	Require credit cards to provide better information to credit card holders.	Do nothing: Expect credit card holders to do the right thing.
economic slowdown	Federal government job programs (e.g., a Works Progress Administration)	Bloc grants to state & local governments to prevent firing of workers; funds for infrastructure contractors	Tax cuts for the rich. Then let the market recover on its own.
budget deficit	Increase taxes.	Design long-term deficit reduction plan acceptable to those affected.	Cut spending.
future Social Security insolvency	Increase taxes.	Design long-term solvency plan acceptable to all those affected.	Privatize Social Security.
future Medicare insolvency	Increase taxes.	Cut health care costs by mandating universal health care insurance.	Privatize Medicare.
improved public health	Government-run health care.	Public-private partnership for universal health care insurance	Leave to the private sector.

175

PROBLEM	LEFT-WING SOLUTIONS	COMMUNITARIAN SOLUTIONS	RIGHT-WING SOLUTIONS
unaffordable health insurance	Single payer plan (Medicaid or Medicare for all)	Employers and employees contribute to insurance plans selected by employees.	Let the market determine prices.
job preparation	Government-funded internships for students	Service learning paid for by private sector firms while students are in school	In-service training after employment
failing public schools	Increase funding to schools and teachers without conditions.	Increase funds to school districts only after they design reforms, including increased pay for better teachers and improved early education programs.	Shut down failing schools. Give parents vouchers so their children can go to private schools.
inadequate educational achievement	Support teachers. Pay them more when they take more college courses.	Private investment in intervention programs for public school districts that pay dividends only if they improve educational outcomes	Standardized tests developed by private firms to goad improvement
global warming	Government regulations + Stiff fines for violations	Private sector alternative energy projects + Tax cuts for efficient energy use + Cap-and-trade	Deny the existence of global warming.

176

Appendix C
Biographies of Barack Obama

Barack Obama is the most misunderstood president in American history because even his biographers have failed to discern basic sources of his personality and political philosophy, leaving readers with a feeling that something about him is missing. That's why I wrote *Barack Obama, The Aloha Zen President* (Praeger, 2011), which identifies the formative ethics and reality of multicultural Hawai'i that he experienced in his early years. Few of his biographers have ever been to Hawai'i, and even fewer have any idea that the culture of the Aloha State is profoundly different from that which they assume to be universal.

A review of biographies, indeed, reveals one characteristic is common: They project their own personalities onto the president, often telling more about themselves than about the president. I am no exception, as I assimilated to the culture of the Aloha State during my thirty-five years living in Honolulu while teaching political science at the main campus of the University of Hawai'i.

Below I analyze various biographies to determine what they consider to be the sources of his personality and political philosophy. By reviewing some of the various biographies, as I do below in alphabetical order, one can find both insights and misinterpretations:

Sasha Abramsky, *Inside Obama's Brain* (New York: Penguin, 2009), attempts to explain influences on Barack Obama's thinking, relying on anecdotes. A journalist, he interviews many persons acquainted with Obama to derive insights, but his remark that Obama was "confined by his many heritages" misses the essential role of multicultural Hawai'i in liberating him from stereotypic thinking of the kind that the author displays. Abramsky assumes that Obama's experience as a community organizer in Chicago is central to his demeanor and outlook. He fails to learn the insight from Emil

Jones, Obama's Illinois political mentor, that Hawai'i primarily influenced him.

Jonathan Alter, *The Promise: President Obama, Year One* (New York: Simon & Schuster, 2009), focuses on how candidate Barack Obama shifted gears to govern as president. A template for the analysis is the author's previous book on the first hundred days in the presidency of Franklin Delano Roosevelt. The narrative ends with passage of Obama's much-sought universal health care bill. Chapter 9 ("Zen Temperament") seeks to describe the personality of President Obama. Quoting two of Obama's Illinois friends, Emil Jones and Eric Whitaker, Alter offers readers the insight that the president's personality was primarily shaped in Hawai'i. A journalist who is a frequent commentator on MSNBC, Alter describes Obama's first year in office as one of frustration—wanting to be inclusive in a bitterly partisan Washington. Alter has written a cover jacket endorsement of my *Barack Obama, The Aloha Zen President*.

Eric Alterman, *Kabuki Democracy: The System vs. Barack Obama* (New York: The Nation Institute, 2011), explains how Obama has been checkmated by societal interests that pressure Congress to do their bidding. A Brooklyn College political science professor, Alterman cites many examples of how Congress has not been the most clever or efficient lawmaking body. Not a biography in the usual sense, the book traces how Obama failed to fulfill various campaign promises because of the dominance of Congress in national governmental decision making. The term "kabuki democracy" refers to the fact that a power game operates in Washington behind the façade of democratic politics. In private conversation, however, Alterman rejects the idea that Obama's personality and philosophy might have been shaped in Hawai'i and does not accept the fact that Obama's willingness to allow compromises is derived from the inclusiveness of the culture of Hawai'i.

Daniel J. Balz and Haynes Johnson, *The Battle for America 2008: The Story of an Extraordinary Election* (New York: Viking, 2009), give an account of the primary and general elections of 2008 by a journalist and a presidential scholar. The aim is to chronicle events and to put them in some context, but neither Obama's personality nor his philosophy are explored in depth.

Marlene Targ Brill, *Barack Obama: Working to Make a Difference* (Minneapolis: Millbrook Press, 2006), in 48 pages writes the shortest biography. Specifically intended for younger readers, Obama's political views are not analyzed. The biographical content seems primarily derived from Obama's *Dreams from My Father* but is also based on interviews in Honolulu and at Harvard. The acknowledgment that Obama grew up "much as a Hawaiian American boy" appropriately gives credit to Obama's formative years in Honolulu. But the term "Hawaiian American" does not apply: The indigenous people are known as "Native Hawaiians," and those in the Islands never use her phrase.

Jack Cashill, *Deconstructing Obama: The Life, Loves, and Letters of America's First Postmodern President* (New York: Threshold Editions, 2011), argues that Barack Obama never wrote *Dreams from My Father* and is a fraud. Executive editor of *Ingram's Magazine,* the Kansas City regional business magazine, with a doctorate in American Studies from Purdue University, Cashill believes that Obama has had a secret life that has been disguised from the public to make him electable. With that premise, there is a lot of make-believe and conspiracy theory in the book.

Jerome R. Corsi, *The Obama Nation: Leftist Politics and the Cult of Personali*ty (New York: Threshold, 2008), a Harvard Ph.D. in political science, twists every possible fact with the aim of defeating Obama even before his nomination. He misses the Hawai'i context, especially the impact of White racism in pre-statehood Hawai'i and of Japanese culture on Obama's best schoolfriend, Keith Kakugawa.

Dinesh D'Souza, *The Roots of Obama's Rage* (Washington, DC: Regnery, 2009), a right-wing ideological thinker, tries to trace the president's views to the ideology of anti-colonialism. D'Souza believes that Obama's father imparted a sinister ideology on his son even though the two hardly knew each another. As evidence, he speculates that his father is his role model, having entitled his book *Dreams from My Father.* D'Souza hunts up essays by his father and insists that the president subscribes to the same views. Although D'Souza's

179

unauthorized political biography is based on conjecture, he is right in detecting an anti-colonial strand within Obama. Contrary to D'Souza, the source of his anti-colonialism can be traced to the bitter memories of non-Whites who were bullied by Whites in pre-statehood Hawai'i. Yet the author dismisses the possibility that Barack Obama was fundamentally influenced by his upbringing in the Aloha State.

William Michael Davis, *Barack Obama: The Politics of Hope* (Stockton, NJ: OTTN Publishing, 2008), offers nearly a magazine with so many pictures and sidebars. A onetime Congressional staffer who once majored in political science, he implies that Obama's life experiences were of much less importance in forging his personality than his racial self-awareness. Otherwise, the biography traces his life competently, with many footnotes.

Mary Lou Décosterd, *Right Brain/Left Brain: Barack Obama's Uncommon Leadership Ability and How We Can Each Develop It* (Westport, CT: Praeger, 2010), assumes that Obama uses both sides of his brain (affective and cognitive) and therefore appeals widely to diverse Americans. However, the book is more about a concept in cognitive psychology than about Obama as a person.

Martin Dupuis and Keith Boeckellman, *Barack Obama, the New Face of America* (Westport, CT: Praeger, 2008), focus on Obama's public career, not his early years. Political scientists, they believe that his formative years began when he threw his hat into the political ring in Chicago and learned to become a master politician in a country where glass ceilings are being shattered by minorities. The authors evidently agree with Obama's political views but fail to analyze his personal or psychological roots anywhere outside Illinois.

Thomas R. Dye, et al., *Obama: Year One*. (Upper Saddle River, NJ: Pearson Education, 2010), compiles seven chapters by political scientists that analyze who voted for Obama in 2008, his unusual campaign strategy, why his message was lost after he was elected, how the White House operates, and the substance of and support for his policies. Organized as a textbook with study questions and a detailed bibliography, Obama is treated as a typical politician.

180

Avner Falk, *The Riddle of Barack Obama: A Psycho-biography* (Praeger 2010), does a thorough job of tracking down personal information about Obama but then draws farfetched inferences about him. A psychiatrist, Falk insists that every situation into which Obama has found himself carries a hidden psychological meaning. At the beginning of the book, Falk admits that the approach called "positive psychology" believes in "cultural universality." After saying that he does not necessarily agree with that claim, he nevertheless uses that template to assess Obama from the standpoint of Western culture (as if Western culture were universal). "Hawai'i," frequently misspelled in the text, is neither recognized in the book's index nor as playing any role in Obama's maturation. Falk starts from the premise that Obama's behavior is a riddle, warranting a psychological analysis. Accordingly, the book fails to perceive cultural explanations, puts far too many thoughts into Obama's head, and praises Obama for meeting Western standards.

Stu Glauberman and Jerry Burris, *The Dream Begins: How Hawai'i Shaped Barack Obama* (Honolulu: Watermark Publishing, 2008), stress that Hawai'i impacts President Obama's personality. The authors interview several persons, including the president's half-sister, to enrich an account of what it was like for young Barry Obama to thrive in a multicultural environment. Journalists, their account is historical, personal, and non-sociological. Although they ably recount some of the political events in Hawai'i during the 1970s, how they impacted Obama's mindset is left unexplained.

Michael Haas, *America's War Crimes Quagmire: From Bush to Obama* (Publishinghouse for Scholars, 2010), analyzes types of war crimes that began in the Bush administration and rolled over to the Obama administration. Most of the 47 chapters deal with Bush-era crimes, but later chapters comment on how Obama has tried to cope with them.

Michael Haas, ed., *Barack Obama, The Aloha Zen President: How a Son of the 50th State May Revitalize America Based on 12 Multicultural Principles* (Praeger, 2011), provides an ethnobiography of Barack Obama in the first chapter. The next thirteen chapters analyze various aspects of the sociology of the Aloha State, indicating wherein Obama was

181

influenced. The last chapter analyzes how Hawai'i has direct-ly influenced his presidency. The coverjacket contains en-dorsements by journalist Jonathan Alter and sociologist Amit-ai Etzioni.

John Heilemann and Mark Halperin, *Game Change: Obama and the Clintons, McCain and Palin, and the Race of a Lifetime* (New York: Harper, 2009), provide a journalistic account of the primary and general elections of 2008. They rely on information, some public and some behind-the-scenes, to explain how the election proceeded. Although more fluent writers than David Plouffe, the latter's book (reviewed below) has much more intimate detail about Barack Obama and the campaign.

Ron Jacobs, *Obamaland: Who Is Barack Obama?* (Hono-lulu: Trade Publishing, 2008), produces more magazine than book in appearance and style. The aim is to provide a guide-book for residents and tourists alike to locate where Barry Obama lived and went to school. Replete with maps and pho-tographs, the publication exudes the richness of the presi-dent's home state. Short comments are written by twenty-two observers, including the current governor, Neil Abercrombie. Although once offered for sale in Waikīkī souvenir shops, sales were reportedly not brisk. Alas, tourists seldom visit Hawai'i to learn about its culture and its people.

Kate Kenski, Bruce W. Hardy, and Kathleen Hall Ja-mieson, *The Obama Victory: How Media, Money, and Mes-sage Shaped the 2008 Election* (New York: Oxford University Press, 2010), explain why Obama won, based in part on poll-ing data during the 2008 election. Three social scientists, they also analyze Obama's support from various interest groups.

James. T. Kloppenberg, *Reading Obama: Dreams, Hope, and the American Political Tradition* (Princeton University Press, 2010), imposes a template on Obama that emerges from the author's quest to write an intellectual history of American politics. Scraps of Barack Obama's writings are seized upon to prove that he is primarily a pragmatist, not just pragmatic. Otherwise, the author finds traces of many intel-lectual schools of American political thought in Obama's prose, though the various isms are not clearly enough pre-sented for those unfamiliar with them. There are two important gaps. One is that the author does not identify Social Darwinism, a major theory espoused by many Republicans, past and present. Kloppenberg thus cannot explain how the different ethnic groups in the State of Hawai'i overcame the ill effects of pre-statehood Social Darwinist Republican rule during the very years when Obama lived in Honolulu. And Kloppenberg's lack of an index entry for "Hawai'i" is indicative of his failure to examine the role of the Aloha State in shaping Obama's fundamental values despite Obama's many statements to that effect. Whereas Kloppenberg talks of "conflicting" intellectual traditions, Obama has praised his exposure to multiple perspectives, which he believes have given him special insights. In Hawai'i the pluralism of views is identified with the existence of alternative cultures that work side by side rather than conflictually. Thus, Kloppenberg views Obama as torn between conflicting philosophical strands, but Obama considers himself enriched by multiple perspectives as a challenge to find "common ground," an assignment that residents of Hawai'i practice daily. Kloppenberg, who takes his own assimilationist monoculturalism for granted, thus cannot explain why Obama is so keen on negotiating compromise.

David Mendell, *Obama: From Promise to Power* (New York: Harper, 2007), a veteran *Chicago Tribune* journalist, interviews Obama's Chicago friends as well as his grandmother and half-sister with the apparent aim of promoting the candidacy of Barack Obama for president by humanizing him. Although he devotes a few pages to those who influenced him personally as he grew up, much of the narrative is devoted to his career in Chicago and Illinois politics as formative in shaping Obama's personality and political style.

Steven J. Niven, *Barack Obama: A Pocket Biography of Our 44th President* (New York: Oxford University Press, 2009), summarizes the life of Barack Obama in 80 pages. Written by a Harvard researcher, the primary focus is on the significance of Obama's rise to prominence as a successful national African American politician. The impact of Hawai'i on Obama, thus, is limited to the facts of his birth and early education in Honolulu. Through the lens of the African Amer-

183

ican experience in America, Niven assumes that race has dominated Obama's political thinking.

Barack Obama, *The Audacity of Hope: Thoughts on Reclaiming the American Dream* (New York: Crown Publishers, 2006), presents the opening statement of someone who ultimately planned to run for president. Although he does not identify a specific guiding political philosophy, the analysis of problems besetting America is mainstream political science. Communitarianism appears to pervade his thinking, though there is no mention of the term in the book and no citation of any famous political theorist. The reader will conclude that important influences on his political thinking must have come long before his candidacy.

Barack Obama, *Dreams from My Father: A Story of Race and Inheritance* (New York: Crown Publishers, 1995), pens an extraordinary autobiography, showing literary talent and introspective soul-searching as he navigates life from birth in 1961 to his marriage to Michelle Robinson in 1992 through experiences in Honolulu, Jakarta, Los Angeles, New York, Chicago, Cambridge, and Kenya. The book was re-issued in 2004 with a new Preface by the author. Although Obama was asked to write a book upon graduation from Harvard Law School in 1991, he delayed writing until he visited Kenya, a trip needed to end his puzzlement over his ancestry and to meet long-lost relatives.

Obama for America, *Change We Can Believe In: Barack Obama's Plan to Renew America's Promise* (New York: Three Rivers Press, 2008), with a Foreword by Barack Obama, reprints seven speeches, and in four chapters outlines a campaign vision relating to the economy, foreign policy, and other issues. Members of the group Obama for America anonymously summarize specific campaign themes. The book is not a biography except insofar as the text serves as a statement of his political ideas.

David Plouffe, *The Audacity to Win: The Inside Story and Lessons of Barack Obama's Historic Victory* (New York: Viking, 2009), offers an account of Barack Obama's campaign for president, as told by his campaign manager. Plouffe clearly admires Obama's determination to win as well as his calm way of dealing with occasional campaign setbacks. Business partner of David Axelrod, Plouffe describes Obama with such adjectives as "humble," and he modestly downplays his own role in the victory of 2008. His account reveals that personal characteristics of the future president sustained his zeal to work tirelessly throughout an exhausting campaign. He does not pause to analyze Obama's personality or his philosophy, preferring a fact-oriented narrative.

Joann F. Price, *Barack Obama: A Biography* (Westport, CA: Greenwood Press, 2008), recapitulates Obama's *Dreams from My Father*. A biographer of Martha Stewart, the author was evidently encouraged by the press to write another in a series of biographies. Although she notes that Hawai'i and Indonesia were "formative" in Obama's life, the book devotes more pages to his political career. An extensive chronology is a major contribution of the book.

David Remnick, *The Bridge: The Life and Rise of Barack Obama* (New York: Knopf, 2009), prepares the longest, best indexed and referenced of all the biographies. Remnick, after interviewing hundreds of persons to find out about Obama, decides to organize the book around the theme that his election is the fulfillment of the dreams of Martin Luther King, Jr. The "bridge" in the title refers to the Edmund Pettus Bridge at Selma crossed on March 7, 1965, by some 600 civil rights advocates, who marched out of Selma to Montgomery to protest the inability of African Americans to register to vote, whereupon they were brutally beaten by state police. Remnick travels to nearly every place where Obama lived for insightful interviews, and his index shows attention to details about what he heard from informants in Honolulu and Jakarta, though with little understanding of either place. Yet when Remnick was interviewed by Charlie Rose, he seemed puzzled about whether he had identified the essence of Barack Obama's personna and political values. At the conclusion of the interview, Rose remarked, "I still do not understand Barack Obama," a critique of Remnick's book that must have rankled him. The biography has a journalistic penchant to focus on symbolic meanings rather than content in dealing with Obama, thereby giving little attention to his underlying personality and philosophy.

Janny Scott, *A Singular Woman: The Untold Story of Barack Obama's Mother* (New York: Riverhead Books, 2011), a *New York Times* reporter, writes primarily about Barack Obama's mother, Stanley Ann Dunham, not him. Yet the motivation for the book is clearly to better understand him, testament to the yearning by many to find some hidden explanation for his unusual behavior. Scott quotes Obama as crediting his mom with inspiring him but also notes that she despaired that her influence ended after he took up residence in Chicago and decided to regard himself as an "African American." After paying considerable attention to his mom's background in Kansas and Seattle, the author describes a woman who must have lived in Honolulu inside an academic ivory tower, ignoring the wider community in Hawai'i. Of the sixteen books cited in the bibliography, most give background on Indonesia and none on Hawai'i. The book has footnotes but lacks an index. Most Honolulu sources are interviews with Caucasians, though she also notes that they are a minority in the Islands and were discriminated against by some Japanese landlords in the early 1960s without inquiring why. In short, the author is oblivious of the role of multicultural Hawai'i on Obama, his mother, and her parents as if the Island state had no history or sociology worth examining. She misses the essence of Barack Obama by looking for clues everywhere but the most obvious place—the Aloha State, which Obama considers the model society.

Dinesh Sharma, *Barack Obama in Hawai'i and Indonesia: The Making of a Global President* (Santa Barbara, CA: ABC-Clio, 2011), writes in an academic term paper style that cites many references but fails to establish a coherent thesis. After identifying more cultural influences on Obama than any other writer, he contradictorily believes that "most social actions stem from the underlying parental influences" (p. 59), and he even spends a fanciful chapter trying to interpret dreams and myths. Although he describes Hawai'i and Indonesia as "competing" with American influences (p. 61), similar to Western monocultural biographers, he nevertheless concedes that the multicultural influence of his Honolulu upbringing "forms the core of Obama's inner self" (p. 136). Although a cultural psychologist, his understanding of Hawai'i's multiculturalism is nonexistent. Whereas he identifies the historical context of Indonesia during Obama's years in Jakarta, Sharma is oblivious of civil rights struggles by Filipinos and Native Hawaiians in the Islands during the 1970s. A few factual errors, incorrect diacritical marks, a pedestrian analysis of world history, and a conspicuous failure to cite the principal source of several ideas indicate some lack of care in the scholarship as well as stereotypic thinking.

Ron Suskind, *Confidence Men: Wall Street, Washington, and the Education of a President* (New York: HarperCollins, 2011), focuses on infighting in the Obama administration among prima donnas in which the president sought common ground, thereby sacrificing policy coherence. Suskind repeatedly expresses frustration with Obama's diffidence, contradicting rosy accounts by Wolffe (reviewed below), and pinning the principal blame on advisers Rahm Emmanuel and Larry Summers for blocking decisions by the president. Suskind, aware that Obama wanted to be president of all the people and thus sought inclusive consensus before definitive action, nevertheless criticizes the president's zen management style. The factual heart of the book is a prolix account, requiring some economic literacy, of the economic crisis that Obama learned about before his nomination and struggled to handle as president amid contending interests. The index contains no reference to Hawai'i. Suskind judges Obama based on Mainland American cultural expectations.

James A. Thurber, ed., *Obama in Office* (Boulder, CO: Paradigm, 2011), compiles essays by sixteen political scientists, who assess Obama's first two years in office, focusing on his relations with other branches of government, the media, and the public. Suitable as an undergraduate textbook, the book is more comprehensive than the one edited by Dye.

John K. Wilson, *Barack Obama: This Improbable Quest* (Boulder, CO: Paradigm Press, 2008), contains eight well-footnoted chapters, tackling issues featured in the campaign of Barack Obama, such as "Is he Black enough?" A former student of the president, he does not, however, identify a fundamental philosophy to which Obama subscribes, instead applying the label "liberal" to his thinking. There is no attention to Obama's personality or formative influences.

Richard Wolffe, *Renegade: The Making of a President* (New York: Crown Publishers, 2009), divulges "exclusive interviews with Barack Obama," according to the cover jacket. A journalist who appears frequently on MSNBC, Wolffe was in the Obama campaign van throughout the 2008 campaign. The word "renegade" is usually used to describe someone who deserts or switches allegiances, so Wolffe's focus in the book is on how Obama began his career by defying his mother—becoming an African American rather than a "citizen of the world"—and then by challenging the heir apparent, Hillary Clinton. Wolffe claims that Obama's experience in New York as a student and later an employee was crucial in his development—not Hawai'i, not Harvard, and not even Chicago, none of which are listed in the index. Specifically inspired by Theodore White's series of books entitled *The Making of the President,* Wolffe describes the 2008 campaign by focusing on Obama's reactions to disappointments and successes without understanding the roots of his Aloha Zen personality.

Richard Wolffe, *Revival: The Struggle for Survival Inside the Obama White House* (New York: Crown Publishers, 2010), summarizes the first years of the Obama's presidency based on inside information. Wolffe identifies how President Obama has dealt with the inevitable infighting within the Obama administration as well as challenges from Congress. The prevailing pressure group model, that political decisions are made in the context of competing forces, is applied to understand Obama's policymaking. Wolffe is impressed by the strength of Obama's character but sees no need to analyze either his personality or his philosophy. He does not identify the impact of Obama's experience in Hawai'i or Indonesia on his policy choices as president, preferring to present facts rather than analyze more deeply.

Richard Wolffe. *Revival 2.0: How the Obama White House Is Making Its Political Comeback* (New York: Crown Publishers, 2011), focuses on the president's role in the killing of Osama Bin Laden, the inside story of the overhaul of top White House staff, the contentious internal debate over the response to the revolutions in Tunisia, Egypt, and Libya, and the campaign strategy for the 2012 election. An update of the author's previous book.

Bob Woodward, *Obama's Wars* (New York: Simon & Schuster, 2010), describes pressures brought to bear on Obama to make crucial decisions, particularly about Afghanistan. Although Woodward utilized his extensive contacts with the military to place wars at the center of his books about President George W. Bush, the narrative in this book is incomplete because Obama's domestic agenda is far more prominent. As with most other journalist biographers, he passes on Obama's personality and political philosophy, preferring a fact-based account.

Bibliographic Essay

Rather than a dry, distracting list of footnotes, I provide below some discussion along with citations to references so that
the interested reader may learn more about the various topics.
References to texts of laws, treaties, or United Nations resolutions are easily searched by title on the Internet and therefore
are not included below.

Chapter 1

Some biographers suggest that his parents and grandparents
shaped him (Scott 2011; Sharma 2011; Wolffe 2009). Another
perspective is that he matured at a very early age (Alter 2010;
O'Reilly 2009; Weisberg 2010). Some, including Hillary
Clinton during the nomination campaign, have claimed that
academic elitism is his main influence (cf. Meacham 2009;
Plouffe 2009:226); Mark Halperin's obsession in this regard
came to light when he called Obama a "dick" (Mak 2011).
Yet another school of thought is that he was largely shaped by
his experience as an African American (Niven 2009; Remnick
2010) or in Chicago (Abramsky 2009; Dupuis and Boeckellman 2008; McClelland 2010; Mendell 2007). His peripa-
tetic mother and four-year Indonesian experience are central,
according to some commentators (Remnick 2010: 430; Scott
2011; Sharma 2011; Zakaria 2009). Some observers believe
Obama, who dedicated one of his books to strong female influences, has feminine traits, yet clearly are unaware that
strict male/female roles are a Western fixation and that
Barack Obama did not live in the dichotomy-prone West during his childhood (cf. Sharma 2011:96). The most extraordinary, culturally myopic, claim is that he has a "Kansas-
Indonesia-Kenya background" (Lelyveld 2010:6)! As his
campaign manager described how he learned to campaign
better, some pundits have understandably sought to explain
changes since he became president as political maturation
(Plouffe 2009:203; Baker 2010; Suskind 2011; Thomas and
Connolly 2010; Wolffe 2010, 2011). For specific comments
on the biographies, see Appendix C.

Sources for most statements in the chapter are found within various chapters of Michael Haas, ed., *Barack Obama, The Aloha Zen President: How a Son of the 50th State May Revitalize America Based on 12 Multicultural Principles* (Santa Barbara, CA: Praeger, 2011). Specific sources for the quoted statements are as follows: Gergen (quoted in Stolberg 2009), Jamieson (quoted in East-West Center 2009), Barack Obama (1999; and quoted in Glaubeman and Burris 2008:4; Honolulu Star-Bulletin 2008; Pang 2004; Walsh 2008; Nakaso and Reyes 2011), Michelle Obama (quoted in Mendel 2007:20), Sotero-Ng (quoted in Thanawala 2008). Although he appears to emulate George Ariyoshi, Sharma (2011:105) reports that he tried to copy Indonesian President Suharto's speechmaking while living there.

The historical section is a summary from Chapter 2 of *Barack Obama, The Aloha Zen President*. The section "The Culture of the Islands" summarizes Chapters 4-7 in that book.

Chapter 2

Sources for most statements in the chapter about Hawai'i are found in Chapters 1, 2, and 14 of *Barack Obama, The Aloha Zen President*. Chapter 3 in the same book provides survey data proving that there is a sharp contrast between attitudes of those in Hawai'i from those on the U.S. Mainland. The same chapter shows that Mainlanders who move to Hawai'i tend to embrace attitudes prevalent in the Aloha State. Suskind (2011:126) identifies Obama's reason to run for the presidency as an answer to a question posed by his spouse.

Pukui's definition of "Aloha Spirit" is found in the Appendix to *Barack Obama, The Aloha Zen President*. The classic explanation of the Bushido Code is by Inazo Nitobe (1902). For a summary, see *thebushidocode.org*. A biography of Barack Obama's mother stresses similar traits (Scott 2011:Chap 4). The view that the American Mainland is hopelessly divided into cultural groups is often taken for granted (Woodward 2011).

Relevant references to Karl Marx are found in Harris (1968), Engels (1884), and Morgan (1870). Regarding inclusiveness, his failure to take definitive stands while advisers disagreed contrasts with his alleged lack of attention to women in policymaking (Suskind 2011:Chap 12-14).

Additional quotes, in order of their appearance, are Ariyoshi (1982); Abercrombie (2008); Obama (quoted in Glauberman and Burris 2008:4; and in Thanawala 2008); Jamieson (quoted in East-West Center 2009); Obama (2004; quoted in Husain and Chang 2005 and in Walsh 2008); O'Reilly (2009); Obama (quoted in MacFarquar 2007; Pang 2004; Glauberman and Burris 2008:4; Zeleny 2008); Obama (2010a; and quoted in Alter 2010:146); Obama (2009a; 1995:270; 2008; 2011). For zen culture, see Nukariya (1913:50-51). Obama's reaction to Reverend Wright is nicely summarized in a report by Ross (2008). Suskind (2011:130,132,141) recounts election night humility. Some journalists, not realizing his background, have described Obama as a "loner" (Wilson 2011a).

For the debt limit debate, see Chapter 9. The use of the "common ground" phrase is reported in Mascaro and Hennessey (2011) and many other sources. Jamieson's study is reported by Fahrenthold (2011b).

Chapter 3

The concept of "political succession" was originally developed by Peter Eisinger (1980). Two excellent histories of political parties in the United States are by Maisel and Barry (2010) and Schlesinger (1980). Political succession in Hawai'i is analyzed in Haas (2010b:Chap 7).

Fears of a dominant group losing political power can even be traced to the early years of North American colonization, as those brought from Africa could have been educated, as were early Irish immigrants, to achieve assimilation. Instead, the English settlers in the southern colonies and their offspring in the later states, doubtless fearing payback from former slaves at the ballot box, erected a host of legal barriers to block their achievement of political power and their social advancement. Among historians who have written on the subject, see Kolchin (2003) and Woodward (2002).

For the events of 1788, see Heintze (2000). The "Patriot Act" of the Adams administration (Miller 1951) was modeled after the crime of lesé majesté. The Burr-Hamilton duel

(Fleming 1999) stimulated a movement to ban the practice. After the "era of good feelings" (Dangerfield 1986), the elections of 1824 and 1828 gave birth to American class politics (Howe 2008). Luebke (1971) analyzes the ethnic vote in the 1860 election. Presidential biographies are legion: Grover Cleveland (Nevins 1932), Woodrow Wilson (Link 1968; cf. Wolgemuth 1959), Franklin Roosevelt (Alter 2006), and John Kennedy (Dallek 2003). President Truman asked Eisenhower to run for president in 1948 (Neal 2001).

Although not always directly concerned with political succession, histories of ethnic and other groups in American politics have been written about African Americans (Davis 2011), Asians (Chang 2001), gays (Rimmerman, Wald, Wilcox 2010), Irish (Dolan 2008), Hispanics (de la Isla 2003), Jews (Fuchs 1956), and women (Krook and Childs 2010).

Woldoff (2011) insightfully traces the impact on a city of "White flight" to the suburbs. More information on the politics of Hawai'i can be found in Haas (2011:Chap 8). Some provisions of the Arizona law have been upheld by the U.S. Supreme Court (Savage 2011). A revision of the 14th Amendment seems unlikely (Somashekhar 2010).

The "socialist" charge is completely refuted in Suskind (2011). The *Daily Show* text can be found on the blog *Finding the Perfect World* (2009). Specific racial animosity directed at Obama has been rare, though present at Tea Party rallies (cf. Maxwell 2011). The Southern Poverty Law Center (2009) has documented a resurgence of racist hate groups (cf. Blow 2009) and a secessionist movement (Smith and Lenz 2011). Fletcher (2009) provides Obama's quotation about race relations.

Opinion surveys on race relations are reported in several sources (Fiorina 2010:9; Balz and Johnson 2009:379; Remnick 2010: 450; Stolberg and Connelly 2009). A more skeptical view emerges from some focus interviews of younger persons (Apollon 2011). Smiley's interview program is broadcast during the week on public television stations. Holder identified civil rights as his number one priority as Attorney General (Kingsbury 2009).

Genealogical reports on Obama have focused on his mother's side of the family (Caplan and Dell 2008; Hammons

2008). One such tracing finds that he is related to several presidents and has royal blood (Morton 2008). The song "Only in America" by Kix Brooks and Ronnie Dunn is a country music song that was originally used by Republicans (Willman 2008).

Chapter 4
Barack Obama's long-form birth certificate was posted by Pfeiffer (2011). For poll results, see Cohen (2011). For a discussion of whether persons born in the United States are considered "natural-born citizens," Wikipedia (2011a) has an excellent article. Milbank (2011a) reports the caper seeking to discredit Marco Rubio and "Bobby" Jindal. Huffington Post (2011a) reports on Georgia.

Chapter 5
The two major scientific publications of Darwin (1859, 1871) were reviewed in layman's language by Thomas Huxley (1860). The classic statement on Social Darwinism in American political history is by Hofstadter (1959). The 144,000 number used by Jehovah's Witnesses is based on a passage in Revelation within the New Testament (see LaHaye 1975).

Libertarian classics are Adam Smith (1776), Ayn Rand (1943), and Milton Friedman (1963), though the latter admitted that his theory of the economy was wrong (Roberts 2008). The triumphalist theory of Hitler (1933) is of course not what Republicans have in mind. For an economist's view of the distinction between what I coin as libertarian and triumphalist economic thinking, see Frank (2011).

Conservative Republican "patron saints" are Barry Goldwater (1960) and William F. Buckley (cf. Edwards 2010). The most recent neo-conservative triumphalist president was George W. Bush (Cohen 2011; Vaïsse 2010).

The McKinley tariff is analyzed by Reitano (1994). Tension between Theodore Roosevelt and William Howard Taft is described in Morris (2010:Chap 8). Wilson segregated the federal government workforce (Wolgemuth 1959).

For Republican policies during the 1920s, see Greenberg (2006) and Smith (1970). Keynes's classic work is *The Economic Consequences of the Peace* (1920). His specific rec-

ommendations for handling the Great Depression were codi-
fied in *The General Theory of Employment, Interest, and
Money* (1936).

Many biographies of recent presidents are available—for
Franklin Delano Roosevelt (Black 2003), Harry Truman (Mc-
Cullough 1992), Dwight Eisenhower (Ambrose 2007), John
Kennedy (Dallek 2003), Lyndon Johnson (Goodwin 1991),
Richard Nixon (Black 2007), Gerald Ford (Brinkley 2007),
Jimmy Carter (Gaillard and Carter 2009), Ronald Reagan
(Morris 1999), George H. W. Bush (Tarpley and Chaitkin
1992), Bill Clinton (Klein 2002), and George W. Bush (Dra-
per 2007).

Obama's economic policies are described in Chapter 9.
His health care plan is discussed in Chapter 10, including reference to the Republican who came up with the idea that was
later attacked as "death panels" (Byrne 2009).

Boehner's speech appears in a television interview with
Brian Williams (First Read 2011). Proposed cuts by Republicans in 2011 were reported on *speaker.gov/blog*, Boehner's
website. The "Let them die!" outburst is reported by Muskal
(2011).

The success of the trade union movement in Hawai'i is
ably described in Beechert (2011). The Social Darwinist ideology of Republicans in Hawai'i is analyzed in Haas
(1992a:Chap 3). For the tension between libertarian and triumphalist Republicans, see Reuters (2011a). On Ron Paul's
comment as an indication of how he is out of touch with reality, see Krugman (2011).

Fannie Mae is the nickname of the Federal National
Mortgage Association. Freddie Mac is colloquial for Federal
Home Loan Mortgage Corporation.

Attitudes about the "American Dream," a view that each
generation in the United States will improve over the previous generation, are measured yearly by Metropolitan Life Insurance Company (2011). Part of the dream, as cultivated in
economic upswings, is that every family will own a house.
The term was coined by James Truslow Adams (1932).

The "American Way" is founded on the notion that the
United States is committed to providing "life, liberty, and the
pursuit of happiness," as stated in the Declaration of Inde-

pendence. Will Herberg (1955) provides the most philosophical statement of its meaning.

To find out which parts of the speech on jobs evoked giggling and guffawing, see Milbank (2011c).

Chapter 6

Many pundits have complained that President Obama is "too cool" and will not "fight" (Brownstein (2010; Cole 2011b; vanden Heuvel 2011; Cole 2011b). West (quoted by Hedges 2011) accuses him of being an Uncle Tom without saying so specifically. For a riposte to West, see Harris-Perry (2011). Decisions that have disappointed Progressive Democrats are identified by Hananel (2001) and Milbank (2011d). Bromwich (2011) provides an acerbic deconstruction of Obama's personality from a conservative viewpoint. Westen (2011) does so from a liberal perspective. After their tirades, I contacted all those mentioned to point out that Obama's personality was fundamentally shaped in Hawai'i. None responded. For Obama's carefully framed definition of "leadership," see Suskind (2011:482).

I also sent unanswered letters regarding several odd reviews in the *New York Review of Books* (Pinckney 2008; Lelyveld 2010; Buruma 2011) for pointedly refusing to recognize his Hawai'i upbringing. Lelyveld gives credit to Indonesia, where he spent 4 years, but not to his 14 years in Honolulu, where he returns annually to be with family and friends. Perhaps the most insensitive suggestion was by journalist Cokie Roberts, who urged him to go on vacation to Myrtle Beach, South Carolina, instead of "exotic" Honolulu (quoted in Boehlert and Foser 2008).

Information about Progressive Democrats of America can be found on its website *pdamerica.org* and its *Facebook* page. The California PDA group also has a website: *pdamerica.org/tag/california*

Citations from Alter, Jamieson, Michelle Obama, and Sotero-Ng are previously listed in Chapter 1. Dukakis contributed the Foreword to my *Barack Obama, The Aloha Zen President*. Amitai Etzioni also wrote a coverjacket endorsement of the book. Jeff Zeleny (2008) based his comment on interviews in Hawai'i, one of which was with my former political science colleague Neil Milner. The as-sessment of the plantation era as "feudal" applied as recently as the mid-1960s (Moore 1969:34).

Axelrod's quote comes from Alter (2010:428). Text of The Aloha Spirit Law is found in the Appendix of my *Barack Obama, The Aloha Zen President*.

Representative Kucinich's opinions about Obamacare have been reported in several places (Ballasy 2010; Egan 2010; Rossomondo 2010; Johnson 2011). For a study of the French and German health care systems, see Giaimo (2002) and Reid (2009).

President Obama rarely draws lines in the sand, but he began doing so during 2011. On April 13, he objected to Ryan's proposal to turn Medicare into a voucher program (Palm Beach Post 2011). During June, he threatened a veto if Congress tied his hands regarding the treatment of prisoners at Guantánamo but compromised in the end (Keneally 2011). He has also pushed back against Republican proposals to extend any more tax cuts to millionaires (Stein 2011).

The analysis of Micah White (2010) may be premature in expecting change from street protest, but the energy of the movement in New York cannot be denied (M. Greenberg 2011).

Pfeiffer's encounter is described by Weiner (2011b). In response to the Republican proposal to cut federal spending (Mascaro 2011), Obama urged Democrats to be flexible (Bacon and Goldfarb 2011). On the merits of Kucinich's lawsuit, Chapter 13 in the present volume provides a legal analysis (cf. Wilson 2011b). Polls on Democrats who do not support Obama are cited in Clement (2011) and McManus (2011b). Caddell and Shoen (2011) want Obama to withdraw in favor of Hillary Clinton, based on their opinion surveys.

Chapter 7
The Boston Tea Party was a protest over a tax on the purchase of tea in order to pay for a war (known as the French and Indian War) that the American colonists had not voted for because they had no delegates in Parliament (Miller 1943:Chap 14).

For information on the origins and composition of today's Tea Party movement, which is not necessarily Republican in loyalty, there are several sources (Good 2009; Easley 2011; Maxwell 2011; Zernike 2010). For a history of conservative Blue Dog Democrats, see Suddath (2009). In October 2010, progressives held a rally at the National Mall in Washington under the banner One Nation, but the rally failed to gain traction. In June 2011 the proposed American Dream Movement sought to emulate the Tea Party by holding rallies around the country but soon fizzled (Weiner 2011a).

Although third parties have a long history in the United States (Green 2010; Rosenstone, Behr, Lazarus 1984), they rarely matter because the main two political parties have either tried to incorporate their ideas into their platforms, have outspent third parties in campaign advertising, or have restricted their ability to qualify for appearance on ballots (Bennett and Nader 2009; Election Law Issues c.2007). A brief summary of modern third parties is provided by Robert Longley (n.d.). Shannon (1955) writes a history of the Socialist Party of America. Chace (2004) offers the best analysis of the 1912 election, a four-party election that some believe to have fundamentally changed the country.

Katz (2005) is a recent advocate of electoral fusion. The concept is briefly explained in an article on Wikipedia (2011b).

McCain, known for many years as a maverick, tilted to the right in primary elections in 2008 but moved to the center in the general election (Novak 2008). He moved to the right again in his 2010 Senatorial re-election campaign because of a Tea Party challenger (Cooper 2010; Condon 2011).

Immobilism has been a problem in Western European multiparty systems (Lijphart 1968; Mair 1990). Contemporary Belgium has set a record for the longest time a legislature has been unable to form a government: Elections held on June 13, 2010, failed to produce a new cabinet one year later. One reason is conflict between Flemish-speaking and French-speaking Belgians (Traynor 2011; cf. Deschouwer 2009).

The tax extension compromise in December 2010 involving Republicans and the White House (Kuhnhenn 2010) excluded House of Representatives Speaker Pelosi and Senate

Majority Leader Reid, both Democrats. They did not attend the signing of the law (Defrank and Bazinet 2010).

Votes on Afghanistan and Libya are analyzed by Fahrenthold (2011c) and Radia and Parkinson (2011). The 17 times where House moderates of both parties prevailed include votes on Libya (HR2278, HJR68, HRCR51, HR292), budget votes (HJR44, HJR48, HR1472, HR754, HR2017, HR1892, HR2218, HR2055, HR3672), extension of the Patriot Act (HR514), the flood insurance program (HR1309), patent reform (HR1249), and the Charter School Act (HR2218). Voting records are at *thomas.loc.gov/home/rollcall votes.html.*

For coverage of negotiations over the debt ceiling, see Mascaro and Parsons (2011), Hennessey and Nicholas (2011a), Silberleib and Cohen (2011), and Sonmez (2011c).

McManus (2011a) and Thompson (2011) report on Americans Elect.

Chapter 8
For an analysis of the 2010 election, see New York Times (2011a). Relevant polls are reported by the New York Times (Connelly and Marsh 2010), University of Maryland (2010), and CBS News (Best 2010).

The classic study positing three basic factors in voting is by three University of Michigan political scientists (Campbell, Converse, Miller 1960). Of course, the state of the economy may influence perception of political parties, issues, and candidates, so cause and effect is not obvious (cf. Haas 1992b:Chap 4).

The role of independents in American elections is disputed (Keith et al. 1992). But there is no doubt that "swing" voters hold the balance of power (Mayer 2008). For public opinion on changes in Medicare and Social Security, see Cohen and Balz (2011).

For Plouffe's four-prong strategy and polls regarding support for Obama, see Calmes and Landler (2011), Cillizza and Blake (2011b), Horowitz (2011), McManus (2011b), Nakamura (2011), and Nicholas (2011b). Immigration problems rose to a higher level of visibility when the Public Television program *Frontline* aired a documentary in October 2011 (Investigative Reporting Workshop 2011).

200

Suskind (2011:478-79) reports that Obama admits that he has not tried to construct a positive narrative, consistent with what pollsters have discovered (Cillizzia and Blake 2011a). Campaign slogans affect voters by giving them a sense of the issues at stake. For a debunking of Obama's so-called "socialist" proclivities, including the charge of "government takeover of health care," see Scherer (2010) and Suskind (2011). Obama's re-election slogan "Winning the Future" has been questioned (Stolberg 2011) and even mocked by Sarah Palin (Jackson 2011). Speculation will continue on his chances for a second term right up to election day 2012 (cf. Motopoli 2011). For poll numbers among his 2008 supporters, see Clement (2011).

The pros (*shouldtrumprun.com*) and cons (Ellis 2011) of Trump's noncandidacy fascinated many, particularly when he joined the birtherists (Knickerbocker 2011), but he lacked basic political knowledge (King 2011). For a British view, see Spillius (2011).

Chapter 9
Reagan is the source of the quote about government as the problem, not the solution. Although he often said so on the campaign trail, he reiterated the point in his 1981 Inaugural Address (cf. Kudlow 2009). Goolsbee, a centrist University of Chicago economist, departed from the Obama administration in mid-2011 (Milbank 2011e).

Obama's views on the economy follow from his ethical principles (see Chapter 2 and Appendix A). For his quotes on "fat cats" and "catalyst," see Jackson (2009) and Nutting (2010). The Chrysler decision is reported in some detail by Suskind (2011:227-30), who also gives a detailed explanation (Chap 18) of how Congress hollowed out the Wall Street reform bill. For cuts in cities' block grants, see Cooper (2011).

Western Europe's social market capitalism was partly a response to the socialist economies of Eastern Europe, which competed for acceptance during the Cold War. The upper classes in Western Europe agreed that they had to ensure that those with lesser incomes would not vote Communist, so they provided welfare benefits which are today the envy of Progressive Democrats of America. For more on the subject, see Hill (2010), Nicholls (1994), and Pontusson (2005).

President Theodore Roosevelt was the first "trustbuster," as described in his biography by Morris (2001). His successor, Taft, vigorously applied the law, and Wilson got Congress to strengthen the law (Arnold 2009). For a history of philanthropocapitalism, see Friedman and McGarvie (2002). Among biographies of Gates, see Lesinski (2009).

The public is unaware of Obama's economic philosophy because the press rarely writes about arcane matters of philosophy and public administration. An exception is David Brooks (2011b), who praises Obama's conservative cost-benefit approach to public policy. Nowadays, few reporters cover federal departments, such as the Department of Commerce. College audiences at talks about my book were amazed that Obama's thinking was so profound.

Pragmatism, which originated in the 1870s, was developed as a philosophy by Pierce, James, and Dewey. Menand (1997) has edited a collection of writings of the early as well as contemporary pragmatists, notably Richard Rorty and Hillary Putnam. A historical view of how pragmatism has been applied in political life is found in Stuhr (2010). Kloppenberg (2010) believes that Obama is primarily a pragmatist but misses his commitment to communitarian philosophy.

The Inaugural Address of Barack Obama (2009b) states his fundamental principles outside economics as well. For Obama on teacher pay, see Associated Press (2009c).

Information is available on race-to-the-top programs for education (SETDA 2010; Crawford 2011), electric vehicles and removal of regulatory barriers (Doggett 2011), juvenile justice (Gramlich 2011), early learning (G. Miller 2011; Wilson 2011c), job training (Georgia 2010), and on the Communities Putting Prevention to Work program (Stier and Miller 2011). One advantage of formula funding, sometimes distributed in block grants, has been that the funds are calibrated to the number of clients served rather than doled out discriminatorily (CPRE 2007).

For results of the stress tests, see Pershing (2009). Journalist Suskind (2011) intimates that Obama wanted Citibank to be broken up, but that Treasury Secretary Timothy

202

Geithner demurred. Suskind's book is the best description of the internal deliberations.

The auto bailouts have been more successful that the bank bailouts (Nicholas 2011d; cf. Kessler 2011), even though both types of loans have nearly been paid back. The bank bailouts were supposed to "help people," as Obama said in his address to Congress on February 24, 2009, but instead banks failed to make sufficient loans to restart the economy (Oral 2010; cf. Wright 2009).

Obama's Social Impact Bonds idea came from England, where the program has been tried to reduce recidivism (Light 2011). A similar effort, without bonds, is the Hawai'i Opportunity for Probation with Enforcement program (Dooley 2009).

For more on the Impact Investment Fund, another idea from Britain, consult Lohr (2011). The Small Business Administration is designated to handle the program. References relating to the infrastructure bank, are found in New America Foundation (2008) and Weber (2010).

The "stimulus" bill was criticized by economist Paul Krugman (2010) because the amount appropriated was too little for the scope of the crisis. Congressional Republicans would not allow the package with a higher price tag (Associated Press 2009a; Meyerson 2011). Job creation was a major goal of the "stimulus" bill, but Congress preferred sending money to the states, leaving the assignment of contractors to unprepared state and local authorities (Nicholas 2011c), which in turn did not always handle the funds in a competent manner (Linthicum 2011). A federal jobs program was ruled out (McEwan 2011) because of the inevitable delay while Washington set up a bureaucracy to handle the funds.

The plot to threaten default in the federal debt as leverage for spending cuts is described by Montgomery et al. (2011). The explanation for Standard & Poors' reduction of the U.S. government credit rating from AAA to AA+ is provided by Bloomberg News (2011). For Obama's proposal to set up a bipartisan debt commission, his comment on the downgrade, and his proposal for a payroll tax cut, see Truth-O-Meter (2010) and Schroeder (2011). John McLaughlin implied that the debt debate was deliberately designed to avoid dealing with the need for job creation during his weekly television program *The McLaughlin Group* on July 29, 2011. For a conservative attack on the Federal Reserve Board, see Ip (2011).

Conservative economist Robert Samuelson (2011; 2008) is the source of statistics on how much revenue results from taxing the rich and of the comment that government can do little to impact an economy. Pros and cons on the cost of government regulation have been argued recently without consensus (Wall Street Journal (2011). For statistics on current hiring practices, see Cappelli (2011). Libertarian economist Allan Greenspan (2007) praised Clinton's economic policies.

For British Petroleum payments, see Hooper (2010). The slow process, however, has received much criticism (Conan 2011).

Lawrence Summers (2011), an initial Obama economic adviser, provided a coherent analysis of how to get the economy to rebound after he left the White House in mid-2011. He is the source of the unemployment statistics in the construction industry and the observation that the tax cuts for the rich do not help to create jobs in the absence of consumer demand.

The Republican-controlled House of Representatives was elected in 2010 after attacking the Obama administration about the failure to produce jobs. But Boehner focused on the deficit when he became Speaker. He even boasted that spending cuts could cost 300,000 jobs, saying, "If federal employees lose jobs because of cuts, so be it" (Caballero 2011).

Deficit figures are from the U.S. Treasury Department (2011) and de Rugy (2009). Some $3 trillion in revenue was lost due to the Bush-era tax cuts for the rich (Jaffe 2011). Statistics on government revenue and spending as a percentage of gross domestic product are from Chantrill (2011a,b). For assessments of the minimal impact of regulations, see Wall Street Journal (2011) and Yang (2011). For a very different view, see Will (2011). The Patriotic Millionaires state their case on the website *patrioticmillionaires.org*

On the limited role of government in the economy, see Samuelson (2008). For the executive orders on refinancing, see Nakamura and Wilson (2011) and Puzzanghera, Lee, Lazo (2011). Many economists find that the more equal the distribution of income, the higher the growth rate and associated increase in employment (Deninger and Squire 1997; Freeman 2004; Kuznets 1955; Oshima 1970; Perotti 1996).

Chapter 10
Candidates Barack Obama and Hillary Clinton announced their health care plans in 2007 (Associated Press 2007; Kornblut and Perry 2007).

Two useful books compare the American health care system with plans in Europe (Giaimo 2002; Reid 2009). The British and Canadian government plans ration care. France and Germany rely on insurance companies, but they are nonprofits because citizens believe that there is a right to health.

For short essays summarizing previous efforts to pass a national health plan, consult Kaiser Family Foundation (2009), Meyer (2009), and Palmer (1999). A more detailed account has been written by several public health professionals (Birn et al. 2003; Committee on the Consequences of Uninsurance 2005). At the state level, summaries exist for Hawai'i (Chong 2008; Harris 2009), Massachusetts (Sack 2009), and Vermont (D.Goodman 2011). Carroll (2009) shows that Hawai'i's health care insurance is the nation's lowest in cost.

Rosko (1994) carefully describes the passage and repeal of the Medicare Catastrophic Health Care law. Dukakis, whose father was a physician, has often stated that his efforts to promote universal health care are based on the Hawai'i model (Dukakis 2011; Hoey 2011).

David Brooks (2008) reveals Clinton's rejection of the bipartisan health care plan. For an analysis of lack of funding for Part D of Medicare, see Bartlett (2009). Borrell (2010) offers a discussion on pros and cons of the individual mandate.

A description of how Obama's mother sought health care insurance appears in her biography (Scott 2011), which partly conflicts with what Obama said on the campaign trail. As a person immediately coming from out of state, she could not obtain health insurance similar to her parents in Hawai'i, where employers are required to provide health care to their employees. Her out-of-state employer's insurance company paid for major hospital expenses but not her considerable disability costs.

Two of Obama's biographers describe the difficulty of passing Obamacare (Alter 2009:Chap 22; Wolffe 2010:Chap 2-3). Tempers flared at many "town hall" meetings during mid-2009, including vitriolic confrontations (Urbina 2009) in which Republicans were following a distinct playbook to disrupt (Fahrenthold 2011a). Republican Senator Isakson's sincere end-of-life counseling proposal of (Klein 2009) was vilified by Palin as "death panels" (Byrne 2009). But amendments demanded by Senators Mary Landrieu and Ben Nelson rankled many as well (Wolffe 2011:109-10). Kucinich (Zeleny and Pear 2010) may have been a thorn in the side of Obamacare, whereas DeMint was out for bigger stakes—limiting Obama to a single term as president by killing his most important legislative priority (Smith 2009).

One of the best summaries of key provisions of Obamacare is provided by Tatarowicz (2010), who laments that Republicans misinform but Democrats do not correct them. Among special provisions are the Minimum Loss Ratio (MediChick 2010), Communities Putting Prevention to Work program (Stier and Miller 2011), the Partnership Program (Nakao 2011), and the cancelled Community Living Assistance Services and Support program (Kliff 2011). For a cautionary scenario about employers paying a fine rather than matching health care for employees, see Johnson and Holtz-Eakin (2011), though the study on which they rely may be flawed (Sargent 2011). For the argument about Obamacare as an incentive, see Leach (2011). The "single payer" plan that was vetoed by Schwartzenegger was introduced into the California Senate again in 2011. Governor Brown seemed determined to give Obamacare a try instead (Hosseini 2010).

Moderate conservative David Brooks (2011a), who believes that ideology is at the root of Republican opposition to Obamacare, contrasts a supposed Democratic top-down approach with a Republican bottom-up solution. He wrongly identifies the 15-member cost containment panel as "top-down," though the body is purely advisory. Although Brooks favors allowing the public to shop around for insurance with high coverage at low cost, presumably the Republican approach, under Obamacare everyone will shop around for a plan in exactly the same manner.

Ryan, concerned about future costs of Medicare and the federal deficit, proposed to turn Medicare into a voucher program (Drum 2011), which was quickly opposed by Republican presidential candidate Newt Gingrich (Silver 2011). At first, Obama spoke against the plan (Gordy 2011), but later he offered various Medicare cuts to be balanced by job-creating spending (New York Times 2011b). Five Republican Senators also voted against Ryan's plan after passage in the House (Nir 2011). Those who voted for the plan knew that they might risk defeat in 2012 by angry voters. The Reagan-era reform of Medicare is described by Millenson (2010).

The "job-killing" claim is refuted by Truth-O-Meter (2011). Predictions about what employers will do have been based on opinion surveys (Turner 2011).

Comparative health data are compiled by the World Health Organization. For a map on life expectancy comparing countries around the world, see *worldlifeexpectancy.com*, which rates the United States below most Western European countries but on a par with health in Libya and Saudi Arabia.

Court challenges to Obamacare have yielded contradictory rulings (Savage and Levey (2011).). The issues involved will have to be resolved by the U. S. Supreme Court (cf. Orange County Register 2011).

Chapter 11
The modern system of individual states, each having with their own sovereignty and recognized borders, was formally recognized in 1648 by two treaties signed in the Westphalian region of what is now Germany (Gross 1948). Principles of international law were developed from that point to bring order to a previously chaotic international system (Brownlie 2008; Shaw 2003).

The Farewell Address of George Washington (1789) is available in book form. He probably had more influence through his *Rules of Civility and Decent Behavior in Company and Conversation* (1746), translated from a set of rules composed by French Jesuits in 1595 (Brookhiser 1996).

Accounts of the War of 1812 differ between Britain, Canada and the United States (Hitsman 1965; Taylor 2010). Britain was trying to cripple Napoléon's France and annoyed that the United States was aiding France with trade. The British also sought a buffer of Native American Nations between Canada and the United States, as some Americans had designs on seizing Canadian territory (Pratt 1925; Smith 1989).

The Monroe Doctrine was actually written by Secretary of State John Quincy Adams but credited to President James Monroe because he articulated the concept in his address to Congress on December 2, 1823 (May 1975; Sexton 2011). British Prime Minister Canning endorsed the Monroe Doctrine, "calling upon the New World to redress the balance of the Old," so that France and Spain would not challenge British world hegemony (cf. Marshall 1938). For Tyler's extension of the Monroe Doctrine to Hawai'i in 1842 and declarations of Britain and France in 1843, see Geschwender (1982:195) and Stevens (1945:18-20).

Conventional accounts of the Mexican War (Tutorow 1979; Lewis 2010) and Spanish-American War (Gould 1982; O'Toole 1986) often ignore possible war crimes and their precedent for future American aggression. But not Bruce Fein (2010), who sees a connection with the Monroe Doctrine, and Walter Karp (1979), who analyzes both conflicts as diversions from domestic problems.

The annexation of Hawai'i is described in Haas, *Barack Obama, The Aloha Zen President*, Chapter 2. The conquest of the Philippines has been described in sanitized versions (Miller 1982), but Philippine leaders had already declared independence from Spain, so McKinley suppressed the country's independence (Agoncillo 1960). In addition, American military forces conquered territories in Mindanao, where Muslims believed that they had never been part of the Spanish colony (Arnold 2011). Similarly, Spain granted independence to Puerto Rico in 1897, which the United States militarily seized during the Spanish-American War (Nelson 1986).

Theodore Roosevelt asserted his Corollary to the Monroe Doctrine because European countries had been attempting to collect their debts with gunboats in Venezuela and were contemplating similar action against the Dominican Republic, which had defaulted in payments (Ricard 2006). But after Roosevelt and Wilson intervened in the Caribbean several times (cf. Cooper 2009), Republican presidents Coolidge and

Hoover repudiated the Corollary, relying on the Clark Memorandum instead (Ferrell 1965).

Wilson's Fourteen Points, perhaps the most comprehensive foreign policy statement of any president, included the need for a League of Nations (Knock 1995). Due to Republican Senate opposition, the United States never joined the League.

The most famous volumes about World War II are by Winston Churchill (Churchill and Keegan 1953). The foreign policies of Franklin Delano Roosevelt and Harry Truman are featured in several books (Dallek 1995; Miscamble 2007; Pierce 2003). Biographies of presidents, from Eisenhower to George W. Bush, are cited in Chapter 5 above. Some publications are specific to their foreign policy doctrines—Eisenhower (Yaqub 2003), Kennedy (FitzSimmons 1972), Johnson (McMaster 1998), Nixon (Litwak 1984), Ford (Mieczkowski 2005), Carter (Korb 2008), Reagan (Burns 1987), George H. W. Bush (Smith 1992), Clinton (Hamilton 2008), George W. Bush (Colucci 2008). For a European view of various doctrines of American foreign policy, see the analysis of Heiko Meiertöns (2010).

The texts of many of Obama's speeches are found on the website *asksam.com*. The UN Human Rights Council superseded UN Human Rights Commission in 2006, but the United States did not participate until after Obama took office (Lynch 2009).

Extrajudicial executions have been in the form of drone attacks, many in Pakistan (Reid 2008). The comments by Brennan, then Deputy National Security Advisor for Homeland Security and Counterterrorism (Collinson 2010), codify what Obama had been saying since his speech to Congress on February 24, 2009 (Zeleny 2009). The arguments in favor of drone attacks are presented by Harold Koh (2010) and reported by Dilanian (2011).

Obama's interviews and speeches abroad have received much press attention—the Al-Arabiya interview (Stein 2009), Cairo (Holzman 2009), Ankara (Parsons and King 2009), Prague (Winfrey 2009), and Strasbourg (Traynor 2009). At the latter venue, he admitted that the United States had "shown arrogance" but he also criticized some Europeans for "casual" if "insidious . . . anti-Americanism."

Other overtures have involved Iran (Athanasiadis 2009), Burma (Bangkok Post 2009), Cuba (Sawyer 2009), Israel (Prusher 2009), North Korea (Labott 2009), Russia (Baker 2009), Sudan (Thompson 2009), and Venezuela (Sawyer 2009; Suggett 2009). Iran (Daragahi and Mostaghim 2009) and Israel (Cowell and Cooper 2009) gave him the most negative responses. The uprising in Iran was in response to rigged elections (Kamalipour 2010).

SEAL (Sea, Air, and Land) teams often operate under uncertain conditions (Fishel 2009). More information is available about the G-20 conference in London (Landler and Sanger 2009), the Copenhagen climate change conference (BBC 2009), and Obama's visit to China (CBS 2009) as well as what he did to address Taiwan's concerns (Adams 2010).

Among Obama's many speeches, two of considerable foreign policy significance in 2009 were at West Point, regarding his decision to send more troops to Afghanistan (Shear 2009), and at Oslo, accepting the Nobel Peace Prize (Thistlewaite 2009). He wrote the quoted essay in *Newsweek* about Haïti (Obama 2010b). The seminal essay of Galtung (1964) has guided much of the spirit of the academic-oriented International Peace Research Association, which he cofounded.

Obama's policy toward nuclear arms reduction, which resulted in the treaty that he signed with Russia's prime minister, was evidently a fulfillment of goals stated in a term paper written while he was a student at Columbia University (Buddenberg 2010). The breakthrough with North Korea is doubtless another example of Obama's quiet diplomacy (Mydans and Choe 2011). For the 47-country conference see Sanger (2010). On Obama's "leading from behind" multilateralism, see Rothkopf (2011). The remarks of Harold Koh (2010) were addressed to the American Society of International Law.

Obama's hesitancy to react to demonstrations in Middle Eastern and North African countries is described in Wolffe (2011). For more on the Libyan intervention and the concepts of humanitarian intervention and R2P (Responsibility to Protect), see Chapter 13 in the present volume. Obama's March

28 speech was delivered at Fort McNair (NPR 2011). For Obama's major speech on uprisings in the Middle East and North Africa on May 19, 2011, and the adverse reaction in that region, see Wyne (2011). Dionne (2011) provides interesting commentary on Obama's speech that announced withdrawals of American troops from Afghanistan. For discussion on various aspects of the Obama Doctrine, see Rogin (2011b) and Zakaria (2011).

Obama does not employ *realpolitik*, a term coined by late nineteenth German Chancellor Otto von Bismarck (Steinberg 2011) to refer to a policy that focuses on material (military) rather than ideological considerations. *Realpolitik* is based on the premise that countries should maintain and expand their power position in the world at all times to avoid being attacked or weakened by other countries. American scholars most closely identified with *realpolitik* are Hans Morgenthau (1948) and Henry Kissinger (2002).

Senator Abraham Akaka's father was a longtime pastor and recognized spiritual leader in Hawai'i (Doo 2009). The Senator's views have been articulated on the Senate floor and in various publications (cf. Akaka 1997). For the "third Senator" comment, see Pang (2004).

The Nobel Committee's statement is on its website (*nobelprize.org*). Dewey's insight is quoted in Sharma (2011: 201).

For the overall assessment, see Ignatius (2011). For polling data showing greatly increased pro-American assessments abroad, see Wike (2011). The quote from Obama is reported by Nakaso and Reyes (2011). For other public opinion data, see Pew Research (2010).

Chapter 12
The problems of Guantánamo, including about 100 war crimes committed at the facility during the Bush administration, are described in Haas (2009:Chap 4; 2010a). The latter reference shows how they rolled over to the Obama administration. For cost estimates, see Rosenberg (2011a). The situation in Gitmo is much better than at Bagram air force base (Hildebrandt 2011), but Geneva Convention violations continue (Associated Press 2011d).

For details on individual prisoners, see Worthington (2007). Displaying photographs of prisoners of war has been banned since the Geneva Convention of 1929. Although Rumsfeld complained when films of American prisoners appeared on television (cf. Hibbits 2003), he did not hesitate to allow photographing of Gitmo prisoners. For the "worst of the worst" quote, see Stein (2011). One observer found that the abuses at Abu Ghraib and Guantánamo were the main reason why jihadists decided to go to Iraq to fight Americans (Alexander 2008).

Campaign promises of McCain (Rosenberg and Youssef 2007) and Obama (White 2007) were similar to George W. Bush's stated desire to close Gitmo (Parker 2006). Congress blocked funding related to Gitmo in 2009 because Obama offered no step-by-step plan for transferring prisoners to close the facility (Espo 2009). The report pursuant to Obama's executive order was submitted by Admiral Patrick M. Walsh (cf. Haas 2009a:Chap 19). Joseph Margulies (2011) attributes improvements in treatment at Gitmo to Supreme Court cases decided in 2006, not to the Obama administration. Nevertheless, solitary confinement continues at Guantánamo (Worthington 2011).

For news about the 68 prisoners transferred out of Guantánamo since Obama took office, see Breaking News items at *USwarcrimes.com*. The plan to send Uighurs to Virginia was evidently designed by Craig and Carter, who resigned after their efforts were leaked and blocked (Bazinet 2009; Bumiller 2009). For Obama's signing statement see Schwinn (2011). Holder's statement is reported in Casert (2011). The unconstitutionality of military commissions is argued in DeVeaux (2011).

My classification of prisoners relies on several sources (Human Rights Watch 2011; Miami Herald 2011; Percival 2008; Weese 2010). Adnan Al-Shar'abi, who was acquitted of any crime in 2010, is still held prisoner at Guantánamo (Anam 2011). The main source of statistics for numbers in each category is from the Human Rights First website, which for some reason does not list the three convicted prisoners in a separate category. See also BBC (2011b) and Finn (2011a).

Current Congressional restrictions are found in Garcia (2011). Frick (2009) explains Obama's petition to have the Supreme Court deny the release of the Uighurs. Three lawyers provide a detailed explanation on the plight of Yemenis, who constitute the largest number of prisoners at Guantánamo today (Wittes, Waxman, Chesney 2011). Herman Cain's gaffe is reported by Altman (2011).

The Convention Relating to the Status of Refugees of 1951 defines the term "refugee." Antónia Guterres is the current UN High Commissioner for Refugees. Since its establishment in 2002, the International Criminal Court only handles cases when the defendant country has ratified the court's statute, known as the Rome Statute. The United States has not ratified the treaty.

Mayor Michael Bloomberg and Senator Charles Schumer strongly objected to trials of 9/11 conspirators in New York (Lisberg, Meek, Katz 2010). Civilian trials sometimes are disrupted by defendants, who are then sent to another room to participate by teleconference (cf. Garofano 2007). Alexander (2011) reported on the veto threat. William Rehnquist (1987: 166) was commenting on Article 1(3) of the Constitution of the United States. Arguments for trials of terrorists in civilian courts, are found in Mikva, Sessions, and Gibbons (2011), PRI (2011) and Wolfson (2011). At least one former Gitmo prisoner who joined the Taliban has already been killed in combat (Bahktar News 2011).

Flaws in the military commissions have been identified by Pitter (2011). The "poisoned tree" argument was invoked unsuccessfully in the case of Omar Khadr (Rosenberg 2010). Those who want Gitmo kept as a permanent facility for terrorists include Senator Mitch McConnell (Lavender 2011). Gitmo was cited as the reason for harsh treatment of the American hikers who strayed into Iran and were arrested and incarcerated (A.Goodman 2011). Other countries have sued the United States in the World Court and won because noncitizens arrested in one of the fifty states have not been allowed to notify their countries' consulates, as required by international law. In some cases the foreigners have been executed without being afforded legal assistance by their consu-

213

lates (Klarevas 2011), which means that Americans traveling abroad may be in jeopardy if other countries do likewise.

Payments to victims of collateral damage have been reviewed by Citizens for Innocent Victims in Conflict (2010). A recent court-martial relating to murdering of an Afghan civilian has been appealed (Graham-Harrison 2011; cf. Kovach 2011). Recent prosecution of civilian contractors for war crimes is reported by Sizemore (2011).

The "national security" and "state secrets" arguments are that revealing some evidence in a trial would disclose names and procedures used by American government officials or contractors, thereby compromising lives and special methods. "Extraordinary rendition" refers to taking a kidnapped person from a civilian setting to a secret prison. For the Italian case, see CNN (2009) and Winfield (2010).

For a discussion of cases brought against Rumsfeld and others for torture under the principle of universal jurisdiction, see Gallagher (2009). Information about court cases inside the United States is found both in press accounts (Agence France Press 2008; Guardian 2005; Horton 2010; Kaye 2011; Reuters 2011b; Stohr 2011; Vicini 2011; Williams 2011; Wittes 2011) and in court documents (479F3rd296; 414 F.Supp.2d 250; 569 F.3d 992). Two of the CIA cases referred to the Justice Department were under investigation by a grand jury during mid-2011 (Daily Mail 2011). Families of three prisoners who committed suicide sued (*Al-Zahrani v Rodriguez*) in a federal court in Seattle during October 2011. Similar cases have been unsuccessful.

The international cases are found in a variety of sources. For the Australian case, see Skibicki (2011). On the British case, see EWCA Civ 1598 Case C/2002/0671A;06117B. The Belgian case for compensation is discussed by Black (2003). The Argentine, German, French, German, and Swedish cases are summarized by the European Center for Constitutional and Human Rights (2011a). For the Pakistani cases, which seek compensation for drone attacks, see Beaumont (2011). Several sources refer to Poland (Agence France Press 2010; Hileman 2011; SAPA 2011; Voice of America 2011a; Williams 2011). For the French case in 2007, see Carvajal (2007). Rumsfeld's escape is reported by AlterNet (2007).

The current French case is reported by Agence France Press (2011a). The Spanish cases are reported by Agence France Press (2011c,d), the Center for Constitutional Rights (2011b), and CNN's Goodman (2011). For Lithuania, see Associated Press (2011b), Canadian Press (2011), and Russian TV (2011). For the Denmark case, consult Press TV (2010). For Macedonia, the news report is from Associated Press (2011a). For the Inter-American Commission on Human Rights cases, see two sources (European Center for Constitutional and Human Rights 2011a; Center for Constitutional Rights 2010). A complaint also has been filed in Canada (Rosenberg 2011b), but no prosecution has resulted.

Many of the same cases are discussed in Haas (2009: Chap 6) and are posted in the Breaking News section of *US-warcrimes.com*. Haas (2010a:Chap 45) has more information on *Vance v Rumsfeld*, which has been accepted by an appeals court for trial (Tarm 2011). The plaintiff in the second case has not been named. For a discussion on both cases, see Szydloski (2011). Ameur's case is reported in Carter (2011). The Obama administration supports Rumsfeld, one of many reasons why the Department of Justice under Eric Holder has been a disappointment to civil libertarians (K. Greenberg 2011).

The Dreyfus Affair is ably described by Bredin (1986). For a similar argument against prosecution in the United States, see Rutten (2009). According to public opinion polls, even after the death of Osama Bin Laden, a majority (57 percent) still favored the use of torture in questioning suspected terrorists (Bedard 2011). A 2009 poll on whether to have a criminal investigation of the use of torture by the Bush administration shows approval by 38 percent, disapproval by 34 percent, though 25 percent were agreeable to a nonpartisan truth commission (Jones 2009). Republicans were most opposed to both types of investigations of alleged American war crimes committed by the Bush administration (54 percent). For Obama's eleven-point plan to gradually end all American war crimes, see Haas (2010a:Chap 42). Holder's determination to close Gitmo was shared with Europeans in September 2011 (Herridge 2011b). Seven former CIA heads wrote President-Elect Obama to warn that prosecutions of Americans for war crimes could lead to major revolts in the agency (Swanson 2011). For perhaps the most thorough assessment, faulting Obama for continuing an assault on civil liberties and international law in the pursuit of Al-Qaeda, see Cole (2011a). One columnist blames Attorney General Eric Holder for gross ineptitude, referring to him as "Obama's albatross" (Thiessen 2011).

Chapter 13
For the attack on Somali pirates, see Walsh (2009). Perspectives on Iraq highlight the differing approaches of Bush (2010) from Obama (2002; cf.Young 2010).

The legality of the Iraq War has been questioned. Ehren Watada, who was ordered for duty in Iraq during 2006, refused to go because he believed the war to be illegal. His military court-martial, however, was ruled a mistrial, and no retrial has occurred. One implication of the Watada case is that a ruling on the law might find the war in Iraq to be illegal, as has been ruled in Germany (Leicht 2005). If so, heirs to American soldiers who have been killed in the Iraq War might sue George W. Bush for murder, an idea that former Los Angeles Assistant District Attorney Vincent Bugliosi has been unable to sell to any district attorney in the United States as a cause of action on behalf of parents, spouses, or children of those who have died in battle in Iraq. For the Watada case, see Barber (2007). Bugliosi's book is *The Prosecution of George W. Bush for Murder* (2008).

Today, a fragile situation remains in Iraq (Mulrine 2011). The change from military to civilian personnel is reported by Bumiller (2011), Denselow (2011), and Sheridan and Zak (2011).

For views on the Afghan War, compare Bush (2010) with Obama (Huffington Post 2011b). Obama's increases in military personnel in Afghanistan during 2009-2010 came primarily from the drawdown from Iraq. Troop withdrawals from Afghanistan were announced on June 22, 2011 (Terkel 2011). For a recent statement by the Taliban leader, see Rashid (2011).

The drone increase (Shane 2009) has definitely annoyed many Pakistanis (SZH/JR 2011a,b; Yusufzai 2011). Yet some drones flew from Pakistani airfields (Miller 2009).

The thesis of Klintworth (1989) was endorsed by Cambodia's Sihanouk (Haas 1991:60). For more on Vietnam's intervention in Cambodia, see Haas (1991). The humanitarian intervention and R2P concepts have been discussed at academic and expert conferences for many years (Evans 2011; Haas 2008:165-67). For an assessment based on the Libyan case, see Bosco (2011).

The tragedies in Kosovo (Judah 2000) and Rwanda (Prunier 1995) offer unclear lessons for Libya. Malic (2005) and Kincaid (2005) question the legality of the bombing of Serbia in the Kosovo War.

Evidence of an impending threat to Benghazi, as stated in Obama's explanation for the operation (Huffington Post 2011c), has been disputed (Chapman 2011). No-fly zones over two parts of Iraq, which had questionable legality (BBC 2001), failed to provide cover for those seeking to force Saddam Hussein from power (Bennis, Honey, Zunes 2001). For Obama's two speeches on Libya, see Reuters (2011c) and NPR (2011).

Objections to the operation in Libya for exceeding the UN mandate came from Brazil, China, India, and Russia (Breaker 2011) as well as the Arab League (Voice of America 2011b). Obama consulted with top Congressional leaders only the day before beginning the Libyan operation (Sonmez 2011b), but he did not report to the entire Congress in accordance with the War Powers Resolution (Taper 2011). Congressional voices of disapproval subsequently emerged (cf. Lugar 2011) as well as votes against the action (Agence France Press 2011e; Fahrenthold 2011c; Geiger 2011; Pace 2011; Steinhauer 2011) and even Kucinich's lawsuit (Sonmez 2011a). For how the court disposed of Kucinich's lawsuit, see Gerstein (2011).

At first, Boehner acknowledged that Obama had not violated the law (Cusack and Hooper 2011), but he later changed his mind (Parsons and Mascaro 2011). For Obama's defense of the operation as "consistent" with the War Powers Resolution, see Wilson (2011b). An alternative argument, that the

UN Security Council authorization freed the president from the need to consult Congress, is found in Whitehouse (2011). Pentagon lawyers, however, disagreed (Savage and Shanker 2011). Two sources report Al-Qadhafi's thanks to Congress for criticizing Obama (Agence France Press 2011b; Dawn 2011). For U.S. military acknowledgement that killing Al-Qadhafi was a goal, see Rogin (2011a). Al-Qadhafi's use of mercenaries is cited by Vogl (2011).

Drone attacks in Yemen started as early as 2009 (Herridge 2011a). Al-Awlaki was identified as responsible for several terrorist attacks inside the United States, namely, the Fort Hood shooting and the underpants bomber, both in 2010 (Shane 2010). Drone attacks also take place in Somalia (G. Miller 2011). For Obama's TV habits, see Haas (2011a:117).

Brown University's Watson Institute for International Studies estimates a $3.7 billion war cost (Byrd 2011), with civilian spending about half that amount (Ukman 2011). Survey data about the wars have fluctuated over time (Craighill 2009; Rasmussen 2011).

The latest bloodbath in Burma, with at least 3,000 dead, occurred in 2007 (Human Rights Watch 2007). Uprisings in Syria (Mazzetti 2011) appear relevant to R2P, but UNSC has not authorized military intervention in that country.

The 700,000 figure is the estimated population of Benghazi. However, a question has been raised whether Al-Qadhafi really contemplated mass murder (Chapman 2011). Blair (2011) contends that the use of drone attacks has discouraged cooperation with Pakistan on counterterrorism. The Obama administration's defense of drones has been succinctly supplied by the legal adviser to the Secretary of State, Harold Koh (2010) despite objections from the civil liberties community (Ratner 2011; cf. Bellinger 2011).

Those who believe that there is a contradiction between Obama's zen personality and his readiness to use military means will find that in Japan the two have historically been entirely compatible (Victoria 1997).

Chapter 14

Scheuer's book *Osama Bin Laden* (2011) is the best biography on the Al-Qaeda leader. Reports on the raid have emerged in pieces (Associated Press 2011c; BBC 2011c; Brown 2011; CNN 2011; Hosenball 2011; Landler and Mazzetti 2011; Sherwell 2011). On OBL's indictment, see Eggen (2006) and Weiser (2011).

The history of the American conflict with the Barbary States is told by Lambert (2005). For Bush's negotiations with the Taliban, see Guardian (2001). Bush's justification for the "war on terror" is stated in his autobiography, *Decision Points* (2010). For the Congressional pushback of the "war on terror" concept in 2001, see PRI (2011). OBL's admission in 2004 that he approved the 9/11 attack is found in Goldenberg (2004). OBL claimed to have gotten the idea for bringing down the World Trade Center towers from Israel's bombing of tall buildings in Beirut during 1982 (Fox News 2004). Associating the United States with its ally Israel prompted OBL's desire for a reprisal.

A senior NATO official disclosed in 2010 that OBL was "living comfortably in a house in the northwest of Pakistan" (Crilly 2010). In 2001, Pakistan's efforts to round up members of Al-Qaeda, with generous American bounties as bait, yielded many Arabic speakers with no connection to Al-Qaeda (Bowers and Tohid 2005; Jones 2008). For Obama's "War on Al-Qaeda" rhetoric, see Washington Times (2009).

The right of reprisal is explained by an American Society of International Law scholar (Kurgis 1998). For Al-Qadhafi's role in the Berlin bombing and the reprisal, see Byrnes (2009). The first UN Security Council resolution supporting military action in Afghanistan, adopted in December 20, 2001, limited the role to protecting Kabul. From October 13, 2003, UNSC resolutions have covered the entire country.

The Panamá intervention is described by Murillo (1995), Eichmann's capture and trial by Sachs (2000).

Arguments that the raid on OBL's compound was legal are advanced by Koh's former colleague at Yale Law School (Rubenfeld 2011). For security considerations that called off Khalid Sheikh Mohammed's civilian trial in New York, see Lisberg, Meek, Katz (2010).

For those who have called for an investigation of OBL's killing, see Hennessy (2011). For Obama's denial that he issued a "kill, not capture" order, see Jordan (2011). The expec-

219

tation of a nuclear reprisal by Al-Qaeda, as disclosed in a "Wikileak," is reported by McCullagh (2011). The website *icasuaties.org/oef* reports civilian deaths in Afghanistan by NATO forces.

Many Pakistanis have reacted negatively to the raid (BBC 2011a,d; Radio Australia 2011; Witte and DeYoung 2011). The decrease in cooperation by Pakistan is exemplified by arrests of CIA officials (BBC 2011d) and by blocking access to the base from which drones have been launched (Crilly 2011).

For the secret memo, see Finn (2011b). David Cole (2011a) makes the progressive case most eloquently, referring to court cases that have continued to allow "state secrets" defenses that block prosecutions regarding torture and criminalization of contributions to charitable organizations in the Muslim world. He cites National Security Adviser Dennis Blair as the source for the estimate that Al Qaeda terrorists number 3,000 to 5,000. Statistics from Baghdad on upticks in terrorist attacks after assassinations are reported by Cockburn (2011).

For analyses of extrajudicial execution by the Bush and Obama administrations, see Cole (2011c) and Ratner (2011). A former high-level Bush-era Justice Department appointee recommends that Congress act to cover the targeted assassination program, which he finds of questionable legality (Bellinger 2011). For Holder's exasperation in being unable to try those at Guantánamo in federal courts, see Lavender (2011). For civil liberties issues with Obama, see Quigley (2011).

Chapter 15
Hoover (2006) ably depicts Ariyoshi's style. Obama's one-term quote came in response to low public opinion poll ratings (Daily Mail 2010). His quiet diplomacy concerning Libya involved getting approval from the Arab League and the UN Security Council before announcing his decision to send American forces to Libya (Kellerhals 2011) on March 28, 2011 (Reuters 2011b). Among comments on Obama's boldness, see Christi (2011) and Youngman (2011).

Gary Wills (2002) ably explains how the Constitution was supposed to work. Although Congress cooperated with presidents during the early years of the Cold War, giving the impression that the legislative branch was subordinate, that changed when Congress began to consider Richard Nixon's impeachment and ways of exercising legislative vetoes of presidential action.

For more on Gitmo, see Chapter 12 above.

The Senate's defeat of proposed legislation that would have allowed judges to modify mortgage loan repayments (Associated Press 2009b) contrasts with the law that allows judges to set terms when companies file for bankruptcy (Efrati and Forsyth 2009). Blocking of appointments by Republican Senators has crippled Obama's nominees for federal courts (O'Keefe 2010; Williams 2010). Civilian deaths in Afghanistan have often been reported (cf. Petras 2011). President Obama has been dismayed by *Citizens United v Federal Election Commission* (558US08-205), decided in 2010.

Iran (Amiri 2011) and Israel (Blomfield 2011) have most blatantly defied Obama. In 2011, he was also defied by the Palestinian Authority, which applied for membership in the UN as a sovereign state,

William Kornhauser (1959) presents the classic political sociological theory of mass society. Most writing about mass society focuses on the corrosive effects of mass media, which are presumed to be manipulated by elites to produce conformity (Horkheimer and Adorno 1947), based on the Nazi use of the media. *Bowling Alone* (Putnam 2000) gives evidence for the current existence of mass society in the United States.

One explanation of voter alienation is presented by Dionne (1992). For the dominance by interest groups, see Alterman (2011).

Sociologist Amitai Etzioni (1993, 2009), who founded an academic communitarian movement, is affiliated with George Washington University. William Galston (1980), who advised President Bill Clinton, is the most prominent philosophical communitarian. Obama's description of the alienation of African Americans in Chicago (Obama 1995:Chap 8-14) has much in common with the thesis of *Bowling Alone*.

For the role of trade unions in Hawai'i, see Beechert (2011). Two quotes on Hawai'i as a model for the rest of the United States appear in Chapter 1 of the present volume, as cited in Glauberman and Burris (2008:4) and in Honolulu Star-Bulletin (2008).

Obama's grassroots mobilization effort is best described by Wolffe (2009:Chap 3). Obama's views on popular uprisings in North Africa, as articulated in his May 19, 2011, speech (cf. Wyne 2011), are written as if fluent in the genre of mass society theory. Obama (2006:Chap 8) has also commented on global mass society.

Some sources provide a longer list of accomplishments (Daily & Sunday Jeffersonian 2010; Rickyrah 2010). In addition to some biographies cited in Appendix C, there are many other analyses of Obama's accomplishments and difficulties (Diehl 2011; Dye 2010; Galston 2010; Haas 2011a:Chap 15; Thurber 2011). For complaints over Obama's policies on civil liberties, see Turley (2011). The Solyndra debacle is examined in Lipton and Broder (2011), Milbank (2011b) and Mufson (2011). Republicans have not been helpful in regard to environmental projects, often attacking the very existence of the Environmental Protection Agency. Recommendations from Obama's national commission on the Gulf of Mexico oil spill have been ignored (Maass 2011).

References

Aaronson, William E., Jacqueline S. Zinn, and Michael D. Rosko (1994). "The Success and Repeal of the Medicare Catastrophic Coverage Act: A Paradoxical Lesson for Health Care Reform," *Journal of Health Politics, Policy, and Law*, 19 (4): 753-771

Abercrombie, Neil (2008). "Foreword." In Stu Glauberman and Jerry Burris, eds., *The Dream Begins: How Hawai'i Shaped Barack Obama*, pp. vi-viii. Honolulu: Watermark

Abramsky, Sasha (2009). *Inside Obama's Brain*. New York: Penguin

Adams, James Truslow (1932). *Epic of America*. Boston: Little, Brown

Adams, Jonathan (2010). "Why US Ignores China and Sells Arms to Taiwan," *Christian Science Monitor*, February 18

Agence France Press (2008). "Iraqi Group Files 200 Lawsuits against Rumsfeld, US Security Firms for Torture," *Agence France Press*, December 15

_____ (2010). "Polish Probe Sought of CIA Secret Prison," *Agence France Press*, December 16

_____ (2011a). "Algerian Sues US for Guantanamo Detention," *Agence France Press*, May 23

_____ (2011b). "Qadhafi Amasses Army of African Mercenaries," *Dawn*, March 3

_____ (2011c). "Spain Drops Case against Bush Officials," *Agence France Press*, April 14

_____ (2011d). "Spain to Probe Guantanamo Torture Claims," *expatica.com*, February 25

_____ (2011e). "US Congress Votes against Libya Funding," *Agence France Press*, June 7

Agoncillo, Teodoro A. (1960). *Malolos: The Crisis of the Republic*. Quezon City: University of the Philippines Press

Ahmad, Sandar (2010). "Taliban Attack Biggest NATO Base in Afghanistan," *Agence France Press*, May 18

Akaka, Abraham (1997). "Remarks of Senator Daniel K. Akaka to the Late Reverend Dr. Abraham Akaka, Pastor

Emeritus, Kawaiahaʻo Church," *akakafoundation.org*, October 21

Alexander, David (2011). "White House Criticizes House Defense Spending Bill," *Reuters*, June 23

Alexander, Matthew (2008). "I'm Still Tortured by What I Saw in Iraq," *Washington Post*, November 30

Alter, Jonathan (2006). *The Defining Moment: FDR's Hundred Days and the Triumph of Hope*. New York: Simon & Schuster

_____ (2009). *The Promise: President Obama, Year One*. New York: Simon & Schuster

Alterman, Eric (2011). *Kabuki Democracy: The System vs. Barack Obama*. New York: Nation Books

AlterNet (2007). "Rumsfeld Flees France, Fearing Arrest," *alternet.org*, October 29

Altman, Joshua (2011). "Cain Backtracks on Trading Gitmo Prisoners," *thehill.org*, October 18

Ambrose, Stephen (2007). *Eisenhower: Soldier and President*. Newtown, CT: American Political Biography Press

Amiri, Mitra (2011). "'No Brake' on Iran Enriching Uranium," *msnbc.msn.com*, June 7

Anam, Fares (2011). "Yemeni Guantanamo Prisoner Held after Acquittal," *yobserver.com*, January 15

Aoudé, Ibrahim (2011). "Political Economy and Contemporary Social Struggles." In Michael Haas, ed., *Barack Obama, The Aloha Zen President: How a Son of the 50th State May Revitalize America Based on 12 Multicultural Principles*, Chap 14. Santa Barbara, CA: Praeger

Apollon, Dom (2011). "Don't Call Them 'Post-Racial': How Young People Actually Think About Race," *AlterNet.org*, June 9

Ariyoshi, George R. (1982). Inaugural Address, December 6. Reprinted in Ariyoshi, *With Obligation to All*. Honolulu: University of Hawaiʻi Press, 1997

Arnold, James R. (2011). *The Moro War: How America Battled a Muslim Insurgency in the Philippine Jungle, 1902-1913*. New York: Bloomsbury Press

Arnold, Peri E. (2009). *Remaking the Presidency: Roosevelt, Taft, and Wilson, 1901-1916*. Lawrence: University Press of Kansas

224

Ask Sam (n.d.). "Barack Obama Speech List, 2002-2009," *asksam.com/ebooks/obama-speeches*

Associated Press (2007). "Clinton Offers Universal Health Care Plan," *Associated Press*, September 17

_____ (2009a). "Dems Power Stimulus Bill through Congress," *msnbc.msn.com*, February 14

_____ (2009b). "Mortgage Bankruptcy Bill Fails in Senate," *msnbc.msn.com*, April 30

_____ (2009c). "Obama Backs Teacher Merit Pay," *USA Today*, March 10

_____ (2011a). "German Sues Macedonia over Alleged CIA Kidnapping," *Associated Press*, February 3

_____ (2011b). "Lithuania: Terrorism Suspect Files Case over C.I.A. Rendition Claim," *New York Times*, October 27

_____ (2011c). "New Details Emerge in Raid to Kill Osama Bin Laden," *Associated Press*, May 3

_____ (2011d). "US Military Denies Claims that Guantanamo Disciplinary Block Violates Geneva Conventions," *Washington Post*, December 9

Athanasiadis, Jason (2009). "Obama Sent Second Letter to Khamenei," *Washington Times*, September 3

Bacon, Perry, Jr., and Zachary A. Goldfarb (2011). "Obama Urges Senate Democrats to Remain Open to Debt-Ceiling Negotiations," *Washington Post*, May 11

Bahktar News (2011). "Released Prisoner of Guantanamo Kills," *bakhtarnews.com.af*, September 3

Baker, Peter (2009). "Obama Offered Deal to Russia in Secret Letter," *New York Times*, March 2

_____ (2010). "Steep Learning Curve as Chief in Time of War," *New York Times*, August 28

Ballasy, Nicholas (2010). "Conyers Admits the Truth about Obamacare," *nation.foxnews.com*, March 15

Balz, Daniel J., and Haynes Johnson (2009). *The Battle for America 2008: The Story of an Extraordinary Election.* New York: Viking

Bangkok Post (2009). "Obama Names Special Rep on Burma," *Bangkok Post*, April 15

Barber, Mike (2007). "Mistrial Ends Watada Court-Martial," *Seattle Post-Intelligencer*, February 6

Bartlett, Bruce (2009). "The 81% Tax Increase," *forbes.com*, May 15

Bazinet, Kenneth R. (2009). "White House Legal Counsel Greg Craig Steps Down Amid Charges He Botched Planned Gitmo Closing," *New York Daily News*, November 13

Beaumont, Peter (2011). "Campaigners Seek Arrest of Former CIA Legal Chief over Pakistan Drone Attacks," *Guardian*, July 15

Bedard, Paul (2011). "Public Backs Torture, Patriot Act," *us-news.com*, May 25

Beechert, Edward D. (2011). "The Strength of Organized Labor." In Michael Haas, ed., *Barack Obama, The Aloha Zen President: How a Son of the 50th State May Revitalize America Based on 12 Multicultural Principles,* Chap. 9. Santa Barbara, CA: Praeger

Bellinger, John B., III, (2011). "Will Drone Strikes Become Obama's Guantanamo?," *Washington Post*, October 3

Bennett, James T., and Ralph Nader (2009). *Not Invited to the Party: How the Demopublicans Have Rigged the System and Left Independents Out in the Cold.* New York: Springer

Bennis, Phyllis, Martha Honey, and Stephen Zunes (2001). "The Failure of U.S. Policy toward Iraq and Proposed Alternatives," *ips-dc.org*, June 1

Best, Samuel J. (2010). "Why Democrats Lost the House to Republicans," *cbsnews.com*, November 3

Birn, Anne-Emanuelle, Theodore M. Brown, Elizabeth Fee, and Walter J. Lear (2009). "Struggles for National Health Reform in the United States," *American Journal of Public Health*, January issue

Black, Conrad (2003). *Franklin Delano Roosevelt: Champion of Freedom*. New York: Public Affairs Press

_____ (2007). *Richard Nixon: A Life in Full*. New York: Public Affairs Press

Black, Ian (2003). "Franks May Face War Crimes Charge," *Guardian*, April 30

Blair, Dennis (2011). "Drones Alone Are Not the Answer," *New York Times*, August 14

Blomfield, Adrian (2011). "Benjamin Netanyahu Defies Barack Obama's Demands over East Jerusalem," *telegraph.co.uk*, April 22

Bloomberg News (2011). "S&P's Beers Discusses U.S. Credit Rating Downgrade," *Washington Post*, August 5

Blow, Charles M. (2009). "Black in the Age of Obama," *New York Times*, December 4

Boehlert, Eric, and Jamison Foser (2008). "Cokie Roberts on Obama's Vacation: 'I Know His Grandmother Lives in Hawaii and I Know Hawaii Is a State,' But It Looks 'Foreign, Exotic'," *mediamatters.org/items/200808100-001*, August 10

Boehner, John (2011). *speaker.gov/blog*

Borrell, Brendan (2010). "Individual Mandate: A Sticking Point in the Health Care Debate," *Los Angeles Times*, February 15

Bosco, David (2011). "Humanitarian Inquisition," *foreignpolicy.com*, September 1

Bowers, Faye, and Owais Tohid (2005). "Al Qaeda's No. 3 a Major Capture," *Christian Science Monitor*, May 5

Breaker, Kenneth (2011). "No Obama Support from Brazil, Russia, China on Libya Front," *forbes.com*, March 25

Bredin, Jean-Denis (1986). *The Affair: The Case of Alfred Dreyfus*. New York: Braziller

Brill, Marlene Targ (2009). *Barack Obama: President for a New Era*. Minneapolis, MN: Lerner Publications

Brinkley, Douglas G. (2007). *Gerald R. Ford*. New York: Holt

British Broadcasting Corporation (2001). "No-Fly Zones: The Legal Position," *bbc.co.uk*, February 19

_____ (2009). "The Copenhagen Climate Summit," *bbc.co.uk*, December 21

_____ (2011a). "Bin Laden: Pakistan Intelligence Agency Admits Failures," *bbc.co.uk*, May 3

_____ (2011b). "Iraq and UN Sign Iranian 'Camp Ashraf' Exile Deal," *bbc.co.uk*, December 26

_____ (2011c). "Osama Bin Laden, Al-Qaeda Leader, Dead—Barack Obama," *bbc.co.uk*, May 2

_____ (2011d). "Pakistan 'Arrests CIA Informants in Bin Laden Raid'," *bbc.co.uk*, June 15

Bromwich, David (2011). "Obama: His Words & His Deeds," *New York Review of Books*, July 14

Brookhiser, Richard (1996). *Founding Father: Rediscovering George Washington*. New York: Simon & Schuster,

Brooks, David (2008). "The Cooper Concerns," *New York Times*, February 5

_____ (2011a). "Where Wisdom Lives," *New York Times*, June 15

_____ (2011b). "The Wonky Liberal," *New York Times*, December 5

Brown, Adrian (2011). "Osama Bin Laden's Death: How It Happened," *bbc.co.uk*, June 7

Brownlie, Ian (2008). *Principles of Public International Law*. New York: Oxford University Press

Brownstein, Donald (2010). "Is Obama Being Too Cool?," *Los Angeles Times*, October 29

Buddenberg, Roger (2009). "A Nuclear-Free World?," *omaha.com*, September 23

Bugliosi, Vincent (2008). *The Prosecution of George W. Bush for Murder*. New York: Vanguard.

Bumiller, Elisabeth (2009). "Official Charged with Closing Guantánamo Quits," *New York Times*, November 24

_____ (2011). "Some Troops to Stay in Iraq as Trainers, Top Officer Says," *New York Times*, November 15

Burns, E. Bradford (1987). *At War in Nicaragua: The Reagan Doctrine and the Politics of Nostalgia*. New York: HarperCollins

Buruma, Ian (2011). "A Free Spirit," *New York Review of Books*, May 26

Bush, George W. (2010). *Decision Points*. New York: Crown Publishers

Bynes, Sholto (2009). "The NS Profile: Muammar Al-Qaddafi," *New Statesman*, August 27

Byrd, David (2011). "Report: Iraq, Afghanistan Wars Cost US Nearly $4 Trillion," *voa.com*, June 29

Byrne, John (2009). "GOP Senator Calls Sarah Palin's 'Death Panel' Remarks 'Nuts'," *AlterNet.org*, August 11

Caballero, Jennifer (2011). "Boehner: If Federal Employees Lose Jobs Because of Cuts, So Be It," *libertypundits.net*, February 15

Caddell, Patrick, and Douglas Shoen (2011). "Hillary's Moment," *Wall Street Journal*, November 21

Calmes, Jackie, and Mark Landler (2011). "Obama Charts a New Route to Re-Election," *New York Times*, September 30

Campaign for Innocent Victims in Conflict (2010). "United States Military Compensation to Civilians in Armed Conflict," *civicworldwide.org*, May

Campbell, Angus, Philip E. Converse, and Warren E. Miller (1960). *The American Voter*. New York: Wiley

Canadian Press, "Rights Groups, Citing Own Evidence, Call for Lithuania to Reopen CIA Prison Investigation," *canadianpress.com*, January 19

Carroll, Susan (2009). "Which State Has the Lowest Health Insurance Premium?," *usahealthcarecosts.blogspot.com*, July 5

Chantrill, Christopher (2011a). "US Government Revenue as Percent of GDP," *usgovernmentrevenue.com*

_____ (2011b). "US Government Spending as Percent of GDP," *usgovernmentspending.com*

Caplan, Jeremy, and Kristina Dell (2008). "The Six Degrees of Obama," *Time*, December 29

Cappelli, Peter (2011). "Why Companies Aren't Getting the Employees They Need," *Wall Street Journal*, October 24

Carnia, Catalina (2011). "Bipartisan House Sends Obama Message on Afghanistan," *Associated Press*, May 26

Casert, Raf (2011). "Eric Holder Vows to Close Guantanamo and End Torture," *Associated Press*, September 11

Carter, Mike (2011). "Former Aid Worker Sues Ex-U.S. Officials," *Seattle Times*, October 6

Carvajal, Doreen (2007). "Groups Tie Rumsfeld to Torture in Complaint," *New York Times*, October 27

Cashill, Jack (2011). *Deconstructing Obama: The Life, Loves, and Letters of America's First Postmodern President.* New York: Threshold Editions

Center for Constitutional Rights (2010). "First Guantánamo Detainee before Inter-American Commission on Human Rights Given Hearing Today," *ccrjustice.org*, October 29

_____ (2011a). "CCR Announced Bush Indictment for Convention against Torture Signatory States," *ccrjustice.org*, February 7

_____ (2011b). "The Spanish Investigation into U.S. Torture," *ccrjustice.org*, n.d.

Chace, James (2004). *1912: Wilson, Roosevelt, Taft & Debs: The Election That Changed the Country*. New York: Simon & Schuster

Chang, Gordon H., ed. (2001). *Asian Americans and Politics: Perspectives, Experiences, Prospects*. Washington, DC: Woodrow Wilson Center Press

Chapman, Steve (2011). "Did Obama Avert a Bloodbath in Libya?," *Chicago Tribune*, April 3

Chong, Frank (2008). "AlohaCare," *alohacare.org*, March 12

Churchill, Winston, and John Keegan (1953). *The Second World War*, 6 volumes. New York: Houghton Mifflin

Cillizza, Chris, and Aaron Blake (2011a). "Barack Obama, the Blurry President," *Washington Post*, November 17

_____ (2011b). "Opposition to Obama Grows—Strongly," *Washington Post*, October 5

Clement, Scott (2011). "Obama Hits New Lows among Strongest 2008 Supporters," *Washington Post*, September 7

CNN (2009). Italy Convicts 'U.S. Agents' in CIA Kidnap Trial," *cnn.com*, November 4

_____ (2011). "Details of Raid on Bin Laden Compound Unfold," *cnn.com*, May 3

Cockburn, Alexander (2011). "Search and Destroy: The Pentagon's Losing War against IUDs," *Harper's Magazine*, November

Cohen, Jon (2011). "Number of 'Birthers' Plummets," *Washington Post*, May 5

Cohen, Jon, and Dan Balz (2011). "Poll Shows Americans Oppose Entitlement Cuts to Deal with Debt Problem," *Washington Post*, April 19

Cohen, Michael A. (2011). "It's Evening in America," *foreignpolicy.com*, June 14

Cole, David (2011a). "After September 11: What We Still Don't Know," *New York Review of Books*, September 29

_____ (2011b). "Guantanamo: The New Challenge to Obama," *New York Review of Books*, June 9

_____ (2011c). "Killing Our Citizens without Trial," *New York Review of Books*, November 24

Collinson, Stephen (2010). "Obama's New Strategy: Terror Is Not Jihad," *middle-east-online.com*, May 27

Colucci, Lamont (2008). *Crusading Realism: The Bush Doctrine and American Core Values after 9/11*. Lanham, MD: University Press of America

ColumbiaBroadcastingCorporation (2009). "Transcript: Obama's Town Hall in China," *cbsnews.com*, November 16

Committee on the Consequences of Uninsurance (2005). *Insuring America's Health: Principles and Recommendations*. Washington, DC: National Academies Press

Conan, Neal (2011). "Many Gulf Residents Still Waiting on BP Fund Relief," *npr.com*, April 20

Condon, Stephanie (2011). "John McCain Ranked Most Conservative Senator in 2010," *cbsnews.com*, February 24

Connelly, Marjorie, and Bill Marsh (2010). "Rightward, March: The Midterm Exit Polls," *New York Times*, November 6

Cooper, John Milton, Jr. (2009). *Woodrow Wilson: A Biography*. New York: Knopf

Cooper, Jonathan J. (2010). "McCain Faces Toughest Re-Election Challenge," *Huffington Post*, February 12

Cooper, Michael (2011). "Cities Face Tough Choices as U.S. Slashes Block Grants Program," *New York Times*, December 21

Copenhagen Press (2010). "Danish Guantanamo Detainee Sues Defense Ministry," *Copenhagen Press*, November 24

Cowell, Alan, and Helene Cooper (2009). "Obama Plays Down Divide with Israel," *New York Times*, June 2

CPRE (2007). "Formula Funding of Schools," Consortium for Policy Research in Education, *cpre.wceruw.org/finance/funding.php*

Craighill, Peyton M. (2009). "Differing Views on Iraq and Afghanistan Wars," *abcnews.go.com*, July 21

Crawford, Patsy (2011). "Race to the Top Initiatives for 2011," *publicconsultinggroup.com*, May 27

Crilly, Rob (2010). "Osama Bin Laden 'Living Comfortably in Pakistan'," *telegraph.co.uk*, October 18

_____ (2011). "Pakistan 'Blocking Supplies to US Base'," *telegraph.co.uk*, June 16

Cusack, Bob, and Molly K. Hooper (2011). "Boehner: Obama Not 'Technically' Violating War Powers Act," *thehill.com*, June 1

D'Souza, Dinesh (2009). *The Roots of Obama's Rage*. Washington, DC: Regnery

Daily & Sunday Jeffersonian (2010). "Obama's Accomplishments," *dailyjeff.com*, July 10

Daily Mail (2010). "Obama: I'd Rather Be a Good One-Term President than a Mediocre Two-Term Leader," *dailymail.co.uk*, January 26

_____ (2011). "Secret Grand Jury Probing Possible CIA War Crimes in Iraq as Investigators Revisit Abu Ghraib Death of 'The Iceman'," *dailymail.co.uk*, June 14

Dallek, Robert (1995). *Franklin D. Roosevelt and American Foreign Policy*. New York: Oxford University Press

_____ (2003). *An Unfinished Life: John F. Kennedy, 1917-1963*. Boston: Little, Brown

Dangerfield, George (1986). *The Era of Good Feelings*. Norwalk, CT: Easton

Daragahi, Borzou, and Ramin Mostaghim (2009). "Iran's Khamenei Rebuffs Obama Overture," *Los Angeles Times*, March 22

Darwin, Charles (1859). *The Origin of Species by Means of Natural Selection, or, the Preservation of Favored Races in the Struggle for Life*. New York: Modern Library, 1998

_____ (1871). *The Descent of Man and Selection in Relation to Sex*. Princeton, NJ: Princeton University Press, 1981

Davis, Theodore J. (2011). *Black Politics Today: The Era of Socioeconomic Transition*. New York: Routledge

Davis, William Michael (2008). *Barack Obama: The Politics of Hope*. Stockton, NJ: OTTN Publishing

Dawn (2011). "Qadhafi Thanks Congress," *Dawn*, June 12

de la Isla, José (2003). *The Rise of Hispanic Political Power*. Los Angeles: Archer Books

de Rugy, Veronique (2009). "Spending under President George W. Bush," *mercatus.org*, March

Décosterd, May Lou (2010). *Right Brain/Left Brain: Barack Obama's Uncommon Leadership Ability and How We Can Each Develop It*. Westport, CT: Praeger

Defrank, Thomas M., and Kenneth R. Bazinet (2010). "President Obama Signs Compromise Bill Extending Bush-Era Tax Cuts; Liberals Angry, GOP Celebrates," *New York Daily News*, December 17

Deninger, Klaus, and Lyn Squire (1997). "Economic Growth and Income Inequality: Reexaming the Links," *Finance & Development*, 34 (1): 38-41

Denselow, James (2011). "The US Departure from Iraq Is an Illusion," *guardian.co.uk*, October 25

Deschouwer, Kris (2009). *The Politics of Belgium: Governing a Divided Society*. New York: Palgrave Macmillan

DeVeaux, Chad (2009). "Rationalizing the Constitution: The Military Commissions Act and the Dubious Legacy of *Ex parte Quirin*," *Akron Law Review*, 41 (1): 13-103

Diehl, Jackson (2011). "South Sudan Shows What Obama Can Do When He Leads," *Washington Post*, July 3

Dilanian, Ken (2011). "U.S. Put New Restrictions on Drone Strikes," *Los Angeles Times*, November 8

Dionne, E. J., Jr. (1992*)*. *Why Americans Hate Politics*. New York: Simon & Schuster

_____ (2011). "Obama's Prudent Policy on Afghanistan," *Washington Post*, June 27

Doggett, Scott (2011). "Obama's 2012 Budget Proposes $7,500 Instant Rebate for EV Buyer," *autoobserver.com*, February 14

Dolan Jay P. (2009). *The Irish Americans: A History*. New York: Bloomsbury Press

Doo, Leigh Wai (2009). "The Day the Aloha State Was Born," *akakafoundation.org*, March 13

Dooley, Jim (2009). "Failures Tarnish Hawaii Program to Rehabilitate Offenders," *Honolulu Advertiser,* November 8

Douthat, Ross (2011). "Not All Choices Are False," *New York Times*, March 29

Draper, Robert (2007). *Dead Certain: The Presidency of George W. Bush*. New York: Simon & Schuster

Drum, Kevin (2011). "Paul Ryan's Voucher Plan for Medicare," *motherjones.com*, April 4

Dukakis, Michael (2011). "Foreword." In Michael Haas, ed., *Barack Obama, The Aloha Zen President: How a Son of the 50th State May Revitalize America Based on 12 Multicultural Principles*, pp. xiii-xv. Santa Barbara, CA: Praeger

Dupuis, Martin, and Keith Boeckellman (2008). *Barack Obama, the New Face of America*. Westport, CT: Praeger

Dye, Thomas R., ed. (2010). *Obama: Year One*. New York: Longman

Easley, Jason (2011). "Tea Party Support for the Republican Congress Drops," *politicsusa.com*, March 22

East-West Center (2009). "Kathleen Hall Jamieson: On the Media, Politics and a President Named Obama," *Observer & EWCA Update*, Spring issue

Edwards, Lee (2010). *William F. Buckley, Jr.: The Maker of a Movement*. Wilmington, DE: ISI Books

Efrati, Amir, and Jennifer F. Forsyth (2009). "Power to Modify Mortgages Sits Well with Judges," *Wall Street Journal*, January 12

Egan, Timothy (2010). "The Purists," *New York Times*, March 17

Eggan, Dan (2006). "Bin Laden, Most Wanted for Embassy Bombings?," *Washington Post*, August 28

Eichensehr, Kristen (2007). "Defending Nationals Abroad: Assessing the Lawfulness of Forcible Hostage Rescues," *Virginia Journal of International Law*, 48 (2): 451-484

Eisinger, Peter K. (1980). *The Politics of Displacement: Racial and Ethnic Transition in Three American Cities*. New York: Academic Press

Election Law Issues (c.2007). "State Regulations That Affect Political Parties," *electionlawissues.org*, Chap. 3

Ellis, John (2011). "Actually, Donald Trump Just Made Himself Look like a Complete Idiot," *businessinsider.com*, April 27

Engels, Friedrich (1884). *The Origin of the Family, Private Property and the State*. New York: Pathfinder, 1972

Espo, David (2009). "Senate Votes to Block Funds for Guantanamo Closure," *Huffington Post*, May 20

Etzioni, Amitai (1993). *The Spirit of Community: Rights, Responsibilities, and the Communitarian Agenda.* New York: Crown Publishers

_____ (2009). *New Common Ground: A New America, a New World.* Washington, DC: Potomac Press

European Center for Constitutional and Human Rights (2011a). "The El Masri Case," *ecchr.eu,* April

_____ (2011b). "Rumsfeld Torture Cases—Criminal Charges Filed," *ecchr.eu,* n.d.

Evans, Gareth (2011). "End of the Argument: How We Won the Debate over Stopping Genocide," *Foreign Policy,* December

Fahrenthold, David A. (2011a). "American Town Halls More Contentious Than Ever, in Part by Design," *Washington Post,* August 28

_____ (2011b). "House Is Having Polite Year, Insult-Wise, According to New Report," *Washington Post,* September 28

_____ (2011c). "House Rebukes Obama on Libya Mission, But Does Not Demand Withdrawal," *Washington Post,* June 3

Falk, Avner (2010). *The Riddle of Barack Obama: A Psychobiography.* Westport, CT: Praeger

Fein, Bruce (2010). *American Empire before the Fall.* Springfield, VA: Campaign for Liberty

Ferrell, Robert H. (1965). "Repudiation of a Repudiation," *Journal of American History,* March issue

Finding the Perfect World (2009). *findingtheperfectworld.blogspot.com/2009/08/raceerase.html,* August 13

Finn, Peter (2011a). "Guantanamo Detainees Cleared for Release But Left in Limbo," *Washington Post,* November 9

_____ (2011b). "Secret U.S. Memo Sanctioned Killing of Awlaqi," *Washington Post,* September 30

Fiorina, Morris P. (2010). "Culture War? The Road to and from 2008." In Thomas R. Dye, ed., *Obama: Year One,* Chap. 1. New York: Longman

First Read (2011). "Boehner Also Talks Budget Cuts, Safety Net," *www.firstread.msnbc.msn.com,* January 6

Fishel, Justin (2009). "Navy Seals Kill Pirates, Rescue American Hostage," *foxnews.com,* April 12

235

FitzSimmons, Louise (1972). *The Kennedy Doctrine*. New York: Random House

Fleming, Thomas (1999). *The Duel: Alexander Hamilton, Aaron Burr, and the Future of America*. New York: Perse-us Books

Fletcher, Michael A. (2009). "President-Elect Sees His Race as an Opportunity," *Washington Post*, January 19

Fox News (2004). "Bin Laden Claims Responsibility for 9/11," *foxnews.com*, October 30

Frank, Robert H. (2011). *The Darwin Economy: Liberty, Competition, and the Common Good*. Princeton, NJ: Princeton University Press

Freeland, Richard M. (1989). *The Truman Doctrine and the Origins of McCarthyism: Foreign Policy, Domestic Policy, and Internal Security, 1946-48*. New York: New York University Press

Freeman, Robert (2004). "The Bush Budget Deficit Death Spiral," *commondreams.org*, October 22

Frick, Ali (2009). "Obama Administration Files Petition to Block Uighurs from Entering U.S., Praises Gitmo Conditions," *thinkprogress.org*, May 30

Friedman, Lawrence J., and Mark D. McGarvie (2002). *Charity, Philanthropy, and Civility in American History*. New York: Cambridge University Press

Friedman, Milton, and Anna J. Schwartz (1963). *A Monetary History of the United States*. Princeton, NJ: Princeton University Press

Fuchs, Lawrence (1956). *The Political Behavior of American Jews*. Glencoe, IL: Free Press

Gaillard, Frye, and David C. Carter (2009). *Prophet from Plaines: Jimmy Carter and His Legacy*. Athens: University of Georgia Press

Gallagher, Katherine (2009). "Universal Jurisdiction in Practice: Efforts to Hold Donald Rumsfeld and Other High-Level United States Officials Accountable for Torture," *Journal of International Criminal Justice*, 7 (5): 1087-1116

Galston, William (1980). *Justice and the Human Good*. Chicago: University of Chicago Press

_____ (2010). "President Barack Obama's First Two Years: Policy Accomplishments, Political Difficulties," *brookings.edu*, November 4

Galtung, Johan (1964). "A Structural Theory of Aggression," *Journal of Conflict Resolution*, 1 (2): 95-119

Garcia, Michael John (2011). *Guantanamo Detention Center: Legislative Activity in the 111th Congress*. Washington, DC: Congressional Research Service

Garofano, Anthony (2007). "Avoiding Virtual Justice: Video-Teleconference Testimony in Federal Criminal Trials," *Catholic University Law Review*, 56 (Winter): 683-714

Geiger, Kim (2011). "House Criticizes Libya Mission But Preserves Funding," *Los Angeles Times*, July 8

Georgia, State of (2010). "Alignment of Georgia Race to the Top and Renaissance™ School Improvement," *Renaissance Learning, doc.renlearn.com/ KMNet/R004554329-GK35ED.pdf*, January 8

Gerstein, Josh (2011). "Judge Zings Lawmakers, Dismisses Lawsuit over Libya Mission," *politico.com*, October 20

Geschwender, James A. (1982). "The Hawaiian Transformation: Class, Submerged Nation, and National Minorities." In *Ascent and Decline in the World-System*, ed. Edward Friedman, Chap. 8. Beverly Hills, CA: Sage Publications

Giaimo, Susan (2002). *Markets and Medicine: The Politics of Health Care Reform in Britain, Germany, and the United States*. Ann Arbor: University of Michigan Press

Glauberman, Stu, and Jerry Burris (2008). *The Dream Begins: How Hawai'i Shaped Barack Obama*. Honolulu: Watermark, 2008

Goldenberg, Suzanne (2004). "Bin Laden Warning to America," *Guardian*, October 30

Goldwater, Barry (1960). *Conscience of a Conservative*. Shepherdsville, KY: Victor Publishing Company

Good, Chris (2009). "The Tea Party Movement: Who's in Charge?," *theatlantic.com*, April 13

Goodman, Al (2011). "3 U.S. Soldiers Indicted in Death of Spanish Journalist," *cnn.com*, October 5

Goodman, Amy (2011). "Freed U.S. Hikers Speak Out: Iranian Guards Cited Guantánamo, CIA Prisons to Justify Mistreatment," *AlterNet.org*, September 26

Goodman, David (2011). "Vermont Passes Single-Payer Health Care, World Doesn't End," *motherjones.com*, May 31

Goodwin, Doris Kerns (1991). *Lyndon Johnson and the American Dream*. New York: St. Martin's Press

Gordy, Cynthia (2011). "Obama Fires Back in Debt Speech," *theroot.com*, April 14

Gould, Lewis L. (1982). *The Spanish-American War and President McKinley*. Lawrence: University Press of Kansas

Graham-Harrison, Emma (2011), "U.S. Soldier Faces Trial for Afghan Civilian Murder," *Reuters*, February 23

Gramlich, John (2011). "Obama Touts New 'Race to the Top' Grants," *westerncitizen.com*, March 2

Green, Donald J. (2010). *Third-Party Matters: Politics, Presidents, and Third Parties in American History*. Santa Barbara, CA: Praeger

Greenberg, David (2006). *Coolidge*. New York: Holt

Greenberg, Karen (2011). "Why Is the Obama Administration Subverting the Rule of Law?," *AlterNet.org*, August 21

Greenberg, Michael (2011). "In Zuccotti Park," *New York Review of Books*, November 10

Greenspan, Allan (2007). *The Age of Turbulence: Adventures in a New World*. New York: Penguin

Gross, Leo (1948). "The Peace of Westphalia, 1648-1948," *American Journal of International Law*, 42 (1): 20-41

Guardian (2001). "Bush Rejects Taliban Offer to Hand Bin Laden Over," *Guardian*, October 14

_____ (2005). "'One of Them Made Cuts in My Penis. I Was in Agony'," *Guardian*, August 2

Haas, Michael (1991). *Genocide by Proxy: Cambodian Pawn on a Superpower Chessboard*. New York: Praeger

_____ (1992a). *Institutional Racism: The Case of Hawai'i*. New York: Praeger

_____ (1992b). *Polity and Society: Philosophical Underpinnings of Social Science Paradigms*. New York: Praeger

_____ (2008). *International Human Rights: A Comprehensive Introduction*. New York: Routledge

_____ (2009). *George W. Bush, War Criminal? The Bush Administration's Liability for 269 War Crimes.* Westport, CT: Praeger

_____ (2010a). *America's War Crimes Quagmire: From Bush to Obama.* Los Angeles: Publishinghouse for Scholars

_____ (2010b). *Looking for the Aloha Spirit: Promoting Ethnic Harmony.* Los Angeles: Publishinghouse for Scholars

_____, ed. (2011a). *Barack Obama, The Aloha Zen President: How a Son of the 50th State May Revitalize America Based on 12 Multicultural Principles.* Santa Barbara, CA: Praeger

_____ (2011b). *Modern Cambodia's Emergence from the Killing Fields: What Happened in the Critical Years?* Los Angeles: Publishinghouse for Scholars

Hamilton, Nigel (2008). *Bill Clinton: Mastering the Presidency.* Washington, DC: Public Affairs Press

Hammons, Steve (2008). "Obama's Scottish, Cherokee Ancestry Has Meaning," *American Chronicle*, October 8

Hananel, Sam (2011). "Obama, Democrats Losing Labor Union Support," *Huffington Post*, September 4

Harris, Gardiner (2009). "In Hawaii's Health System, Lessons for Lawmakers," *New York Times*, October 16

Harris, Marvin (1968). *The Rise of Anthropological Theory: A History of Theories of Culture.* New York: Crowell

Harris-Perry, Melissa (2011). "Cornel West v. Barack Obama," *The Nation*, May 16

Hedges, Chris (2011). "The Obama Deception: Why Cornel West Went Ballistic," *truthdig.com*, May 16

Heilemann, John, and Mark Halperin (2009). *Game Change: Obama and the Clintons, McCain and Palin, and the Race of a Lifetime.* New York: HarperCollins

Heintze, James R. (2000). "Fourth of July Celebrations Database," *www1.american.edu/heintze*, July 4

Hennessey, Kathleen, and Peter Nicholas (2011). "Default Risk Widens Rift within GOP," *Los Angeles Times*, July 14

Hennessy, Selah (2011). "UN Investigators Call for More Facts on Bin Laden Death," *voanews.com*, May 6

239

Herberg, Will (1955). *Protestant, Catholic, Jew: An Essay in American Religious Sociology*. Chicago: University of Chicago Press

Herridge, Catherine (2011a). "CIA Preparing Secret Drone Strikes in Yemen," *foxnews.com*, June 14

_____ (2011b). "Obama Administration Seeks to Close Gitmo before 2012 Elections," *foxnews.com*, September 20

Hibbitts, Bernard (2003). "Iraq TV Display of US Soldiers Violates Geneva Convention—Rumsfeld," *jurist.com*, March 23

Hildebrandt, Amber (2011). "Bagram Prison: The 'Other Guantanamo'," *cbc.ca/news*, September 21

Hileman, Ashley (2011). "Poland Prosecutors Ask US to Question Guantanamo Detainees over Secret CIA Prison," *jurist.com*, March 28

Hill, Steven (2010). *Europe's Promise: Why the European Way Is the Best Hope in an Insecure Age*. Berkeley: University of California Press

Hitler, Adolf (1933). *Mein Kampf.* New York, Reynal & Hitchcock, 1939

Hitsman, J. Mackay (1965). *The Incredible War of 1812*. Toronto: University of Toronto Press

Hoey, Dennis (2011). "Dukakis Pushes Health Care for All," *Portland Press Herald*, April 27

Hofstadter, Richard (1959). *Social Darwinism in American Thought*. New York: Braziller

Holzman, Todd (2009). "Obama Seeks 'New Beginning' with Muslim World," *npr.org*, June 4

Honolulu Star-Bulletin (2008). "Obama Greets Supporters at Keehi Lagoon Park," *Honolulu Star-Bulletin*, August 8

Hooper, Molly K. (2010). "Feinberg Ordered by Obama to Get BP Claims Paid 'Quickly'," *thehill.com*, June 20

Hoover, Will (2006). "George Ariyoshi," *Honolulu Advertiser*, July 2

Horkheimer, Max, and Theodore W. Adorno (1947). *Dialectic of Enlightenment*. New York: Herder and Herder, 1972

Horowitz, Jason (2011). "For David Plouffe, a Top Obama Adviser, a New Strategy and Old Doubts," *Washington Post*, September 27

Horton, Scott (2010). "The El-Masri Cable," *Harper's Magazine*, November 29

Hosenball, Mark (2011). "U.S. Commandos Knew Bin Laden Likely Would Die," *Reuters*, May 2

Hosseini, Raheem F. (2010). "Single Payer, New Player," *newsreview.com*, November 18

Howe, Daniel Walker (2008). *What Hath God Wrought: The Transformation of America, 1815-1848*. New York: Oxford University Press

Huffington Post (2011a). "Georgia Birthers Challenge Obama's Placement On Presidential Ballot," *Huffington Post*, December 16

_____ (2011b). "Obama: Afghanistan War to See Transition," *Huffington Post*, January 25

_____ (2011c). "Obama Libya Speech Strongly Defends Intervention," *Huffington Post*, March 29

Human Rights Watch (2007). "Burma: Crackdown Bloodier than Government Admits," *hrw.com*, December 7

_____ (2011). "Resettlement of Guantanamo Bay Detainees," *hrw.org*, February 25

Husain, Laurel Bowers, and Laurie Uemoto Chang (2005). "Obama Encourages Students to 'Dream Big'," *Punahou Bulletin*, Spring issue

Huxley, Thomas H. (1860). "The Origin of Species." In *Collected Essays, Darwiniana*, pp. 71-79. London: Macmillan, 1860. Reprinted in Michael Ruse, *But Is It Science?*, volume 2, pp. 106-9. Amherst, NY: Prometheus Books, 1996

Ignatius, David (2011). "A Successful Post-Bush Foreign Policy," *Washington Post*, September 4

Investigative Reporting Workshop (2011). "Lost in Detention," *Frontline*, October 18

Ip, Greg (2011) "The Republicans' New Voodoo Economics," *Washington Post*, August 21

Jackson, David (2009). "Obama: 'Fat-Cat' Bankers Owe Help to U.S. Taxpayers," *USA Today*, December 18

_____ (2011). "For Palin, Obama's 'Winning the Future' Phrase Is WTF," *USA Today*, January 27

Jacobs, Ron (2008). *Obamaland*. Honolulu: Trade Publishing

Jaffe, Sarah (2011). "The Bush Tax Cuts Turn 10; Let's Look at the Damage They've Caused," *AlterNet.org*, June 8

Johnson, Bridget (2011). "Kucinich: GOP Push against Healthcare Law Could Revive Single-Payer Push," *thehill.com*, January 1

Johnson, Ron, and Douglas Holtz-Eakin (2011). "Coming Soon: A Bigger, Costlier Obamacare," *Washington Post*, June 16

Jones, Jeffrey M. (2009). "No Mandate for Criminal Probes of Bush Administration," *gallup.com*, February 12

Jones, Kristin (2008). "Uighurs Sold to U.S. Military for Bounty?," *propublica.org*, October 9

Jordan, Bryant (2011). "Obama Denies 'Kill Not Capture' Mission," *military.com*, June 29

Judah, Tim (2000). *Kosovo: War and Revenge*. New Haven, CT: Yale University Press

Kaiser Family Foundation (2009). "National Health Insurance—A Brief History of Reform Efforts in the U.S.," *kff.org*

Kamalipour, Yahya R. (2010). *Media, Power, and Politics in the Digital Age: The 2009 Presidential Election Uprising in Iran*. Lanham, MD: Rowman & Littlefield

Karp, Walter. (1979). *Politics of War: The Story of Two Wars Which Altered Forever the Political Life of the American Republic*. New York: Harper & Row

Karvelas, Patricia (2011). "Downer Amazed by Payment to Former Detainee Mandouh Habib," *The Australian*, January 10

Katz, Alyssa (2005). "The Power of Fusion Politics," *The Nation*, September 12

Kaye, Jeff (2011). "CCR Files Al-Zahrani v Rumsfeld Appeal on Behalf of Detainees' Families," *firedoglake.com*, June 14

Keith, Bruce E., et al. (1992). *The Myth of the Independent Voter*. Berkeley: University of California Press

Kellerhals, Merle, Jr. (2011). "Obama Welcomes Arab League Support for Libyan People," *scoop.co.nz*, March 14

Keneally, Meghan (2011). "Will Obama Send U.S. Citizens to Guantanamo? Outrage as President Signs off Law to De-

242

tain Home-Grown Terror Suspects Indefinitely," *Daily Mail*, December 15

Kenski, Kate, Bruce W. Hardy, and Kathleen Hall Jamieson (2010). *The Obama Victory: How Media, Money, and Message Shaped the 2008 Election*. New York: Oxford University Press

Kessler, Glenn (2011). "President Obama's Phony Accounting on the Auto Industry Bailout," *Washington Post*, June 9

Keynes, John Maynard (1920). *The Economic Consequences of the Peace*. New York: Harcourt, Brace, and Howe
_____ (1936).*The General Theory of Employment, Interest, and Money*. London: Macmillan

Kincaid, Cliff (2005). "Bush Critics Ignore Clinton's Illegal Pro-Muslim War in Kosovo," *aim.org*, December 19

King, John (2011). "Trump Stumbles over Abortion Issue," *johnkingusablogs.cnn.com*, April 19

Kingsbury, Alex (2009). "Why Eric Holder Says Civil Rights Is His Top Priority after the Bush Years," *usnews.com*, March 12

Kissinger, Henry (2002). *Does America Need a Foreign Policy?: Toward a Diplomacy for the 21st Century*. New York: Simon & Schuster

Klaveras, Louis (2011). "Locked up Abroad," *foreignpolicy.com*, October 4

Klein, Ezra (2009). "More on Isakson and End-of-Life Counseling," *Washington Post*, August 11

Klein, Joe (2002). *The Natural: The Misunderstood Presidency of Bill Clinton*. New York: Random House

Kliff, Sarah (2011). "White House Kills CLASS," *Washington Post*, October 14

Klintworth, Gary (1989). *Vietnam's Intervention in Cambodia under International Law*. Canberra: Australian Government Publishing Service

Kloppenberg, James T. (2010). *Reading Obama: Dreams, Hope, and the American Political Tradition*. Princeton, NJ: Princeton University Press

Knickerbocker, Brad (2011). "Are Donald Trump and His Fellow 'Birthers' Racist?," *Christian Science Monitor*, April 30

Knock, Thomas J. (1995). *To End All Wars: Woodrow Wilson and the Quest for a New World Order*. Princeton, NJ: Princeton University Press

Koh, Harold H. (2010). "The Obama Administration and International Law." Speech to the American Society of International Law, *airforce-magazine.com*, March 25

Kolchin, Peter (2003). *American Slavery, 1619-1877*. New York: Hill and Wang

Korb, Lawrence J. (2008). *Moving Beyond the Carter Doctrine: The U.S. Military Presence in the Persian Gulf*. New York: Century Foundation

Kornblut, Anne E., and Perry Bacon, Jr. (2007). "Obama Says Washington Is Ready for Health Plan," *Washington Post*, May 30

Kornhauser, William (1959). *The Politics of Mass Society*. New York: Free Press

Kovach, Gretel C. (2011). "Dismissal of Major Iraq War Crimes Case Cast in Doubt," *signonsandiego.com*, January 12

Krook, Mona Lena, and Sarah Childs, eds. (2010). *Women, Gender, and Politics: A Reader*. New York: Oxford University Press

Krugman, Paul (2010). "How Did We Know the Stimulus Was Too Small?," *New York Times*, July 28

_____ (2011). "Free to Die," *New York Times*, September 15

Kudlow, Larry (2009). "What Did Reagan's Inaugural Say?," *nationalreview.com*, January 19

Kuhnhenn, Jim (2010). "Obama Salutes Spirit of Compromise, Signs Tax Bill," *Associated Press*, December 17

Kuznets, Simon (1955). "Economic Growth and Income Inequality," *American Economic Review*, 45 (1): 1-28

Kurgis, Frederick L. (1998). "Cruise Missile Strikes in Afghanistan and Sudan," *asil.org*, August

Labott, Elise (2009). "U.S. Envoy for North Korea May Visit Pyongyang," *cnn.com*, February 26

LaHaye, Tim (1975). *Revelation: Illustrated and Made Plain*. Grand Rapids, MI: Zondervan

Lambert, Frank (2005). *The Barbary Wars: American Independence in the Atlantic World*. New York: Hill and Wang

Landler, Mark, and Mark Mazzetti (2011). "Account Tells of One-Sided Battle in Bin Laden Raid," *New York Times*, May 4

Landler, Mark, and David Sanger (2009). "World Leaders Pledge $1.1 Trillion for Crisis," *New York Times*, April 2

Lavender, Paige (2011). "Eric Holder Defends Civilian Trials for Terrorists," *Huffington Post*, June 16

Leach, William D. (2011). "An Odious Mandate?," *Los Angeles Times*, October 7

Leicht, Justus (2005). "German Court Declares Iraq War Violated International Law," *globalresearch.ca*, September 28

Lelyveld, Joseph (2010). "Who Is Barack Obama?," *New York Review of Books*, May 13

Lesinski, Jeanne M. (2009). *Bill Gates: Entrepreneur and Philanthropist*. Minneapolis, MN: Lerner Publishing Group

Lewis, Felice Flanery (2010). *Trailing Clouds of Glory: Zachary Taylor's Mexican War Campaign and His Emerging Civil Leaders*. Tuscaloosa: University of Alabama Press

Light, Paul (2011). "The Best Idea in Obama's Budget (Hint: It's Not a Cut)," *Washington Post*, February 18

Lijphart, Arend (1968). "Typologies of Democratic Systems," *Comparative Political Studies*, 1 (1): 3-44

Link, Arthur S. (1968). *Woodrow Wilson: A Profile*. New York: Hill and Wang

Linthicum, Kate (2011). "U.S. Stimulus Funds at Risk," *Los Angeles Times*, July 12

Lipton, Eric, and John M. Broder (2011). "E-Mail Shows Senior Official Pushed Solyndra Loan," *New York Times*, October 8

Lisberg, Adam, James Gordon Meek, and Celeste Katz (2010). "Sens. Schumer, Gillibrand OK Moving 9/11 Trial Out of New York City," *New York Daily News*, January 28

Litwak, Robert S. (1984). *Détente and the Nixon Doctrine: American Foreign Policy and the Pursuit of Stability, 1969-1976*. New York: Cambridge University Press

Lohr, Steve (2011). "The Administration Starts Its Start-Up Policy," *New York Times*, January 31

Longley, Robert (2011). "Why Third Parties? They Rarely Win, But 3rd Party Candidates Are Essential," *usgov-info.about.com*

Luebke, Frederick C. (1971). *Ethnic Voters and the Election of Lincoln*. Lincoln: University of Nebraska Press

Lugar, Richard M. (2011). "Obama's Risky Course on Libya," *Washington Post*, June 6

Lynch, Colum (2009). "U.S. to Join U.N. Human Rights Council, Reversing Bush Policy," *Washington Post*, March 31

Maass, Peter (2011). "What Happened at the Macondo Well?," *New York Review of Books*, September 29

MacFarquhar, Larissa (2007). "The Conciliator," *newyorker.com*, May 7

Mair, Peter (1990). *The West European Party System*. New York: Oxford University Press

Maisel, L. Sandy, and Jeffrey M. Barry, eds. (2010). *The Oxford Handbook of American Political Parties and Interest Groups*. New York: Oxford University Press

Mak, Jim (2011). "Mark Halperin Suspended for Obama Remark on Morning Joe," *politico.com*, June 30

Margulies, Joseph (2011). "Trapped in Guantanamo," *Los Angeles Times*, September 29

Marshall, Dorothy (1938). *The Rise of George Canning*. London: Longmans

Mascaro, Lisa (2011). "Reid Rejects Boehner Proposal for $2 Trillion in Spending Cuts," *Los Angeles Times*, May 19

Mascaro, Lisa, and Kathleen Hennessey (2011). "Republicans in Congress Soften Their Tone, If Not Their Positions," *Los Angeles Times*, September 16

Mascaro, Lisa, and Christi Parsons (2011). "Obama Ends Debt Meeting with Warning," *Los Angeles Times*, July 14

May, Ernest R. (1975). *The Making of the Monroe Doctrine*. Cambridge, MA: Harvard University Press

Mayer, William G., ed. (2008). *The Swing Voter in American Politics*. Washington, DC: Brookings Institution

Maxwell, Angie (2011). "Tea Party Distinguished by Racial Views and Fear of the Future," *ark.edu/rd_arsc/blair-rockefellerpoll/5293.php*, June 21

Mazzetti, Mark (2011). "U.S. Is Intensifying a Secret Campaign of Yemen Airstrikes," *New York Times*, June 9

McClelland, Edward (2010). *Young Mr. Obama: Chicago and the Making of a President*. New York: Bloombury

McCullagh, Declan (2011). "Wikileaks Doc: Nuclear Reprisals If Bin Laden Killed," *cnet.com*, May 3

McCullough, David (1992). *Truman*. New York: Simon & Schuster

McEwan, Melissa (2011). "Obama Administration Has No Use for WPA-Type Programs That Would Help Poor and Unemployed," *AlterNet.org*, May 31

McManus, Doyle (2011a). "Another Presidential Gene Pool," *Los Angeles Times*, November 29

_____ (2011b). "Team Obama's Victory Plan," *Los Angeles Times*, July 7

McMaster, H. R. (1998). *Dereliction of Duty: Lyndon Johnson, Robert McNamara, the Joint Chiefs of Staff, and the Lies That Led to Vietnam*. New York: HarperCollins

Meacham, Jon (2009). "Realism We Can Believe in," *Newsweek*, December 14

MediCheck (2010). "Minimum Loss Ratio (MLR) Requirement," *medibid.com*, November 4

Meiertöns, Heiko (2010). *The Doctrines of US Security Policy—An Evaluation under International Law*. New York: Cambridge University Press

Menand, Louis, ed. (1997). *Pragmatism: A Reader*. New York: Knopf

Mendel, David (2007). *Obama: From Promise to Power*. New York: Amistad/HarperCollins

Metropolitan Life Insurance Company (2011). *2011 MetLife Study of the American Dream*. New York: MetLife

Meyer, Bill (2009). "National Health Care Debate Goes Back to Theodore Roosevelt Plan in 1912: Analysis," *Cleveland Plain Dealer*, August 12

Meyerson, Harold (2011). "How Will History Judge Obama's Economic Policy?," *Washington Post*, June 8

Miami Herald (2011). "By the Numbers," *Miami Herald*, June 29

Mieczkowski, Yanek (2005). *Gerald Ford and the Challenges of the 1970s*. Lexington: University Press of Kentucky

Mikva, Abner, William S. Sessions, and John J. Gibbons (2011). "Beyond Guantanamo," *Chicago Tribune*, October 7

Milbank, Dana (2011a). "The Birthers Eat Their Own," *Washington Post*, October 21

_____ (2011b). "The Birthing of Solyndra," *Washington Post*, September 26

_____ (2011c). "The Irrelevancy of the Obama Presidency," *Washington Post*, September 9

_____ (2011d). "Squawk Treatment: Progressives Voice Their Anger at Obama," *Washington Post*, June 24

_____ (2011e). "With Goolsbee's Departure, Obama Losing a Voice of Reason," *Washington Post*, June 11

Millenson, Michael L. (2010). "Bipartisan Health Reform Shocker: Reagan Was a Rino!," *Huffington Post*, February 16

Miller, George (2011). "Miller Applauds Race to the Top Announcement," Committee on Education and the Workforce, House of Representatives, *democrats.edworkforce.house.gov/newsroom/2011/05/millerapplauds-race-to-the-top.html*, May 25

Miller, Greg (2009). "Feinstein Comment on U.S. Drones Likely to Embarrass Pakistan," *Los Angeles Times*, February 13

_____ (2011). "CIA to Operate Drones over Yemen," *Washington Post*, June 13

Miller, John C. (1943). *Origins of the American Revolution*. Boston: Little, Brown

_____ (1951). *Crisis in Freedom: The Alien and Sedition Acts*. New York: Little Brown

Miller, Stuart Creighton (1982). *Benevolent Assimilation: The American Conquest of the Philippines, 1899-1903*. New Haven, CT: Yale University Press

Miscamble, Wilson D. (2007). *From Roosevelt to Truman: Potsdam, Hiroshima and the Cold War*. Cambridge, UK: Cambridge University Press

Montgomery, Lori, et al. (2011). "Origins of the Debt Deal," *Washington Post*, August 7

Montopoli, Brian (2011). "How Good Are Obama's Re-election Chances?," *cbsnews.com*, April 4

Moore, Richard A. (1969). *Lanai Management and Development Study*. Honolulu: Richard Moore Associates

Morgan, Lewis Henry (1870). *Systems of Consanguinity and Affinity*. Washington, DC: Smithsonian Institution

Morgenthau, Hans J. (1948). *Politics Among Nations: The Struggle for Power and Peace*. New York: Knopf

Morris, Edmund (1999). *Dutch: A Memoir of Ronald Reagan*. New York: Random House

_____ (2010). *Colonel Roosevelt*. New York: Random House

_____ (2011). *Theodore Rex*. New York: Random House

Morton, J. (2008). "Obama's Background—Impressive Royal and Presidential Connections," *jmortonmusings.blogspot.com/2008/10/obamasbackgroundimpressive-royal-and.html*, October 25

Mufson, Steven (2011). "Solyndra Investment Was Tough Call, Says Former Bush Official Turned Energy Investor," *Washington Post*, October 4

Mulrine, Anna (2011). "Pentagon Fears Iraq Is Becoming 'Forgotten War'," *Christian Science Monitor*, February 4

Murillo, Luis E. (1995). *The Noriega Mess: The Drugs, the Canal, and Why America Invaded*. Berkeley, CA: Video Books

Muruyama, Milton (1975). *All I Asking for Is My Body*. San Francisco: Supa Press

Muscal, Michael. "Support at GOP Debate for Letting the Uninsured Die," *Los Angeles Times*, September 13

Mydans, Seth, and Choe Sang-Hun (2011). "North Korea Is Said to Consider Nuclear Weapons Test Moratorium," *New York Times*, August 24

Nakamura, David (2011). "Axelrod: Obama in Good Position for 2012 with Liberal Base, Electorate," *Washington Post*," September 16

Nakamura, David, and Scott Wilson (2011). "Obama Unveils Student Loan Aid," *Washington Post*, October 27

Nakao, John (2011). "Hawaii Missing Its Chance to Promote Long-Term Care Insurance," *Honolulu Star-Advertiser*, June 5

Nakaso, Dan, and B. J. Reyes (2011). "Obama Evokes Island Spirit as Model," *Honolulu Star-Advertiser*, November 13

National Public Radio (2011). "Obama's Speech on Libya: 'A Responsibility to Act'," *npr.org*, March 28

Neal, Steve (2001). *Harry and Ike: The Partnership That Remade the Postwar World*. New York: Simon & Schuster

Nebojsa, Malic (2005). "NATO's Illegal and Criminal Intervention in Kosovo," *globalresearch.com*, March 26

Nelson, Anne (1986). *Murder under Two Flags: The U.S., Puerto Rico, and the Cerro Maravilla Cover-Up*. New York: Ticknor & Fields

Nevins, Allan (1932). *Grover Cleveland: A Study in Courage*. New York: Dodd, Mead

New America Foundation (2008). *Financing America's Infrastructure*. Washington, DC: New America Foundation, June 9

New York Times (2008). "Obama's Remarks on Iraq and Afghanistan," *New York Times*, July 15

_____ (2011a). "Barack Obama," *New York Times*, April 8

_____ (2011b). "President Obama's Medicare Proposals." *New York Times*, September 26

Nicholas, Peter (2011a). "Deficit Talks Strain Obama's Goal of Bipartisan Politics," *Los Angeles Times*, July 24

_____ (2011b). "Obama Says He's a 'Warrior' for the Middle Class," *Los Angeles Times*, September 28

_____ (2011c). "Obama Seeks Ways around Congress to Boost Economy," *Los Angeles Times*, June 14

_____ (2011d). "With Economy Stumbling, Obama Hails Auto Industry Bailout," *Chicago Tribune*, June 3

Nicholls, A. J. (1994). *Freedom with Responsibility: The Social Market Economy in Germany, 1918-1963*. Oxford: Clarendon Press

Nir, David (2011). "Ryan Budget Fails in Senate: Five Republicans Defect," *dailykos.com*, May 25

Nitobe, Inazo (1902). *Bushido: Samurai Ethics and the Soul of Japan*. 10th ed. Mineola, NY: Dover, 2004

Niven, Steven J. (2009). *Barack Obama: A Pocket Biography of Our 44th President*. New York: Oxford University Press

Novak, Robert (2008). "Is McCain a Conservative?," *Washington Post*, January 31

Nukariya, Kaiten (1913). *The Religion of the Samurai: A Study of Zen Philosophy and Discipline in China and Japan*. Totowa, NJ: Rowen & Littlefield

Nutting, Rex (2010). "I'm No Socialist, Obama Tells CEOs," *marketwatch.com*, February 24

O'Brien, Natalie (2011). "Habib to Sue US and Egypt over Torture Case," *Sydney Morning Herald*, January 9

O'Keefe, Ed (2010). "Sen. Richard Shelby Blocking Obama Nominees," *Washington Post*, February 5

O'Reilly, Bill (2009). "What President Obama Can Teach America's Kids," *Parade*, August 5

O'Toole, G. J. A. (1986). *The Spanish-American War: An America Epic 1898*. New York: Norton

Obama, Barack (1995). *Dreams from My Father: A Story of Race and Inheritance*. New York: Crown Publishers

_____ (1999). "A Life's Calling to Public Service," *Punahou Bulletin*, Fall issue

_____ (2002). "Obama's Speech against the Iraq War," *npr.com*, January 20, 2008

_____ (2004). Keynote Speech, Democratic National Convention, July 27. Text at *Washington Post*, July 27

_____ (2006). *The Audacity of Hope: Thoughts on Reclaiming the American Dream*. New York: Crown Publishers

_____ (2008). "A More Perfect Union." Speech delivered at Constitution Center, Philadelphia, May 18. Text in Obama for America, *Change We Can Believe in: Barack Obama's Plan to Renew America's Promise*, pp. 215-32. New York: Three Rivers Press

_____ (2009a). Address to Joint Session of Congress, February 24. Text in *Washington Post*, February 24

_____ (2009b). Inaugural Address, January 20. Text in *New York Times*, January 20

_____ (2010a). Address at Vermont Avenue Baptist Church, Washington, DC, January 17. Text at *www.scribd.com*

_____ (2010b). "Why Haiti Matters," *Newsweek*, January 25

_____ (2011). Speech at the Memorial Service for the Victims of the Shooting in Tucson, Arizona, January 12. Text at *www.cbsnews.com*

Obama for America (2008). *Change We Can Believe In: Barack Obama's Plan to Renew America's Promise*. New York: Three Rivers Press

Oral, Ronald D. (2010). "TARP Overseer Says Bank Bailout Program Has Mixed Results," *marketwatch.com*, January 31

Orange Country Register (2011). "Obamacare Closer to Supreme Court," *Orange Country Register*, February 1

Oshima, Harry (1970). "Income Inequality and Economic Growth: The Postwar Experience of Asian Countries," *Malayan Economic Review*, 15 (2): 7-41

Pace, Julie (2011). "Obama Report on Libya Fails to Appease Lawmakers," *Honolulu Star-Advertiser*, June 16

Palm Beach Post (2011). "Neither Obama Nor Ryan Gets Serious about Medicare, So Maybe Start with Social Security?," *Palm Beach Post*, April 14

Palmer, Karen (1999). "A Brief History: Universal Health Care in the US," Physicians for a National Health Program, *pnhp.org*

Pang, Gordon Y. K. (2004). "Democrats Call Obama Hawai'i's Third Senator," *Honolulu Advertiser*, December 17

Parker, Laura (2006). "Bush: Guantanamo's Future up to Supreme Court," *usatoday.com*, June 14

Parsons, Christi (2011). "Obama Turns to His Instincts," *Los Angeles Times*, June 28

Parsons, Christi, and Laura King (2009). "Obama: The U.S. Is Not at War with Islam," *Los Angeles Times*, April 7

Parsons, Christi, and Lisa Mascaro (2011). "GOP Unity Fraying over War Policy," *Los Angeles Times*, June 20

Percival, Jenny (2008). "Guantánamo Jury Jails Bin Laden Media Chief for Life," *Guardian*, November 4

Perotti, Roberto (1996). "Growth, Income Distribution, and Democracy: What the Data Says," *Journal of Economic Growth*, 1 (2): 149-187

Pershing, Ben (2009). "Bank Stress Tests: Good News for Obama?," *Washington Post*, May 7

Pew Research (2010). "Obama More Popular Abroad than at Home, Global Image of U.S. Continues to Benefit," *pewresearch,org*, June 17

Petras, James (2011). "Why Civilians Are Killed in Afghanistan?," *Tehran Times*, June 12

Pfeiffer, Dan (2011). "President Obama's Long Form Birth Certificate," April 27. Transcript at *whitehouse.gov/blog/2011/04/27/presidentobamas-long-form-birth-certificate*, April 27

Pierce, Anne R. (2003). *Woodrow Wilson and Harry Truman: Mission and Power in American Foreign Policy*. Westport, CT: Praeger

Pinckney, Darryl (2008). "Dreams from Obama," *New York Review of Books*, March 6

Pitter, Laura (2011). "Guantánamo's Simulacrum of Justice," *Guardian*, February 21

Plouffe, David (2009). *The Audacity to Win: The Inside Story and Lessons of Barack Obama's Historic Victory*. New York: Viking

Pontusson, Jonas (2005). *Inequality and Prosperity: Social Europe vs. Liberal America*. Ithaca, NY: Cornell University Press

Pratt, Julius W. (1925). *Expansionists of 1812*. New York: Macmillan

Press TV (2010). "Pakistani to Sue CIA over Drone Strikes," *presstv.ir*, November 29

Price, Joann F. (2008). *Barack Obama: A Biography.* Westport, CT: Greenwood

Prunier, Gérard (1995). *The Rwanda Crisis: History of a Genocide*. New York: Columbia University Press

Prusher, Ilene R. (2009). "Mitchell Visit to Israel: Does Obama's Path to Iran Pass through Jewish Settlements?," *New York Times*, April 16

Public Radio International (2011). "Guantanamo Bay and an Unending War on Terror," *pri.org*, September 20

Putnam, Robert (2000). *Bowling Alone: The Collapse and Revival of American Community*. New York: Simon & Schuster

Puzzanghera, Jim, Don Lee, and Alejandro Lazo (2011). "Plan Would Help More Refinance," *Los Angeles Times*, October 25

Quigley, Bill (2011). "20 Ways the Obama Administration Has Intruded on Your Rights," *AlterNet.org*, December 4

Radia, Kirit, and John Parkinson (2011). "Libya: House Rejects Obama Authorizing U.S. Strikes, Threatens to Cut Funding," *abcnews.go.com*, June 24

Radio Australia (2011). "Hundreds Protest in Pakistan over Bin Laden's Death," *radioaustralianews.net.au*, May 3

Rand, Ayn (1943). *The Fountainhead*. Philadelphia, PA: Blakiston

Rashid, Ahmed (2011). "What the Taliban Say They Want," *New York Review of Books*, September 29

Rassmussen Reports (2011). "Voters Grow Pessimistic Again about Afghanistan, Iraq," *rasmussenreports.com*, June 10

Ratner, Michael (2011). "The Extrajudicial Drone Murder of US Citizen Anwar Al-Awlaki," *AlterNet.org*, October 2

Rehnquist, William H. (1987). *The Supreme Court*. New York: Vintage

Reid, T. R. (2009). *The Healing of America: A Global Quest for Better, Cheaper, and Fairer Health Care*. New York: Penguin

Reid, Tim (2009). "President Obama 'Orders Pakistan Drone Attacks'," *Sunday Times* (London), January 23

Reitano, Joanne (1994). *The Tariff Question in the Gilded Age: The Great Debate of 1888*. University Park: Pennsylvania State University Press

Remnick, David (2010). *The Bridge: The Life and Rise of Barack Obama*. New York: Knopf

Reuters (2011a). "John Boehner Stuck Between Tea Party and a Hard Place," *Reuters*, May 17

_____ (2011b). "Obama Administration Wants Guantanamo Suit Tossed," *Reuters*, June 29

_____ (2011c). "Obama Speaks on Libya, Says U.S. Ready to Enforce Sanctions," *Huffington Post*, March 18

Ricard, Serge (2006). "The Roosevelt Corollary," *Presidential Studies Quarterly*, 36 (1): 17-26

Rickyrah (2010). "President Obama's 244 Accomplishments, Part 4," *jackandjillpolitics.com*, October 28

Rimmerman, Craig A., Kenneth D. Wald, and Clyde Wilcox, eds. (2000). *The Politics of Gay Rights*. Chicago: University of Chicago Press

Roberts, Russ (2008). "Milton Friedman Admits Entire Life Was a Lie," *cafehayek.com*, October 23

Rogin, Josh (2011a). "Top U.S. Admiral Admits We Are Trying to Kill Qaddafi," *thecable.foreignpolicy.com*, June 24

_____ (2011b). "White House: Obama Method for Regime Change Better than Bush Method," *foreignpolicy.com*, August 24

Rosenberg, Carol (2010). "Changes to Key Guantanamo Evidence Innocent, Officer Says," *Miami Herald*, May 1

_____ (2011a). "Annual Cost to House a Captive at Guantanamo Bay Is $800,000," *Stars and Stripes*, November 9

_____ (2011b). "At Canadian Economics Summit, Bush Confronted with Guantanamo Torture Complaint," *Sacramento Bee*, October 20

Rosenberg, Carol, and Nancy A. Youssef (2008). "Kansas GOP Senators Slam McCain Guantanamo Plan," *Miami Herald*, June 25

Rosenstone, Steven J., Roy L. Behr, and Edward H. Lazarus (1984). *Third Parties in America*. Princeton, NJ: Princeton University Press

Ross, Brian (2008). "Obama's Pastor: God Damn America, U.S. to Blame for 9/11," *abcnews.go.com*, March 13

Rossomondo, John (2010). "Liberal Kucinich Plans Vote against Obamacare," *newsmax.com*, March 9

Rothkopf, David (2011). "On the Economic Roots of Leading from Behind . . . ," *foreignpolicy.com*, August 23

Rubenfeld, Jed (2011). "His Killing Was Lawful," *Los Angeles Times*, May 16

Russian TV (2011). "Lithuania: A Gitmo on the Baltic?," *rt.com*, November 25

Rutten, Tim (2009). "We Don't Need the Pain of Torture Indictments," *Los Angeles Times*, August 26

Sachs, Ruth (2000). *Adolf Eichmann: Engineer of Death.* Costa Mesa, CA: Saddleback Press

Sack, Kevin (2009). "A Lesson on Health Care from Massachusetts," *New York Times*, March 28

Samuelson, Robert J. (2008). "Why It's Not the Economy," *Washington Post*, February 6

_____ (2011). "Busting the Budget Myths," *Washington Post*, November 7

Sanger, David E. (2010). "Obama Vows Free Proliferation Push as Summit Ends," *New York Times*, April 13

SAPA (2011). "CIA Prisons in Poland 'Illegal'," *news24.com*, May 30

Sargent, Greg (2011). "McKinsey Releases Methodology; Firm Concedes Study Not Predictive," *Washington Post*, June 20

Savage, Charlie, and Thom Shanker (2011). "Scores of U.S. Strikes in Libya Followed Handoff to NATO," *New York Times*, June 20

Savage, David G. (2011). "Supreme Court Upholds Arizona Immigration Law Targeting Employees," *Los Angeles Times*, May 26

Savage, David G., and Noam M. Levey (2011). "Obama Health Care Law Reaches High Court," *Los Angeles Times*, November 13

Sawyer, Diane (2009). "Obama Deals with Cuba, Venezuela—as Chavez Gives Him Book Assailing U.S.," *abcnews.go.com*, April 18

Scherer, Ron (2010). "Is Obama a Socialist? What Does the Evidence Say?," *Christian Science Monitor*, July 1

Scheuer, Michael (2011). *Osama Bin Laden.* New York: Oxford University Press

Schlesinger, Arthur M. (1980). *History of U.S. Political Parties*, 4 volumes. New York: Chelsea House

Schroeder, Robert (2011). "U.S. Will Always Be Triple A Country, Obama Says," *foxbusiness.com*, August 8

Schwinn, Steven D. (2011). "President Obama's Signing Statement on Guantanamo Restrictions," *lawprofessors.typepad.com*, January 9

Scott, Janny (2011). *A Singular Woman: The Untold Story of Barack Obama's Mother.* New York: Riverhead Books

SETDA (2010). "Race to the Top News." State Educational Technology Directors Association, *setda.org*

Sexton, Jay (2011). *The Monroe Doctrine: Empire and Nation in Nineteenth-Century America*. New York: Hill and Wang

Shane, Scott (2009). "C.I.A. to Expand Use of Drones in Pakistan," *New York Times*, December 3

_____ (2010). "U.S. Approves Targeting Killing of American Cleric," *New York Times*, April 6

Shannon, David A. (1955). *The Socialist Party of America*. New York: Macmillan

Sharma, Dinesh (2011). *Barack Obama in Hawai'i and Indonesia: The Making of a Global President*. Santa Barbara, CA: Praeger

Shaw, Malcolm N. (2003). *International Law*. New York: Cambridge University Press

Shear, Margot (2009). "At West Point, Obama Talks of a New 'International Order'," *Washington Post*, May 22

Sheridan, Mary Beth, and Dan Zak (2011). "State Department Readies Iraq Operation," *Washington Post*, October 7

Sherwell, Philip (2011). "Osama Bin Laden Killed: Behind the Scenes of the Deadly Raid," *telegraph.co.uk*, May 7

Should Trump Run (2011). "Should Donald Trump Run for President," *shouldtrumprun.com*

Silberleib, Alan, and Tom Cohen (2011). "Obama Signs Debt Ceiling Bill, Ends Crisis," *cnn.com*, August 2

Silver, Nate (2011). "The Ryan Budget Tipping Point," *New York Times*, May 24

Sizemore, Bill (2011). "2nd Ex-Blackwater Contractor Gets 30 Months for Manslaughter," *The Virginia Pilot, hamptonroads.com*, June 28

Skibicki, Stefan (2011). "David Hicks Launches UN Human Rights Case against Australia," *greenleft.org*, September 3

Smith, Adam (1776). *An Inquiry into the Nature and Causes of the Wealth of Nations*. London: Dent, 1904

Smith, Ben (2009). "Heath Reform Foes Plan Obama's 'Waterloo'," *politico.com*, July 17

Smith, Dwight L. (1989). "A North American Neutral Indian Zone: Persistence of a British Idea," *Northwest Ohio Quarterly*, 61 (Autumn): 46-63

Smith, Gene (1970). *The Shattered Dream: Herbert Hoover and the Great Depression*. New York: Morrow

Smith, Janet, and Ryan Lenz (2011). "Meet the Secessionist Group Waiting for the Collapse of US Empire So the 'South Can Rise Again'," *AlterNet.org*, November 30

Smith, Jean Edward (1992). *George Bush's War*. New York: Holt

Somashekhar, Sandhya (2010). "GOP Push to Revise 14th Amendment Not Gaining Steam," *Washington Post*, August 8

Sonmez, Felicia (2011a). "Kucinich, Other House Members File Lawsuit against Obama on Libya Military Mission," *Washington Post*, June 15

_____ (2011b). "Obama Consults with Congressional Leaders on Libya," *Washington Post*, March 18

_____ (2011c). "The Senate Debt-Ceiling Vote: Behind the Numbers—and Inside the Chamber," *Washington Post*, August 2

Southern Poverty Law Center (2009). "Militia Movement Resurgent, Infused with Racism," *SPLC Report*, 39 (3): 1-4

Spillius, Alex (2011). "Donald Trump Not Running for President," *telegraph.co.uk*, May 16

Stein, Jeff (2011). "Rumsfeld Complained of 'Low Level' GTMO Prisoners, Memo Reveals," *Washington Post*, March 3

Stein, Sam (2009). "Obama on Al-Arabiya: First Formal Interview as President with Arab TV Network," *Huffington Post*, January 26

_____ (2011). "Obama Debt Speech: Tax Increases, Medicare Changes Included in President's Plan," *Huffington Post*, April 13

Steinberg, Jonathan (2011). *Bismarck: A Life*. New York: Oxford University Press

Steinhauer, Jennifer (2011). "House Spurns Obama on Libya, But Does Not Cut Funds," *New York Times*, June 24

Stevens, Sylvester K. (1945). *American Expansion in Hawaii, 1842-1898*. Harrisburg: Archives Publishing Company of Pennsylvania.

Stier, Jeff, and Henry I. Miller (2011). "Government, Heal Thyself," *Los Angeles Times*, June 3

Stohr, Greg (2011). "Abu Ghraib Inmates Lose U.S. High Court Bid to Sue Contractors," *bloomberg.com*, June 27

Stolberg, Sheryl Gay (2009). "White House Unbuttons Formal Dress Code," *New York Times*, January 28.

_____ (2011). "A 'Winning Slogan' for the History Books?," *New York Times*, February 10

Stolberg, Sheryl Gay, and Marjorie Connelly (2009). "Obama Is Nudging Views on Race, a Survey Finds," *New York Times*, April 28

Stuhr, John J., ed. (2010). *One Hundred Years of Pragmatism: William James's Revolutionary Philosophy*. Bloomington: Indiana University Press

Suddath, Claire (2009). "A Brief History of Blue Dog Democrats," *Time*, July 28

Suggett, James (2009). "Obama Nominates New Ambassador to Venezuela," *venezuelanalyis.com*, June 30

Summers, Lawrence (2011). "How to Avoid a Lost Decade," *Washington Post*, June 13

Suskind, Ron (2011). *Confidence Men: Wall Street, Washington, and the Education of a President*. New York: HarperCollins

Swanson, David (2011). "Obama Transition Team Member Explains Why Administration Chose Not to Prosecute Torture," *truthout.org*, September 6

SZH/JR (2011a). "Pakistanis Protest US Drones," *presstv.ir*, October 22

_____ (2011b). "US Drone Strikes Violate International Law," *presstv.ir*, October 28

Szyldoski, David (2011). "How U.S. Citizens are Suing Rumsfeld for Torture," *inthesetimes.com*, August 22

Tapper, Jake (2011). "White House on War Powers Deadline: 'Limited' US Role in Libya Means No Need to Get Congressional Authorization," *abcnews.com*, May 20

Tarm, Michael (2011). "Court Allows Torture Lawsuit against Rumsfeld," *Associated Press*, August 8

Tarpley, Webster Griffin, and Anton Chaitkin (1992). *George Bush: The Unauthorized Biography*. Washington, DC: Executive Intelligence Review

Tatarowicz, David (2010). "Just What Is in Obama Care—Provisions That May Surprise You," *shorewoodnow.com*, October 24

Taylor, Alan (2010). *The Civil War of 1812: American Citizens, British Subjects, Irish Rebels, & Indian Allies*. New York: Knopf Doubleday

Thanawala, Sudhin (2008). "Sister: Obama's Success Rooted in Hawaii," *Associated Press*, February 14

Thiessen, Marc A. (2011). "Eric Holder, Obama's Albatross," *Washington Post*, October 10

Thistlethwaite, Susan Brooks (2009). "Obama's New 'Just War' Peace Policy," *Washington Post*, December 11

Thomas, Evan, and Kate Connelly (2010). "Learning from LBJ: Obama Is More of a Persuader than a Fighter—But He's Still a Work in Progress," *Newsweek*, April 5

Thompson, Ginger (2009). "Sudan's Critics Relieved That Obama Chose a Middle Course," *New York Times*, October 17

Thompson, Krissah (2011). "Moderate Americans Elect Group Hoping to Add Third Candidate to 2012 Election Ballot," *Washington Post*, November 24

Thurber, James A., ed. (2011). *Obama in Office*. Boulder, CO: Paradigm

Traynor, Ian (2009). "Barack Obama Emphasises Shared Responsibility in Strasbourg Speech," *Guardian*, April 4

_____ (2011). "Some Streak: Belgium Marks 250 Days with No Government, *Guardian*, February 18

Truth-O-Meter (2010). "DNC Chairman Says Republicans Blocked Move to Cut the Deficit," *politifact.com*, August 15

_____ (2011). "The CBO, the Congressional Budget Office, Has Said That Obamacare Will Kill 800,000 Jobs," *politifact.com*, June 13

Turkel, Amanda (2011). "Obama Announces Afghanistan Troop Withdrawal in Speech to Nation," *Huffington Post*, June 22

Turley, Jonathan (2011). "Taking Liberties," *Los Angeles Times*, September 29

Turner, Grace-Marie (2011). "Losing Your Coverage under Obamacare," *nationalreview.com*, June 22

Tutorow, Norman E. (1979). *Texas Annexation and the Mexican War: A Political Study of the Old Northwest*. Palo Alto, CA: Chadwick House Publishers

Ukman, Jason (2011). "Cost of Civilian 'Surge' in Afghanistan: $1.7 Billion," *Washington Post*, September 8

United States, Department of the Treasury (2011). "US National Debt during George W. Bush," *metricmash.com*, May 5

University of Maryland (2010). "Voters Say Election Full of Misleading and False Information," *worldopinion.org*, December 9

Urbina, Ian (2009). "Beyond Beltway, Health Debate Turns Hostile," *New York Times*, August 7

Vaïsse, Justin (2010). *Neoconservatism: The Biography of a Movement*. Cambridge, MA: Harvard University Press

vanden Heuvel, Christina (2011). "Obama Should Fight for 'People's Budget'," *The Nation*, April 15

Vicini, James (2011). "U.S. Court Dismisses Iraq Contractor Torture Cases," *reuters.com*, September 21

Victoria, Brian A. (1997). *Zen at War*. New York: Weatherhill

Vogl, Martin (2011). "Tuaregs 'Join Gaddafi's Mercenaries'," *bbc.co.uk*, March 4

Voice of America (2011a). "Al-Qaida Suspect Files Human Rights Case against Poland," *voanews.com*, May 10

_____ (2011b). "Arab League Criticizes Libya No-Fly Zone Implementation," *voanews.com*, March 20

Wall Street Journal (2011). "Are Excessive Regulations Holding Back the U.S. Economic Recovery?," *Wall Street Journal*, October 26

Walsh, Kenneth T. (2008). "Becoming Barack Obama," *usnews.com*, May 31

_____ (2009). "Why Obama's Action against the Somali Pirates Matters," *usnews.com*, April 23

Washington, George (1748). *George Washington's Rules of Civility and Decent Behavior in Company and Conversation*. Boston: Houghton Mifflin, 1926

_____ (1789). *Washington's Farewell Address to the People of the United States.* Washington, DC: Government Printing Office, 1966

Washington Times (2009). "White House: 'War on Terrorism' Is Over," *Washington Times*, August 6

Weber, Joseph (2010). "Obama to Propose $50B in Infrastructure Projects," *Washington Times*, September 6

Weese, Bryn (2010). "Omar Khadr Gets 40 Years," *Toronto Sun*, November 1

Weiner, Rachel (2011a). "Can Liberals Start Their Own Tea Party?," *Washington Post*, June 25

_____ (2011b). "Dan Pfeiffer Gets Chilly Reception at Liberal Conference," *Washington Post*, June 17

Weisberg, Jacob (2010). "Alone in a Crowd," *Newsweek*, January 22

Weiser, Benjamin (2011). "Federal Court Drops Charges against Bin Laden," *New York Times*, June 18

Westen, Drew (2011). "What Happened to Obama?," *New York Times*, August 7

White, Elizabeth (2007). "Obama Says Gitmo Facility Should Close," *Washington Post*, June 24

White, Micah (2010). "Clicktivism Is Ruining Leftist Activism," *guardian.co.uk*, August 12

Whitehouse, John (2011). "A Legal War: The United Nations Participation Act and Libya," *jenkinsear.com*, March 19

Wike, Richard (2011). "From Hyperpower to Declining Power: Changing Global Perceptions of the U.S. in the Post-Sept. 11 Era," *pewglobal.org*, September 7

Wikipedia (2011a). "Natural-Born Citizen Clause of the U.S. Constitution," *en.wikipedia.org*, September 17

_____ (2011b). "Political Fusion," *en.wikipedia.org*, September 4

Will, George F. (2011). "Choking on Obamacare," *Washington Post*, December 2

Williams, Carole J. (2010). "Political Logjam on Federal Judges," *Los Angeles Times*, August 31

_____ (2011). "Five Foreign Men Lose 'Extraordinary Rendition' Case," *Los Angeles Times*, May 17

Willman, Christ (2008). "'Only in America' Could Obama Borrow the GOP's Favorite Brooks & Dunn Song," *popwatch.ew.com*, August 29

Wills, Gary (2002). *James Madison*. New York: Macmillan

Wilson, John K. (2008). *Barack Obama: This Improbable Quest*. Boulder, CO: Paradigm Press

Wilson, Scott (2011a). "Obama, the Loner President," *Washington Post*, October 8

_____ (2011b). "Obama Administration: Libya Action Does Not Require Congressional Approval," *Washington Post*, June 15

_____ (2011c). "Obama to Announce Changes to Head Start Funding during Philadelphia Visit," *Washington Post*, November 8

Winfield, Nicole (2010). "Italy Appeals Court Ups US Sentences in CIA Trial," *boston.com*, December 15

Winfrey, Michael (2009). "Obama in Prague Echoes Famous Cold War Speeches," *Reuters*, April 5

Witte, Griff, and Karen DeYoung (2011). "Arrest Indicates Pakistan Leaders Face Rising Pressure to Curb U.S. Role," *Washington Post*, June 15

Wittes, Benjamin (2011). "D.C. Circuit Argument in al-Zahrani," *lawfareblog.com*, October 4

Wittes, Benjamin, Matthew Waxman, and Robert Chesney (2011). "Transfers of Guantánamo Detainees to Yemen: Policy Continuity between Administrations," *brookings.edu*, June 16

Woldoff, Rachel A. (2011). *White Flight/Black Flight: The Dynamics of Racial Change in an American Neighborhood*. Ithaca, NY: Cornell University Press

Wolffe, Richard (2009). *Renegade: The Making of a President*. New York: Crown Publishers

_____ (2010). *Revival: The Struggle for Survival Inside the Obama White House*. New York: Crown Publishers

_____ (2011). *Revival 2.0: How the Obama White House Is Making Its Political Comeback*. New York: Crown Publishers

Wolfson, Andrew (2011). "U.S. Attorney Says Civilian Courts Pose No Security Risk in Terror *Trials*," *Louisville Courier-Journal*, June 17

Wolgemuth, Kathleen L. (1959). "Woodrow Wilson and Federal Segregation," *Journal of Negro History*, 44 (April): 158ff

Woodward, Bob (2010). *Obama's Wars*. New York: Simon & Schuster

Woodward, C. Vann (2002). *The Strange Career of Jim Crow*. New York: Oxford University Press

Woodward, Colin (2011). *American Nations: A History of the Eleven Rival Regional Cultures of North America*. New York: Viking

Worthington, Andy (2007). *The Guantánamo Files: The Stories of the 774 Detainees in America's Illegal Prison*. London: Pluto Press

_____ (2011). "UN Torture Expert Calls for End to Solitary Confinement, Discusses Bradley Manning," *eurasianreview.com*, October 24

Wright, Robert E., ed. (2009). *Bailouts: Public Money, Private Profit*. New York: Columbia University Press

Wyne, Hisham (2011). "Obama: The King's Speech of May 19, 2011," *Huffington Post*, May 20

Yaqub, Salim (2003). *Containing Arab Nationalism: The Eisenhower Doctrine and the Middle East*. Chapel Hill: University of North Carolina Press

Yang, Jia Lin (2011). "Does Government Regulation Really Kill Jobs? Economists Say Overall Effect Minimal," *Washington Post*, November 13

Young, Jim (2010). "Obama Speech, August 31: Pays Tribute to Troops, Refocuses on Economy," *Christian Science Monitor*, August 31

Youngman, Sam (2011). "Bin Laden's Death a Transformative Moment for Obama's White House," *thehill.com*, May 3

Yusufzai, Rahimullah (2011). "US Drone Strikes," *asianaffairs.in*, May

Zakaria, Fareed (2009). "Obama: The Anti-Churchill," *Washington Post*, December 7

_____ (2011). A New Era in U.S. Foreign Policy," *cnn.com*, August 23

Zeleny, Jeff (2008). "Obama's Zen State, Well, It's Hawaiian," *New York Times*, December 25

_____ (2009). "Obama Vows, 'We Will Rebuild' and 'Recover'," *New York Times*, February 24

Zeleny, Jeff, and Robert Pear (2010). "Kucinich Switches Vote on Health Care," *New York Times*, March 17

Zernike, Kate (2010). *Boiling Mad: Inside Tea Party America*. New York: Times Books

Index

Abercrombie, Neil, 17, 28, 182

Abramsky, Sasha, 177-78

absentee ballots 68

Ackerman, Peter, 62-63

acute health conditions 95

Adams, James Truslow, 196

Adams, John, 26, 193

Adams, John Quincy, 26, 56, 207

Afghan War 21, 22, 52, 61, 71, 106, 108, 109, 112, 116, 119, 121, 125, 131, 135-36, 141, 145, 146, 149, 150, 157, 158, 200, 210, 213, 216, 219, 221. See also Taliban

Afghanistan 121, 123, 125, 131, 135, 136, 141, 144, 145, 146, 149, 157, 158, 189, 210, 213, 216, 219, 221. See also Taliban

African Americans 25, 27, 29, 31, 65, 155, 183, 184, 185, 186, 188, 191, 194, 221

Africa 193. See also North Africa; specific countries

African culture 47

Akaka, Daniel, 119, 211

Air Force One 49

Al-Arabiya 111, 209

Al-Awlaki, Anwar, 140, 149-50, 217

Al-Bahlul, Ali Hamza Ahmad Suliman, 123

Al-Qadhafi, Muammar, 115, 138, 140, 146, 158, 217, 218, 219. See also Libya

Al-Qaeda 22, 109, 110, 112, 117, 119, 121, 128, 130, 133, 135, 136, 140, 142, 143, 145, 146, 148, 149, 150, 151, 157, 215, 218, 219. See also Bin Laden, Osama

Al-Shar'abi, Adnan, 123, 212

Alabama. See Edmund Pettus Bridge

Albany, New York, 26

All I Asking for Is My Body (1975) 8

alliances 103, 106, 109, 115, 119, 150, 219. See also North Atlantic Treaty Organization

Aloha Spirit 3, 4, 10, 13, 15-16, 17, 22, 23, 44, 48, 119, 166, 192

265

Arthur, Chester Alan, 33
Asia-Pacific Economic Cooperation 119
Asian Americans. See specific groups
assimilation 5, 6, 13, 16, 21, 108, 171, 177, 183, 193
Australia 117, 131, 132, 137, 159, 214. See also Evans, Gareth
Authorization for the Use of Military Force Resolution (2001) 135, 140
automobile emissions. See carbon emissions
Axelrod, David, 49, 69, 70, 185, 198

Bahrain 116
bailouts 21, 41, 75, 112, 156, 157, 170, 202-3
Balz, Daniel J., 178-79
bankruptcy 75, 76, 85, 95, 102, 162, 170, 217
banks 14, 21, 41, 61, 74, 75, 76, 79, 81, 86, 166, 174, 221
Bar Associations 173
Barack Obama, The Aloha Zen President (2011) vii, viii, 1, 4, 9, 33, 34, 48, 51, 67, 72, 177, 174, 177, 178, 181, 192, 197, 198
Barbary States 144, 218
Battle of New Orleans (1815) 56
Beirut, Lebanon, 219
Belgium 59, 132, 199, 214
Bell, John, 56
Benghazi 115, 138, 158, 217, 218. See also Libya
Berlin Wall. See Germany
Biden, Joseph, Jr., 73
Bill of Attainder 127
Bill of Rights 131, 150. See also civil liberties
Bin Laden, Osama, 22, 71, 117, 136, 141, 143-49, 151, 153, 158, 188, 215
bipartisanship 10, 59, 61, 63, 69, 70, 81-82, 89, 91, 92, 122, 133, 157, 159, 203, 205
birth records 33-35, 72, 195
"birtherists" 33-34, 35, 72, 201
Bismarck, Otto von, 211
Blacks. See African Americans
Blair, Dennis, 141, 218, 220
block grants 77, 202

Bush, George W. (continued)
132, 133, 135, 145, 146, 150, 162, 168, 181, 189, 195,
196, 204, 209, 211, 212, 215, 216, 218, 220
Bush Doctrine 108, 209
Bushido Code 13, 14, 16, 192

Cain, Herman, 31, 124, 212
California 29, 104
    Democratic Party 50, 51, 59, 99, 100, 197
    legislature 59, 99, 206
    Los Angeles vii, 5, 29, 67, 184, 216
    Palm Springs 28
    San Francisco 28, 29, 114
Cambodia 137, 216
Cambridge, Massachusetts. See Massachusetts
Camp Cropper. See Iraq
Canada 50, 103, 123, 131, 205, 207, 215
cancer 90
Canning, George, 103-4, 208
capitalism 14, 41, 76, 85, 86. See also humanistic capitalism;
    philanthrocapitalism; social market capitalism
carbon emissions 157. See also global warming
Carender, Keli, 55
Carnegie, Andrew, 76
Carpenter, Tim, 45, 100
Carter, Jimmy, 40, 106-7, 196
Carter, Philip, 122, 212
Carter Doctrine 106-7, 209
Cashill, Jack, 179
Castro, Fidel, 106
Catholic Americans 27, 65
Caucasian Americans 3, 6, 8, 14, 15, 16, 22, 25, 27, 28, 30,
    31, 44, 47, 48, 49, 179, 180, 186, 194
Cayetano, Ben, 8
centrism 10, 46, 55, 59, 62-63, 201
charisma 17-18, 167
Charter School Act (2011) 200
Chávez, Hugo, 111
Cherokees 31

269

271

drones (unmanned aerial vehicles) 22, 52, 110, 115, 136, 140,
141, 149, 157, 209, 214, 216, 217, 218, 220
drug trafficking 107
dueling 26, 194
Dukakis, Michael, vii, 48, 67, 89, 90, 197, 205
Dunham, Stanley Ann, 20, 33, 34, 50, 90, 186, 188, 191, 192,
194, 205
Dunn, Ronnie, 195
Dupuis, Martin, 176
Dutch Americans 31
Dye, Thomas R., 180

East Coast of the United States, 46, 72. See also Washington,
D.C.; New York City
Economic Consequences of the Peace, The (1920), 195
economic exploitation 5, 6, 14
economic rights 113
economic "stimulus" 41, 65, 71, 77, 79, 80, 81, 82, 83, 90,
161, 162, 203. See also American Recovery and Reinvestment Act (2009)
economics 37, 40, 41, 42, 71, 75-86, 202. See also classical
economics; Keynsian economics; social investment economics; supply-side economics
economy, American, 6, 37-39, 40-41, 43, 66, 68, 69, 72, 73,
75, 76, 78-79, 80-85, 86, 117, 162, 163, 173-76, 184, 195,
200, 201, 203, 204. See also Hawai'i, economy
education 1, 9, 26, 61, 72, 73-74, 154, 172, 180, 189, 198
Egypt 105, 106, 111, 115, 132, 188, 209
Eichmann, Adolf, 146, 219
Eisenhower, Dwight, 27, 39, 88, 105, 112, 117, 194, 196, 209
Eisenhower Doctrine 105, 117, 209
Eisinger, Peter, 193
elections, American, 8, 25-30, 39-41, 56-59, 68-69, 200
1800 26
1824 26, 56, 194
1828 26, 194
1860 26, 56, 194
1884 27
1892 27
1900 57

Geneva. See Switzerland

Geneva Convention (Convention Relative to the Treatment of Prisoners of War) (1929) 121, 211

Geneva Conventions (1949) 110, 121-23, 125, 130-31, 133, 156, 211

George W. Bush, War Criminal? 121, 124

George Washington University 221

Georgia 36, 91, 195

Gergen, David, 3

German Americans 31

Germany 38, 51, 87, 96, 105, 132, 146, 198, 205, 207, 214, 216

Giffords, Gabrielle, 23, 60

Gingrich, Newt, 71, 179

glass ceilings 29, 180

Glauberman, Stu, 181

global warming 109, 171, 176. See also carbon emissions; greenhouse gasses

God 19, 37, 168

Goldwater, Barry, 195

Goolsbee, Austan, 75, 201

Gore, Al, 57

government bonds 61, 78, 80, 203

government regulation 37, 38-39, 41, 76, 83, 96, 101, 157-58, 174, 175, 176, 204. See also anti-trust laws

Grand Bargain (2011) 62

Grassley, Chuck, 92

Great Depression 39

Great Society 40

Greece 105

Green Party 55, 57, 62

greenhouse gasses 112, 157. See also global warming

Greenspan, Allan, 204

Guam 126

Guantánamo Bay Naval Base 22, 49, 52, 110, 121-30, 131, 132-33, 145, 149, 154, 156, 198, 211, 212, 220

Gulf of Mexico 79, 222

Haas, Michael, vii-viii, 1, 5, 6, 10, 15-16, 17, 33, 34-35, 45-46, 47, 50-51, 52, 66, 67-68, 70, 88, 97, 100, 121-22, 177, 181-81, 197
habeas corpus 129
Hagel, Chuck, 80
Hague, The. See the Netherlands
Haïti 125, 160, 161, 2210
Halperin, Mark, 182, 191
Hamdan, Salim, 126
Hamilton, Alexander, 26, 194
Hardy, Bruce W., 182
harmoniousness 3, 4, 6, 15, 19-20, 47, 150, 169
Harris-Perry, Melissa, 47
Harvard University 3, 179, 183, 184, 188
Hawai'i 1, 4, 5, 9, 10, 13, 19, 21, 22, 32, 46, 86, 87, 115, 173, 175, 176, 177-78, 179, 182, 188
   annexation 6, 14, 44, 104, 208
   criminal justice system 9, 78
   culture vii, 1-5, 6-10, 13-23, 45, 47-48, 49, 67, 71, 72, 76, 108, 153, 165-71, 177, 178, 179, 181, 182, 183, 186
   Department of Health 33-34
   economy 5-6, 8, 13-14, 43-44, 48, 76, 90, 182
   education 7, 182, 184
   health care 50-51, 88-89, 100, 155, 205
   history 5-6, 8-9, 14-16
   Honolulu vii, 1, 5, 13, 15, 17, 20, 23, 33, 34, 43, 44, 47, 48, 49, 67, 108, 141, 153, 170, 177, 179, 183, 184, 185, 186, 197
   immigrants 14, 15
   Kapi'olani Medical Center for Women & Children 34
   Kingdom of Hawai'i 5-6, 13-14, 104
   linguistic diversity 4, 6-7, 8, 9, 13
   literature 7-8
   "locals" 16
   media 7, 33
   military bases 5, 22
   music 8
   Pearl Harbor 105
   plantations 6, 7, 9, 14, 19, 41, 42, 46, 198

humanistic capitalism 75-76, 79, 84, 170
humanitarian intervention 112, 116, 137-39, 210, 216
humility 15, 17-18, 108, 163, 167, 185, 193
humor 7, 18, 30, 167. See also joviality
Huntsman, John, 31
Hussein, Saddam, 108, 131, 135, 217
Huxley, Thomas, 37, 195

Idaho 58
ideology 10, 19, 50, 51, 75, 76, 80, 101, 108, 112, 117, 170, 179, 196, 206, 211. See also conservatives; communists; leftists; libertarianism; Progressive Democrats; Social Darwinism
Ignatius, David, 119
Illinois 56, 178, 180, 183. See also Chicago
immigrants, American, 29, 35, 70, 161, 193, 200. See also Hawai'i, immigrants
immobilism 59, 62, 63, 133, 199
Impact Investment Fund (IIF) 80, 203
impeachment 30, 88, 127, 220
imperialism 38, 104, 111, 156. See also anti-colonialism; colonialism
inclusiveness 2, 8, 9, 17, 112, 166, 178, 187, 192-93
incumbent candidates vii, 27, 39, 40, 41, 57, 58, 59, 68, 69, 72, 85, 92, 153, 162, 199, 201
indefinite detention 110, 124
Independent Payments Advisory Board 94, 96
independent voters 65, 66, 68, 69, 200. See also swing voters
India 217
Indian Americans 28
Indian Nations of North America 103. See also French and Indian War; Native Americans
Indiana 126
individual mandate 87, 90, 91, 92, 93, 98, 100, 101, 102, 201, 205
individualism 19, 75, 169
Indonesia 15, 22, 108, 184, 185, 186, 187, 188, 191, 192, 197
inequality 61, 85-86, 204
infrastructure 41, 43, 78, 80, 81, 82, 175. See also National Infrastructure Reinvestment Bank

281

Ingram's Magazine 179
Inouye, Daniel, 28
insolvency 41, 75, 96, 174, 175
insurance industry. See flood insurance; health insurance; motor vehicle insurance
Inter-American Commission on Human Rights 122, 214
interculturalism 4, 16, 22
interest groups 7, 88, 100, 155, 178, 182, 189, 221. See also pressure group model
International Court of Justice 137, 149
International Covenant on Civil and Political Rights (1967) 110, 121, 125, 147
International Criminal Court (ICC) 125, 213
international law 110, 115, 127-28, 131, 137-38, 144, 145, 148, 207, 213, 215, 219
International Peace Research Association 206
Iran 111, 119, 154-55, 209, 210, 213, 221
Iraq 38, 107, 108, 109, 121, 131, 135, 141, 148, 158, 212, 216, 217, 220
Isakson, Johnny, 91, 206
Ireland 31
Irish Americans 27, 31, 193, 194
irritability 20, 170
Islam 110, 111. See also Muslim world
isolationism 38, 58
Israel 76, 106, 111, 119, 143, 145, 155, 209, 210, 219, 221. See also kibbutz system
Italy 132, 138, 214

Jackson, Andrew, 26, 56
Jacobs, Ron, 182
Jakarta. See Indonesia
James, William, 72-73, 198
Jamieson, Kathleen Hall, 2, 17, 23, 48, 182
Japan 6, 7, 14, 15, 218
Japanese Americans 3, 7-8, 14-15, 16, 18, 19, 20, 21, 28, 47, 49, 153, 186
Japanese culture 4, 6, 10, 13, 16, 18, 19, 20, 21, 47, 48, 153, 166, 179
Japanese language 6-7

Los Angeles. See California
Los Angeles Times Festival of Books 45
Louisiana 28, 35, 56, 92

Macedonia 132, 214
Mainlanders, U.S., vii, 5, 6, 8, 9, 13, 14, 15, 16, 17, 18, 19,
    20, 21, 47, 48, 67, 124, 165, 166-71, 192
Making Home Affordable plan 156
Making of the President series 188
Margulies, Joseph, 212
Marshall Plan 105
Marx, Karl, 13, 192
mass society 155-56, 221. See also civil society
Massachusetts 28, 89, 90, 205
    Boston 27, 55, 198
    Cambridge 184
Maugham, Somerset, 7
McCain, John, iii, 29, 33, 38, 58, 59, 122, 199, 212
McConnell, Mitch, 59, 61, 213
McKinley, William, 38
McKinley Tariff 38, 195
McLaughlin, John, 203
McLaughlin Group, The, 203
media 7, 31, 68, 133, 148, 187, 221
    Internet vii, 30, 33, 51, 63, 191
    newspapers vi, viii, 7, 33
    radio 7
    television 7, 31, 45, 111, 160, 194, 196, 200, 203-4, 211
    See also Hawai'i, media
Media Council Hawai'i 7
Medicaid 42, 84, 86, 88-89, 93, 94, 95, 97, 100, 176
Medicare 40, 42, 44, 69, 71, 80, 84, 88-89, 90, 91, 94, 95-96,
    97, 99, 100, 159, 161, 175-76, 198, 200, 205, 206, 207
Medicare Advantage 91, 95
Medicare Beneficiaries and Pension Relief Act (2010) 161
Medicare Catastrophic Health Care Act (1988) 89, 205
Medicare Physician Payment Reform Act (2009) 159
Medigap plans 96
Medvedev, Dmitry, 111, 114
Mendell, David, 183

285

political parties. See third parties or specific political parties

political science viii, 5, 68, 89, 177, 178, 179, 180, 184, 187, 198, 200

political succession 25-32, 193

Portuguese Americans 6

Portuguese language 6

poverty 40, 90, 93, 94

pragmatism 10, 21, 76-80, 84, 85-86, 116, 117, 182, 202

Prague. See Czech Republic

predatory lending 174

preemptive war 108, 118

Prepaid Health Care Act (1974) 88

Preservation of Access to Care for Medicare Beneficiaries and Pension Relief Act (2010) 161

pressure group model 188. See also interest groups

Price, Joann F., 185

primitive communism 13

Princeton University 45

private property 14

private sector 19, 78, 79, 84, 173, 174, 175, 176

privatization 175

pro bono attorneys 173

Progressive Democrats of America (PDA) 24, 45-54, 55, 58, 60, 61, 62, 67, 69, 70, 71, 92, 99, 100, 139, 150, 156, 197, 199, 201, 220

Progressive Democrats of California 99, 100

Progressive Democrats of Los Angeles 51-52, 99, 100

Progressive Party (La Follette) 57, 58

Progressive Party (Roosevelt) 57

Prosecution of George W. Bush for Murder, The (2008), 216

protectionism. See tariffs

psychiatry 181

psychology 180, 187

public displays 121

public health 102, 175, 205. See also health care

public opinion surveys 65-66, 133, 141, 200, 215, 220

"public option" 49, 92

Puerto Rico 104, 208

Pukui, Mary Kawena, 15, 17, 192

Punahou 7

show trials 130
Signa Health Insurance Company 90
Sihanouk, Norodom, 137, 216
"single payer" health insurance 49, 50, 51, 59, 99-100, 176, 206
Six Day War (1967) 106
slavery 38, 56
Smiley, Tavis, 31, 194
Smith, Adam, 195
Smith, Alfred E., 27
Social Darwinism 37-44, 75, 76, 81, 84-85, 183, 195, 196
Social Impact Bonds (SIBs) 78, 203
social investment 76-80, 94, 96
social market capitalism 76, 201
social safety net 40
Social Security 39, 42, 44, 69, 84, 175, 200
Social Security Act (1935) 87
socialism 27, 30, 41, 69, 85, 88, 194, 201. See also democratic socialists
Socialist Party (United States) 57, 58, 60, 92, 199
solitary confinement 122, 131, 212
Solyndra Corporation 162
Somalia 140, 144, 218
South Africa 112
South Carolina 58, 92, 197
South China Sea 117
South Korea. See Korea
South Sudan, Republic of, 158. See also Sudan
Southern Poverty Law Center 194
Southerners, U.S., 26, 56, 57, 193
"sovereign citizens" 30
sovereignty 6, 9, 14, 38, 104, 146-47, 148, 149, 207, 221
Spain 5, 103, 132, 208, 214
Spanish-American War (1898) 104, 208
Standard & Poors 82
standardized tests 176
Star Trek 141
State Children's Health Insurance Program (SCHIP) (1997) 90, 199
State Health Insurance Program Act (1989) 88-89

www.ingramcontent.com/pod-product-compliance
Lightning Source LLC
Chambersburg PA
CBHW062200270326
41930CB00009B/1592